John Burns has spent over forty years exploring Britain's mountains. He has walked and climbed in the American and Canadian Rockies, Kenya, the Alps and the Pyrenees. John was a member of the Cairngorm Mountain Rescue Team and is an award-winning mountain writer. He has written, and still regularly performs, two one-man plays – *Mallory: Beyond Everest* and *Aleister Crowley: A Passion for Evil.* His popular blog receives many thousand visits and John continues to develop his career as a writer and outdoor storyteller.

THE
LAST
HILLWALKER

A sideways look at forty years in
Britain's mountains

JOHN D BURNS

JOHNDBURNS.COM

The Last Hillwalker

Published in 2017

www.johndburns.com
Copyright © John Burns

Edited by Pinnacle Editorial
www.alexroddie.com/pinnacle-editorial

Cover design, illustration & interior formatting by
Mark Thomas / coverness.com

First Paperback Edition
The author asserts the moral right under the Copyright,
Designs and Patents Act 1988 to be identified as the author of
this work.

British Library CIP
A CIP catalogue record for this title is available from the
British Library

ISBN: 978-0-9955958-0-4

CONTENTS

Acknowledgements

Writing this book has been a great journey and there have been times I have stumbled along the way. I have only reached this point in my travels because of the support and encouragement of a great many people, some of whom I would like to thank here.

My thanks to Peter J Biggar, editor of The Scottish Mountaineering Club Journal, without whose encouragement I would never have written at all. Thanks also to Austin J Low, who helped me to believe in myself and to Peter Urpeth, Director, Emergents Creatives, who invested a great deal of professional support. Finally, thanks to Alex Roddie for his services as an editor, and his advice as a friend.

~

To the memory of my father,
whose love of nature inspired me.
And for
Joe, Martin, John and Steve.
Who shared the best and the worst of it.

~

1
Psycho Killer

We are vain and we are blind...

Fulfilling my hope, I throw myself towards glory

Talking Heads

I have climbed into a place where nothing works. The veneer of ice glazing the rock is too thin to allow me to drive in my ice axes, yet too thick to allow me to climb the rock. I'm high on the cliffs of Ben Nevis, Britain's highest mountain; it's cold, it's going dark, and I struggle to contain the rising panic. Once again I turn towards the louring wall, once more I summon all my determination. All my years of climbing experience tell me that the next few feet of rock are close to impossible – but there is no other way, so that is the route I have to follow. I curse myself for my stupidity in getting me and my climbing partner, Joe, into this position. I think about my two girls, my wife, and then take the only option there is: I keep moving. Hooking my ice tools over the top of the small overhang in front of me, I struggle for some kind of purchase with my feet. The snow is sugary and soft and offers little security for the steel talons of my tools. Scouring the rock walls above me for a crack to take a piton or a nut, anything to give me some defence against plunging into the abyss below, I find nothing but blank walls.

Oh God, this is desperate.

A few feet below me, Joe, whom I've known since I was a teenager and climbed with for almost twenty years, is shivering on a small ledge. Nervously, he watches me struggle from the insecure belay as I probe for angles on the rock, trying to find holds for my ice tools over and over again. The rope moves out a few inches only to slip back as I try repeatedly to make the move over the small overhanging bulge. He must know I'm in trouble. I'm more experienced in these conditions than he is, so I do the leading – but if I can't climb it, he can't take over. Stupidly, I hadn't brought enough rope to allow us to retreat.

"It's only Green Gully," I'd responded to Joe's concerned questioning of the need for more than one rope. "How hard can it be?"

I had climbed the route before and found it easy in perfect conditions. But today we are climbing a different Green Gully and this one is lean, mean and nasty. I should have known that when looking up at the route from its base, but somehow I hadn't seen the obvious signs of a Scottish ice climb being out of condition, as it's called in climbing circles, or unclimbable. I was so desperate to climb I had seen what I wanted to see: a thin white line of imagined ice, all the way up the route. Now I was about to find out how hard it could be.

Suddenly both my ice tools break free and the crampon spikes on my right foot rip through the ice. Fear surges through me. *I'm coming off!* If the belay fails the fall will kill us both; if it holds, I could smash a few bones and, trapped on that ice-wreathed face overnight, the cold might get the job done. Somehow, inexplicably, I don't plunge to an icy grave. Moments later, I'm still there, trembling like a terrified spider, embracing the small overhang. Something is keeping me in that precarious position – I just can't figure out what it is. Then I realise that one point of the crampon on my left foot is still holding in something. Between me and an early grave are 5mm of jagged metal wedged into an icicle the size of a child's lollipop. The laws of physics suggest that I should have fallen, but I'm lucky; perhaps gravity is having a day off. I hardly dare blink in case the fluttering of an eyelid is enough to disturb the strange equilibrium of my position.

"Watch the rope," I call down to Joe, as though he needs reminding that our fates are joined by a 9mm nylon cord and the one thing that might save both our lives is prompt action on his part to control the rope should I fall. I think it unlikely that this has slipped his mind, but I feel the need to call to him – perhaps I just want the reassurance of human contact at that moment, to remind myself that I am not alone in that savage place.

I don't want to be here. I want to go home and sit with a beer by the fireside. Please let me get out of this.

Joe's voice drifts up to me: "Can you get some protection in?" He's trying to sound calm but the anxiety is obvious.

Just now my mind is focused on only two things – not falling off and finding protection. Joe knows that but can't help reminding me as he watches helpless from the stance below. Green Gully and I slug it out. The leader's mind is focused on what he is doing, sometimes even to the exclusion of fear, but it is the curse of the second man on the rope that his imagination has the time to torture him with endless permutations of disaster. I long to swing my picks into the snow above the overhang in some vain hope that I might find solid ice, but any violent movement could sever my fragile connection with the mountain. Working blind, unable to see my feet, I probe the rock below me for some kind of hold. My crampons bounce off rock every time I kick. I try over and over again, searching for some security, and eventually find the same tiny icicle that holds my left foot. It's not much but it's something.

I begin to gingerly probe the snow above the bulge for something to hook into. At last my pick sticks. It feels loose, insubstantial, but it's all there is. I don't know if my tools will hold but it's now or never. I take a deep breath and lunge for the overhang.

* * *

Mountains have been at the centre of my life for the twenty years that have led to this moment of terror. I had moved to Sheffield and spent my summer evenings learning to climb on the Gritstone edges of Derbyshire and my weekends wandering the rolling hills of the Peak District. In winter my weekends were spent camped in Lake District snow, summer holidays backpacking across the wastes of the Scottish Highlands or in frantic attempts to climb in the Alps. I fell in love with the remoteness of Scotland and finally moved north and made my home there all so I could spend time in the mountains and, best of all, climb on Scottish ice. Climbing was my pressure valve, my release; it got me through bad days at work and the mundane dreary days. I didn't think of it as an escape from real life. It was life, and everything else just got in the way.

As the years passed, however, my priorities began to change. I married and, in what seemed a fraction of time, became a father. I found a new kind of fulfilment in my children and I loved being a family man. I got promoted at work and moved up the ladder as a Local Authority Social Worker. Gradually I spent less and less time in the hills, less time in the world that I loved. At first I thought that it didn't matter; I had a new life with new challenges. My children brought me endless joy and I thought I did not need the mountains, I thought it was a chapter of my life I could close. Inevitably, as life moves on, pressures build and I needed my safety valve more than ever – but it wasn't there. That weekend would be my only free time for most of the year. I didn't *want* to climb, I *had* to. What keeps you alive in the mountains isn't climbing skill, or fitness, or navigational skill, in the end it's judgement – the ability to assess risks and to analyse situations. That day on Ben Nevis my judgement had failed.

* * *

High on the face, reality checks in to my head with a sudden jolt. I replay the steep, thinly iced pitches I have climbed to get to this point. My mind fills with images of iced rock, patches of soft powder snow and belay slings ten feet out of reach, hanging where snow should have been if this had been an average winter. When you are climbing at your limit the brain sometimes disengages the memory and focuses all its attention on what's about to happen. History has little use in a survival situation: the last move doesn't matter, it's only the next that counts. Some sections of the climb are crystal clear to me, others I can only vaguely remember, if at all. Like waking from a dream, I realise the climb I thought I was on didn't exist that day. I'm on the back of a very different monster.

I take a deep breath and lunge for the overhang. For a moment my body sways in and out of balance, feet scratching for holds, pegs and ice screws jangling on my belt. Then, suddenly, I'm over the overhang and standing on a small platform. It's perhaps only a foot wide, but after the insecurity of the last few moments, it feels like a football field. The little overhang holds a sting in its tail. From the small platform a smooth slab of ice-glazed rock leads up to an easy section of thick ice, a place where I will be able to use my ice tools, a place where I will be back on the kind of climbing I know. If I can make the ice, the battle will be over... if.

The sight of that rock slab churns my stomach. It looks unclimbable, no holds for ice axes and the ice too thin for crampon points to hold. *Oh God, I don't want to be here, I can't get up that.* Then I make myself look at that slab again, really hard, harder than I've ever looked at any section of a climb before. As I look I begin to see, here and there, places where the ice thickens slightly – perhaps, just perhaps, thick enough to let me climb it. I step up onto the slab, expecting my crampons to shear through the ice and hurl me backwards over the overhang below. To my intense relief, they hold. Now I tiptoe up the slab, my ice axes sinking in only three or four millimetres, more points of balance than anchors. My crampon points do the same. I can see the thick ice above now – it feels very close, yet there are still a few heart-stopping moves left. With no runners and a lot of hard rock below me, one slip will bring disaster.

Suddenly I'm close to the ice bulge. One lunge and I can drive a pick in and be safe, but if I lunge now my feet will slip and I'll never make to the ice. It's a trap. *Just keep doing what you are doing. Don't fail now.*

One more teetering move and I am close enough to make my swing. I raise the axe gently and let its own weight carry it into the ice. Until I can drive the picks home, I'm not safe; close is not enough. The pick sinks into the ice with a reassuring thud and suddenly I'm in a world I understand. The ice is steep but feels easy and I can breathe again. Ten minutes later I swing my axe for the last time, and it shudders as it buries itself deep into the hard ice of Ben Nevis's summit plateau.

"I'm up," I yell down to Joe.

"Thank God." His voice echoes in the darkening corrie.

I silently respond in thought. *Yes. Thank God.*

* * *

A couple of days later, on the last day of my weekend of freedom, my friend Robert and I return to Ben Nevis with thoughts of climbing Tower Ridge. As we sit beside the Charles Inglis Clark Hut – the climber's refuge on the mountain – an icy wind drives those ideas from our minds and we begin to think of excuses to go down. A bearded youth, swathed in blue fibre pile, emerges from the hut drinking tea. We discuss the climbing conditions and he declares, with all the solemn authority that only the young possess, that Green Gully is unclimbable. I delight in informing him that I climbed it a few days before, but agree that the climb is way out of condition and make the point that

I wouldn't recommend it to anyone. At first he doesn't believe me, but then he decides I'm telling the truth and vanishes back into the ice-wreathed hut. Moments later he returns, still in silence, this time with half a dozen of his friends, who line up a respectful distance away and stand staring at me. At first I think that this must be out of respect for my climbing skills, but then I begin to realise they are looking at me like an exhibit in a zoo. They've come to see the lunatic who climbed the unclimbable. They are staring at a psycho killer.

2

American Pie

Candles flicker in the snug of the Rose and Crown, the old pub at the centre of my home town of Bebington. The lights are out, the TV dead and the jukebox silent. Darkness has settled across this Liverpudlian suburb, merging softly with the Mersey fog. The town is in the grip of a power cut, a national crisis – although, for me and my small group of friends, darkness is our ally. Customers appear only as vague silhouettes in the candlelight and our secret is safe. Every now and again the suspicious landlord pauses from glass polishing and peers through the gloom towards our table.

Outside the cosy snug of the Rose and Crown, a battle is raging between the miners and Ted Heath's government. Both are deeply entrenched in a strike about wages and conditions, neither side will back down, so every possible step is being taken to conserve power. Power cuts are frequent but, far worse than the darkness, the TV goes off at 10.30 and everyone has to go to bed. Halfway through our second pint the lights flicker back on, the TV crackles into life, and Dolly Parton resumes *Stand by Your Man*. Our little group freezes in the merciless glare of a 60W bulb. The landlord's eyes grow wide as he spots my diminutive mate Andy.

"What's your date of birth?" the landlord barks.

The game works like this; when the landlord demands to

know your age, you have to lie convincingly enough to get past his built-in truth detector. This is easy in darkness, but Andy – who is all of sixteen but looks twelve – panics in the full glare of the electric light. He blurts out a date that would make him forty-seven.

"You lot," the landlord roars, "out!"

Sadly, for us juvenile beer drinkers, the power cuts are short lived.

It is 1972 and every day the news seems to bring details of new conflict both home and abroad. The miner's strike dominates the national news, while internationally the Olympics are marred by Black September's massacre of eleven Israeli athletes. The Watergate scandal threatens to bring down US president Nixon and, in a bizarre twist, the eyes of the world focus on a game of chess. Russian Boris Spassky is facing American Bobby Fischer, who is attempting to wrestle the world championship from him.

In 1972, however, crises across the world don't concern me much. I am seventeen, there is music, flared trousers, wide-collared shirts, beer and, better than everything else, girls. The whole of my life has been spent on the Wirral peninsula, a small finger of land poking into the Irish Sea, bounded on one side by the River Mersey and on the other by the River Dee. My home is a small semi-detached house in the suburb of Bebington, a short boat ride across the Mersey to the city of Liverpool. The city's importance as a port, though declining, still dominates Merseyside. My home town is wedged between the giant shipbuilding cranes of Birkenhead and the fairy-tale village of Port Sunlight. Birkenhead is back-to-back terraces and vast shipyards; Port Sunlight, the vision of industrialist William Lever, is a model village, with wide boulevards, an art gallery and swimming pools. The village was constructed by Lever for his workers, with every house different from its neighbour, at a time when most employers were content to house their workers in endless rows of identical rabbit hutches.

At seventeen my only adventures beyond the boundaries of my Wirral home have been family outings to places like Rhyl and Towyn on the North Welsh coast. As a small boy these were long journeys on terrifying steam trains to seaside resorts already in decline; my gran, cousin and aunty all crammed into tiny chalets that stood in serried ranks along with thousands of other such dwellings in fenced-in parks. Picture a kind of Auschwitz by the sea. For years my Merseyside home has felt safe and comfortable but now, in my teenage years, it increasingly feels claustrophobic. I am desperate to find some kind of escape.

One morning, just after school assembly, my eye is drawn to a sign pinned to the notice board announcing plans for a youth hostelling trip to the Lake District. It occurs to me that here at last is my chance to branch out from the little peninsula that has been my home for so long.

I have only a vague idea of where the Lake District is – there are mountains there, I am fairly sure of that – but otherwise I haven't much of a clue. For advice I turn to Martin Jones, a gangly teenager a year older than me whom I have known since primary school. Martin and I attended St Andrew's, a small Church of England primary with an ancient heating system that spluttered and gurgled around the classrooms, feeding hot water into monumental cast-iron radiators. As a young boy I began my early climbing career devising elaborate low-level traverses round the window ledges and guttering systems of the Victorian school building.

A year is a big age difference in primary school so Martin and I have only been brief acquaintances. One of my greatest friends, in that small school, is an intelligent, awkward boy called Alex. He and I have similarly vivid imaginations and we spend all our break times acting out scenarios where he is the evil green alien, the Mekon, and I am his brave nemesis, Dan Dare. Both characters feature in the *Eagle* comic we both read avidly. Alex is endlessly inventive and prompts me to act out stories – the roof of the school's coke-burning boiler house becomes our silver-clad rocket ship, and the coke pile an arid Venusian landscape. Alex, whose surname is Cox, goes on to become a film director, best known for his creation of the films *Sid and Nancy* and *The Repo Men*. It feels odd watching those films years later and seeing his quirky personality emerge through them. I was the first actor he ever directed.

Martin, whose father owns a chemist's shop, has been on family trips with his father to places like the Lake District and Wales, and has some basic experience of hillwalking. Apart from a rudimentary interest in the hills, he and I have something else in common: we have been judged as failures by an education system that assesses children at age eleven for educational success or failure. This Dickensian system grades children like eggs. Those judged bright are allowed through the gates of Wirral Grammar school, which boasts Prime Minister Harold Wilson amongst its alumni, whilst the rest of us hapless illiterates are consigned to our local single-sex Secondary

Modern School in New Ferry.

Bebington Secondary Modern School for Boys is designed to be a machine for producing apprentices. As a result, woodwork, metalwork and technical drawing are given high priority. Martin and I are amongst the few who aspire to a university education, despite a system that works against us. In our school it is impossible to study both history and geography – you have to make a choice between the subjects, presumably because apprentices don't need to know where they are going or understand where they have come from. Foreign languages are not on offer at all. As these are an entry requirement of most universities, I go to evening classes at the local technical college in an attempt to gain a basic language qualification. Martin and I, with our academic aspirations, are oddities – and being odd brings us together.

Martin reads the notice thoughtfully. "Looks pretty good. Maybe we could get off on our own, do some hills."

* * *

The bus stands outside the school gates, diesel engine throbbing, in the heat of the July morning. Most of the other boys have little in the way of anything that could be described as hill gear. I at least look the part. I have boots, bought for weekend fishing trips with my father. They are sturdy black things with an unusual seam up the middle of the toe, manufactured in Czechoslovakia. It's a sobering thought that I once owned a pair of boots made in a country that no longer exists. I carry my father's World War II parachute regiment rucksack. It's made of canvas, with an A-shaped frame and loads of leather straps that have mysterious functions like carrying mortar rounds and entrenching tools. It has been designed by someone who has never seen a real human being and was working from a sketch made by a drunken miner in a bar in some far-flung galaxy. As a result it doesn't really fit anywhere and drives sharp angles of metal into my body at every step.

My proudest possession, however, is a pair of brand new climbing breeches, tucked in to thick hiking socks that connect up with the Czech boots. Despite the fact that the temperature is in the mid-seventies and climbing, I stoically remain equipped for the North Face of the Eiger. Sweat trickles down my back. The bus has a unique smell: a mixture of diesel fuel, leather and stale cigarette smoke. Gleaming chrome rails run along the back of each seat at exactly the right height to collide with your head should the bus stop suddenly. The rails throb with the pulse of the diesel engine as we climb on board and into the sweltering heat.

Don MacLean's *American Pie*, number one in the charts, blares out of the bus's speakers as we fight for seats. The seats at the back are, of course, sought after by those who want to indulge in some form of clandestine activity. To be fair there isn't much you could get up to on the back seat of a bus, and those amongst the criminal classes mainly have to content themselves with pulling faces and giving V signs to drivers following behind.

"Now then, tha best listen t'me," says Mally, our geography teacher, addressing us from the front of the bus in his broad Yorkshire accent.

Mally is popular with the handful of us who occupy the sixth form, largely because of his down-to-earth Northern attitude and dry sense of humour. He's in his early thirties, sports huge sideburns and is beading with sweat in the inferno of the bus's interior. During lessons he often pops out for a quick five-minute cigarette, like many of the teachers, although over the last few months he's been struggling to quit and has replaced his Number 6 cigarettes with Mars bars, consumed surreptitiously in the store cupboard. This, and his fondness for beer, explain his rapidly expanding waistline.

Mally goes on to give the standard warning about anyone 'showing us up' by misbehaving with dire threats about being sent home for disgracing the school. I'm not sure that our rather down-at-heel school could have its reputation lowered much further than it already has. We spend much of the journey trying to out-cool each other by interpreting the almost incomprehensible lyrics of *American Pie*. Years later I learned that the lyrics are apparently inspired by Buddy Holly's death in a plane crash in 1959, although you would be hard put to understand that if you listen to the track. When someone asked MacLean what the song meant to him, he replied, "It means I never have to work again."

* * *

Martin spreads the map out across the table. "We are here." He points to a square on the map. "And we want to get here, but there's this hill in the way." He is pointing at the map again now, this time to a mass of squiggly lines. I try to make them look like a hill but no matter how I try they still look like the workings of a deranged spider.

"Oh yes, I see," I respond, not seeing at all.

"If we follow this path here, we can cut the corner off," – more spiders – "and we'll be at Kirkstone Pass for lunchtime." Martin looks at us, seeking approval for his plan, but I stare earnestly at the spiders.

"We'll do that, then." I haven't the faintest idea what I have just agreed to.

There is a lot riding on this. Mally has agreed that, if we manage to navigate the team over the hill through the winding paths to Kirkstone Pass, we wouldn't have to peel spuds that evening and we could go off on our own the following day. Kirkstone Pass is one of the most significant high passes in the Lake District. From Windermere the old road winds its way between Red Screes and Stony Cove Pike, climbing some 1,500 feet to a small white inn which has served ale and pies to weary travellers for over five hundred years. There's a name for this road over Kirkstone Pass: 'The Struggle'. As Martin and I lead a procession of boys, staggering under unfamiliar backpacks, up the road through the heat of this July day we both know how it got its name.

The heat takes hold in my thick hiking socks. Inside my climbing breeches I am reaching boiling point. This is not how it is supposed to be – I imagined braving the savage cold of mountain tops snug in my Alpine gear, but in reality I am melting. I think the sweat running down my legs is beginning to ferment. As our little group climbs higher the backpacks grow heavier, our legs weaker, and another obsession takes over: thirst. Our meagre supplies of water are rapidly consumed. Many of the boys carry no water at all, having never strayed this far from a tap before. In my bizarre assortment of equipment I carry a small glass bottle that may once have contained gin, with a metal cup that screws over the top so you can drink from it. As mountaineering equipment it is a failure and was probably designed so that maiden aunts could secretly swig from it in church on Sundays, a role in which I'm sure it excelled. Gin bottle empty, legs weary, dripping with sweat, I toil on towards the summit of our Lakeland Everest. The little white inn draws slowly and painfully closer.

Mally stands at the bar, moist and swaying, sweat sticking his Bri-Nylon shirt firmly his back. Bri-Nylon has one major advantage: you don't have to iron it, you just wash it and hang it up to dry. The fact that it scratches against your skin like sandpaper and generates masses of static electricity seems irrelevant. I have Bri-Nylon sheets on my bed, and as I slip between them they crackle with static – you can actually see sparks. Despite the fact that Mally's shirt is soaked in sweat, and he must have generated enough static electricity walking the pass to power a small town, he remains impeccably pressed. Mally steadies himself against the bar reverentially. He is like a priest who, after a long pilgrimage, has finally reached the altar.

"Give me two pints," he gasps. "Put one there and one there." He points to two very specific spots on the old polished wood. The first pint he downs in one, this one for the fluid; the second he cherishes and savours, this one for the taste.

The view from the top of the pass seems endless, the trials of the ascent forgotten, as the Lakeland fells unroll beneath me – a patchwork of green hills topped with summits of broken rock and endless fields of scree. Travellers on coach trips throughout the length of Britain see only 'scenery', a green video that plays on the television screens of their bus windows. Only someone who walks through a landscape can understand it, have a relationship with it, each footfall is a contact with the land, part of a conversation. Now that I have taken my first faltering steps into this upland world I begin to see things differently. My eyes follow the roll of the hills cut by the straight lines of dry-stone walls that divide the Cumbrian hills. At the top of the pass there is a cool breeze, and to a boy from industrial Merseyside the air feels fresh, clean and alive. I am fascinated by the vastness of the landscape, with its green hills and sparkling blue tarns. From the height of the pass my imagination wanders through dales, over hillsides, and across the cool Lakeland water. Here, there is a place of endless possibilities.

"I thought me and Martin might go over Red Screes and meet the rest of you at Patterdale Hostel, sir?" I tentatively enquire of Mally after my second pint of cider, Martin and I having fulfilled our part of the navigational bargain.

By this point, Mally, leaning in rapture against the bar, is on his third pint of bitter and so much at peace with the world that I doubt he would have demurred if I had requested permission to climb the North Face of the Eiger. Another of our friends, Phil Harris, asks if he can come with us. Mally agrees with enthusiasm.

Red Screes, it must be said, is a long way from the Eiger in both technical difficulty and aesthetic beauty. It is a cone-shaped hill, a pile of stones, like the rubble remaining from the demolition of an old derelict mountain. I suppose geologically that's what it is: the remains of a much higher and once majestic peak. But the moment has arrived and we are free. It matters little to us that we are climbing a small nondescript Lakeland hill – we are on our own at last, able to enjoy ourselves in the great wilderness of the Lakes. Before we depart from the hotel I am forced to capitulate in my attempt at looking like Edmund Hillary and replace my overheated climbing breeches with shorts. Despite the indignity, the current of cool air around my pale spindly legs is delightful.

Our euphoria is, however, short lived. The hill grows quickly steeper, the day hotter, and the scree looser with every step. In the ever-increasing heat we take one step only to slide back down to where we started, as though on some kind of mountain treadmill. Soon we are all sweating and struggling under our sacks. Phil, who is at that awkward teenage stage when the length of his limbs exceeds his ability to control them, quickly begins to lag behind. After a few hundred feet, poor Phil drops his rucksack and begins vomiting into the scree.

"What did you have to drink?" I ask him, thinking a surfeit of cider might be to blame.

"Just tea!" Then, heaving again: "Well… then I had some milk."

"That shouldn't—"

"Then, I think, there was another tea."

"Well, it is hot," I suggest, trying to offer moral support in that typically English way of stating the bleeding obvious.

"Yes, it is," he burps, "so I had some fizzy orange."

"Ah." Dr Burns is beginning to form a diagnosis. "Perhaps it was the fizzy orange."

"But I don't think it was the orange. No, I think it might have been the pot of tea I had after that."

He totters on his feet before collapsing back onto the hillside with a grimace. Martin and I exchange glances over our fallen comrade. We'd both felt a bit reckless having two pints of cider each, but our alcoholic excesses are nothing compared to Phil's soft drink cocktail. We are halfway up our first mountain and, with a man down, this is a bit more adventure than we bargained for. Suddenly we feel very alone.

Uncertain of what to do, and worried that we might do the wrong thing, we do nothing – which proves to be the right thing. After half an hour, Phil feels able to rise, head down, his legs even more deer-like and wobbly than usual. Martin supports him, and I – feeling more than a little heroic – strap his rucksack on top of mine. My rucksack takes the added weight as a cue to drive every sharp bit of metal on its frame into my body with an evil delight. Heroism, I discover, is bloody uncomfortable.

The descent is almost as tortuous as the ascent. This is my first encounter with scree and by now I am hoping it will be my last. You don't really *climb* scree, I discover, as I step on to the mound of small stones and push it down the mountain. It seems to me that I remain where I am whilst the hill moves downwards. Perhaps if I do this long enough I might be able to lower the mountain sufficiently to step on to its summit as it falls past.

I had been looking forward to the descent, thinking it would be easier than the climb up; but now I realise that scree can be just as treacherous on the way down. Nothing I step on seems solid. Every footstep gives way, sending me and my two rucksacks careering towards the valley while I frantically try to remain upright. I twist my ankles painfully every other step. This is not what I had in mind when I signed up for this trip, and on the way down the hill I begin to seriously doubt if mountaineering is for me at all.

I stagger, slip and stumble down. By some miracle there is an ice cream van parked on the road at the foot of the hill. Now my sole aim in life is to reach it. My greatest fear is that it might drive away before I get there, its chimes ringing out, and leave me sobbing by the roadside.

"I'll have a 99," I say to the large bald-headed man in the ice cream van.

The cold, white, sweet creamy heaven that I hold in my sweating hand is the most delicious thing I have ever tasted. I drop the rucksacks and perch on the dry-stone wall beside the road. My feet swinging in mid-air, I enjoy my ice cream while Phil and Martin approach a few minutes later. I'm sitting in an earthly paradise, in a place where all is joy. I take in the sweeping hills around me, enjoy the smell of the sheep and the grass. I begin to think that, perhaps, this mountain business might be something I can enjoy after all. I forget the hours spent sweating up the steep scree, the ankle-wrenching descent, the heat, the sunburn, the exhaustion. Images fill my mind – the endless peaks I saw briefly from the summit, the outlines of ridges and hills, villages nestling beneath green slopes. In my imagination I stand again on the top of the hill we have just climbed and glimpse a new world that draws me to it. It is a trick that mountains have: they rob you of the memory of all the pain and leave you with this romantic image of enjoyment. I am being seduced.

* * *

Ting, ting, ting, ting, the sound of a huge Youth Hostel teapot being struck with a spoon rings out through the hubbub of voices in the dining room. All eyes turn to the hostel warden who is battering the crockery for all he is worth. The room falls silent.

"There have been several cases of people collapsing through salt deficiency due to the heat," he announces as if informing us of an outbreak of the Black Death. "Also, some people have been making themselves very ill by drinking beck water."

"He's talking about streams," Martin whispers, the soup spoon in his hand suspended between the bowl and his lips.

"Make sure you take on extra salt and don't drink beck water. Thank you," the warden adds before rustling off in his khaki shorts, having just delivered the judgement of Solomon.

I pick up the salt cellar from the plastic-covered table and dutifully pour a large measure of the stuff into the lukewarm pond water that is pretending to be vegetable soup. The warden has spoken, and I am quickly beginning to realise that, in the land of the youth hostel, the warden's word is law. His words, in fact, are everywhere. I find them in the dormitories, and there are hundreds in the kitchen relating to the use of pots and pans and dire warnings about washing up. On the main door of the hostel there is a sign insisting everyone be back by ten. Alcohol is, of course, prohibited. Even car ownership is frowned upon; this rule comes from the YHA handbook.

Youth Hostels are for the use of members who travel on foot, by bicycle, or canoe; they are not for members touring by motor car, motor cycle, or any power-assisted vehicle.

That evening, as the day begins to cool, Martin and I explore the little village and find respite in a local pub. The landlord asks me my date of birth, I lie well, and we spend the evening filling up on cider. We pass an hour trying to decide the origin of the village's name, Patterdale. With the profound insight that comes from slight inebriation, I pronounce that it must come from times when the weather was wetter. Hence, the patter of raindrops in the valley or dale, Patterdale, you see? I am rather pleased with my logical analysis until a local explains that the village name came from the pilgrims who passed through the place hundreds of years ago. They would recite the Lord's Prayer, or Pater Noster, abbreviated to Paters. I think my explanation, though wrong, makes more sense. That night we sleep in the rickety hostel bunk beds that are refugees from Second World War army barracks, and lie on plastic-covered waterproof mattresses that make everything stick to you. Despite the endless squeaking from the beds of other occupants I eventually doze off, my head full of the adventures of the coming days.

Helvellyn is one of the finest hills in the Lake District, or so Martin said when he persuaded me to climb it. The path ahead, leading up and away from Patterdale towards Grisedale Tarn, shimmers in the heat as Martin and I slowly make our way towards the start of the ridge. This is going to be our first real mountain and I am more than a little apprehensive. Martin, more experienced and more confident, leads the way up the path that follows the small stream towards the tarn. Phil, mindful of his gastric disaster on Red Screes, has wisely decided to confine himself to an easier day in the valley.

As we climb higher, a gentle breeze picks up and brings some relief from the heat. Every now and then as we pause for breath Martin brings out the map and identifies the ridges, paths and streams we can see below. I am still bemused by the mass of squiggles I saw on our first day, but I begin to be able to make sense of the map and catch the odd glimpse of the landscape it is trying to depict. After a couple of hours Grisedale tarn lies far below us, a shimmering blue disc set deep in the rolling green of the hills. Higher still we pass over the minor summits of the range, Dollywaggon Pike and Nethermost Pike, whose wild names conjure images of an ancient world peopled by men whose language is long lost.

Finally we pant to the summit and sit admiring the view, delighting in the mountain gods we have become. We both feel we've achieved something important by making our way unaided to the summit of Helvellyn and, despite our aching legs, are happy to reach the top. Martin opens up our rucksack, home to our precious lunches, and immediately upturns it. To Martin's amazement, our food and spare clothes fall out on to the rocky summit. Martin and physics don't really get on.

We then devour our standard-issue YHA lunches:

White rolls, with spread, x 2

Crisps, packet of, 1

Biscuit, chocolate covered (melted), 1

At last we decided to head down. "It's this way," Martin declares and walks over a cliff.

I manage a panic-stricken "Are you sure?" before he vanishes over the edge to certain death.

"Oh, yes. This is Striding Edge," comes his disembodied voice, obviously not dead.

I follow the sound of the voice and an impossibly narrow ridge appears before me. Trembling with fear I follow Martin, convinced that he is leading us on some suicidal path that no human being can survive. I feel as though I am standing on a tightrope with nothing but space all around me, and my legs shake uncontrollably. It's only when we reach the summit of High Spying Howe that my legs begin to obey me again.

"My God that was narrow," I exclaim.

"Yes, good wasn't it," Martin replies. Obviously this is some new use of the term good I am unfamiliar with. Below us I can see the tiny village of Patterdale nestling in the folds of the Cumbrian hills. Down there I know there will be hot food, beds, cider and, above all, running water. Martin and I have run out of drinking water. As I have consumed enough salt to melt an ice cap, thirst is becoming a major issue. After our journey into the unknown it feels good to be returning to the domestic security of the hostel and, after Striding Edge, back to the security of the horizontal. A couple of miles before the village we encounter a small bubbling stream, one of the infamous becks the warden warned us about. I look longingly at the sparkling, cool, clear water.

"Do you think it would be okay to drink it?" I ask Martin as he lowers his pack to the ground.

"Better not, remember what the warden—"

But before he can finish the sentence I am face deep in the beck, gulping up as much of the toxic water as I can. I might die but at least I won't die thirsty.

The hot weather finally breaks a day or so later. We are engulfed in mist and rain, and I can at last wear my Alpine hero breeches. We attempt to conquer another Lakeland giant. Martin adjusts the compass, another mystery to me, and sets off into the mist. The Lakeland weather, benign to the point of generosity until today, has finally revealed its true nature and is now giving us a soaking.

Martin points to an indeterminate spot somewhere out in the fog. "The trig point must be over there."

I look at the map and try to appear knowledgeable, but the mist and the hill's level top defeat my fledgling map-reading skills. High Street is an odd name for a hill, made even stranger by the fact that the Romans built a road along the top of it. Martin and I can find no real evidence of the road and so far we are having difficulty finding evidence of the summit. Martin sets off into the mist, guided by the mysterious force of the compass needle; I follow guided by an intense desire to go home. In Northern vernacular, High Street is known as a 'fell'. I can never understand how anyone could call a hill a 'fell' – a rise perhaps, a climb, an up even – unless, of course, it's because people 'fell' off them.

"There it is," Martin cries in triumph.

Sure enough, there, standing in the mist like a solitary obelisk erected by an ancient civilisation, is the concrete pillar marking the summit.

Pride, they say, often comes before a fall. Towards the end of our holiday Martin and I are becoming increasingly confident in our ramblings. At first we set out tentatively, feeling our way in the unfamiliar landscape; but now, with several mountain conquests under our belts, our ambitions are growing. On the last day of our holiday, we hatch a plan to travel up Langdale, walk to Great Gable, then Scafell and return via Bowfell. The hostel warden laughs when we ask his advice about our chosen route and wishes us luck with a sarcastic grin. Later that day we begin to understand why.

We catch the little maroon Ribble bus at the end of Langdale, and weave along the valley heading for road's end at Dungeon Ghyll. Langdale is one of the gems of the Lake District, always green and verdant, and the crags that surround it give some of the finest rock climbing in the National Park. We follow the path up the valley climbing up beside Rossett Ghyll, a small fast-flowing stream, and arrived at Angle Tarn already way behind schedule.

This small lake has something magical about it. It has a sense of remoteness, and I feel as though I am at the very heart of the mountains, the centre of the Lake District. Just above Angle Tarn we arrive at Esk Hause, a spaghetti junction where paths converge from all points of the compass and valleys radiate like the spokes of a wheel. At three o'clock we arrive, exhausted, on the summit of Great Gable. We instantly abandon any plans to go on to Scafell and Bowfell. Our chances of catching the last bus down the valley have vanished and our over-ambitious plan now lies in tatters. At around seven in the evening we finally find ourselves back at Dungeon Ghyll, barely able to take another step. The bus departed long ago, but a phone call to the hostel brings a good-natured Mally, in his Austin 1100, to collect us.

I feel a sense of achievement as I climb back in to the diesel-fumed interior of our chartered bus for the return journey. I could tell you that in total we have walked just under a hundred miles in our week in the Lakes; I can list the hills we've climbed, point out the routes; I know all that. What I didn't know was that this week has changed me, opened up a new chapter, a relationship with the landscape that will leave an indelible mark on my life.

Oh, I almost forgot, but you must have worked it out by now – the beck water didn't kill me.

3
Horizontal Everest

I sigh. "Well, there it is."

Martin, a gangly youth with the aquiline features of a Viking, stands beside me on the lawn. We both stare at a strange orange construction of canvas and elastic.

"Yes, there it is."

We circle the object in silence, peering at it from different angles. There's a wooden pole at each end, joined in the middle by an aluminium sleeve. From the top of each pole two sheets of fragile material, separated by cotton reels, extend out at an angle secured to the grass by an assortment of string and elastic. I take hold of the top of one of the poles and gently shake it. The material flaps alarmingly but, to our surprise, the structure remains upright.

Martin drops to his hands and knees and crawls cautiously towards one end. "Best try it out, then."

Joe is a slim youth with a mop of curly red hair. We're in his garden, and he watches our deliberations with an air of amused curiosity, as though Martin and I are about to perform a bizarre circus act. I follow Martin's example and we lie side by side under the sheets of material, watching the breeze billow the fabric back and forth.

"It *is* a tent," I declare, as if by making the statement I will imbue the flimsy structure with solidity.

Martin doesn't look convinced. The fact that he and I are about to embark on a walk of over two hundred and seventy miles up the Pennine spine of Britain, with this rickety structure as our only means of shelter, inspires neither of us with confidence.

"I think there's something you should know," Joe informs us from his vantage point outside the tent.

As soon as I stick my head out of the flaps that form a door, the 'something' becomes immediately obvious. There, on the grass outside, is a pair of large feet. Martin's, to be precise. The tent is six feet long, two inches longer than me; but, sadly for Martin's extremities, three inches shorter than him. Martin's feet, we decide, will have to suffer the indignity of sleeping outside the tent in a plastic bag.

This is 1974 and Britain is torn by conflict. The IRA bombs the UK mainland. Ted Heath, the Tory Prime Minister, and Joe Gormley, the coal miners' leader, are squaring up for yet another slugfest that will put out the lights in our Merseyside semi. Heath hurls down the gauntlet and calls a general election focused around the question of who governs Britain. The government tries to maximise coal reserves by reducing many non-essential factories to working three days a week. Worse than that, to save power, the TV goes off at 10.30 and everyone has to go to bed. On cold, dark, winter evenings I huddle near the coal fire with my parents. Our Jack Russell sleeps contentedly before the hearth. All is usually peaceful until the BBC News, when Gormley appears, making statements about the miners' solidarity; at that point, my father, a staunch Conservative, rises like a man possessed to hurl abuse at the telly. Our dog, convinced we are under attack, leaps up and barks furiously, searching for unseen assailants. In the mayhem, my mother and I exchange glances.

"Dad, he can't hear you."

She rolls her eyes in despair; this is family life.

Despite the strife surrounding me, I don't worry about politics in 1974. I am nineteen; I have long hair, flared trousers and wing-collar shirts; there are girls and cider; and I am about to go to university. I'd spent the past year in what would today be called a gap year. I'd worked as a volunteer organiser and then at Kelvinators Fridge factory in Bromborough trying to earn some cash to help me get through university. Working in the factory had several results: I can now fit a fridge door in less than forty seconds, my legs are strong from walking miles every day carrying heavy doors, and I now have a burning desire never to return to the inhuman drudgery of the line.

* * *

Full of the optimism of youth, tinged with trepidation, Martin and I board a train and set off for the small Derbyshire village of Edale where the Pennine Way begins. I was at a party the night before and am desperately hung over. My first priority, on arrival, is to find a cafe and force some breakfast down me. That summer's day the small village is full of establishments perfect for reviving the weary traveller, but there is one problem – most of them make it clear we are not welcome. In the small pub and in three cafes we visit there are signs like 'NO BOOTS' or 'CAR DRIVERS ONLY'. We trek around the village until at last we find one small teashop that isn't set to repel borders.

Inside, the place smells of paint and new Formica and it has only recently been opened. Behind the counter a tiny middle-aged woman glares at Martin and me as we trudge through the door, her eyes fixed firmly on my boots. Perhaps she has forgotten to put up her sign.

"Yes?" she barks, as formidable as she is rotund. I am all for sprinting for the door but Martin, older than me, in his second year at Manchester College of Music, and more confident, is determined to see the thing through and orders tea.

"How many sugars?" the woman demands. Clearly young men with long hair, Pink Floyd T-shirts and flared trousers aren't allowed to sugar their own tea. Perhaps she's afraid we might make off with the teaspoon and perform some psychedelic ritual with it.

"Five," Martin replies.

His appetite for all kinds of food is legendary. In an Indian restaurant he recently ordered a curry with a side order of another curry and a plate of chips to go with the rice.

The waitress looks at him, outraged, as though the whole fabric of society will collapse if she gives him five sugars. "How many?" she asks again, making it clear that she had heard the first time, but hoping he might give ground and perhaps reduce the demand to three.

"Five."

Disgusted, the woman spoons in two sugars and stirs vigorously. She then raps the spoon loudly on the cup, wipes it on her apron and places it in a drawer, which she slams shut. The subject of the sweetness of Martin's tea is now closed. This is the first time we have encountered open hostility towards the outdoor fraternity but, as we are later to discover, it is by no means rare in the early seventies.

Most walkers and climbers possess odd assortments of clothes, hijacked from everyday use and pressed into service in the hills. Old jumpers, ragged-arsed trousers, and battered boots are the uniform of the outdoor brigade. In contrast, magazine adverts show smartly dressed young men with Brylcreemed hair helping elegant young women into shiny new cars. The outdoor community is a counter culture, glorying in its raggedness as a mark of experience on the hills and a rejection of what the marketing men tell us we should aspire to be. Hostelry owners take one look at the holes in our jumpers and the rips in our trousers, decide we have no money, and take steps to keep us out.

Taking refuge at the table furthest from the glare of the waitress, Martin and I huddle round a small plastic-backed book that is to become our bible for the next two weeks. The book is a guide to the Pennine Way published only a handful of years earlier, in 1968, by the man we regard as a hillwalking guru, Alfred Wainwright. The Borough Treasurer for Kendal, Wainwright spent his every free moment wandering the fells of northern Britain as an antidote to the tedium of his working days. As I turn the pages of the book, day after day of long hard stages of hillwalking are revealed, all of which we will have to complete carrying our makeshift home.

"Do you think we can do it?" I say as I finish my tea. The pounding in my head gradually begins to subside.

"According to Wainwright we should be able to do it in fourteen days," Martin declares.

I find this a little bit strange. As far as I know, Alfred Wainwright has no idea how far I can walk. In an act of generosity, Mr Wainwright himself has established a fund to buy walkers of the Way a drink at the end of the walk. Shops and pubs stamp your book which, when presented at the inn in Kirk Yetholm, entitles you to a pint of ale. Martin heads towards the Gorgon at the counter to get his first stamp. When I thumb through the book I notice a paragraph that declares the total height climbed over the whole route is 32,000 feet. We are about to climb a horizontal Everest, but I don't mention that bit to Martin.

* * *

The first few miles are easy. We climb beside the babbling waters of Grinds Brook in the green valley that leads away from Edale and on towards the plateau of Kinder Scout, the first hill of many that the Pennine Way has to surmount. The dale is warm and pleasant, the air full of the grassy smells of the meadows and the bleating of hill sheep. The first few miles pass swiftly and Martin and I are unaware of what awaits us higher on the hill.

Soon we are climbing up into the clouds that sit on the top of Kinder, hiding it from view. As we climb it begins to drizzle and the unfamiliar weight of our packs grows with each step. The drizzle soon gives way to rain and we are forced to put on our rain gear. The only thing my meagre budget would allow was a PVC contraption known as a 'Pac-A-Mac'. In 21st century Britain these are all but extinct, but appear to be alive and well in the USA; you will occasionally see herds of American tourists being shepherded round Edinburgh wearing their regulation beige outfits and sporting Pac-A-Macs to keep out the Scottish weather. They are totally waterproof but fragile and cleverly designed to hold in every drop of condensation and press it as close to the body as possible.

For protection against the rain Martin has somehow acquired a voluminous yellow cycle cape complete with matching sou'wester. The cape is fine as long as there is no wind, but should there be even the suggestion of a breeze the yellow covering inverts itself and, if it can't actually carry Marin away, it tries to throttle him. After half an hour in the deluge we are soaked and struggling to make headway against the wind and rain. What we don't know is that there is far worse to come – we are about to encounter the black beast at the heart of Kinder Scout.

I'm following the twists and turns of the vague path, head down, trying to keep the rain out of my face when the ground gives way below me and I sink up to my knees in a black slimy soup. My feet have stopped but the weight of my rucksack keeps my upper body moving and hurls me face forward into a pool of blackness. Martin laughs. I try to get up but can't get any purchase in the mire and the weight of my pack pushes me deeper. I lie, face down, swearing for a moment. Martin laughs again. When I wriggle out of my rucksack and manage to regain the vertical, black ooze drips from the shiny surface of my Pac-A-Mac. We have entered the peat – Kinder's secret weapon. Nothing in our Lake District travels has prepared us for this. The path is dissolving into an organic black custard, a sort of liquid coal that fills my boots and squeegees between my toes with every step.

Kinder Scout doesn't really have a summit; it's like a mountain with the top cut off. What's left, on this stump of a hill, is a plateau of peat hags – mounds of peat topped with grass, conveniently the height of a man so you can't see over them. In thick mist and rain, like it is today, it's a navigation nightmare.

As we huddle round the map I drip black sludge onto the contours. Martin wipes the map clean wordlessly and tries to line the compass up with a feature neither of us can see. I'm beginning to make some sense of maps now, but here, in this featureless wilderness, my fledgling skills desert me.

Martin takes a bearing, then passes me the compass and map so I can check it. "What do you think?"

I look to my left – rain and peat – to my right, more rain and more peat; in fact that's all either of us can see in any direction.

I have no idea where we are or which direction we should go. So I say with confidence, "Looks about right to me," and pass the sodden map back to Martin.

Martin sets off. "All right then. According to Wainwright it's this way."

The god has spoken. Something tells me I am going to hear the phrase "according to Wainwright" a lot over the next two weeks. Following the needle, Martin makes three strides before the peat gets him. Down he goes, face down, unable to get up. I'm too wet and tired to laugh.

This happens over and over again to us both. After a couple of hours we are coated in black sludge to the waist, and my boots gurgle, full of black water. We aren't laughing now. Just as I'm thinking things can't get any worse, Martin's shoes come off completely when he tries to pull his feet out of the muck. Shoeless, he teeters for a moment before falling back into the mud. At least I have my Czechoslovakian boots that stay on my feet; all Martin has is his street shoes. They are branded Tuff by their manufacturers, who claim they are the 'go anywhere shoes'. I don't think they had 270 miles of peat in mind when they said that.

Our progress is painfully slow but eventually we emerge from the mist on the far side of Kinder, wet, filthy and exhausted. That night, under the shelter of our improvised tent, we reflect on the fact that we only covered half the distance planned for that day. Kirk Yetholm, the village at the end of the Way, feels further away than ever.

"This isn't going well," I point out before we drift off to sleep. Martin doesn't respond but I'm sure his feet, outside in the rain, wouldn't disagree.

* * *

The following day we try to pack up our saturated tent. There's a problem: the rain has swelled the wooden sections of the poles and now they won't come apart. Martin pulls with all his might on one end of the pole while I heave at the pointed end. We wrestle back and forth but it resists all our efforts.

We are struggling away when the tousled head of a Boy Scout pops up from behind a wall, his eyes growing wide with alarm. "Mr Walters! Mr Walters!" he yells. "Come quick, there's two men here trying to stab each other." The Boy Scout is immediately joined by several more startled Scouts and, finally, by a concerned Mr Walters. Mr Walters grasps the situation instantly and clips the tousled head behind the ear.

"Idiot." The Scout Master glares at his errant charge. "Have you tried heating it up?" he enquires of us. We hadn't. When we try this, it comes apart. Obviously years of experience in the tented world of the Boy Scouts have not been wasted on Mr Walters.

Yesterday we battled with one dark peat monster. Today we must face a bigger one – Bleaklow. The clue about the nature of Bleaklow is in its name. If you look up 'Godforsaken place' you'll find a photo of the hill. Even Wainwright himself, the man whose love of the hills is legendary, has little time for it. He wrote:

Nobody loves Bleaklow. All who get on it are glad to get off it. This section is commonly considered the toughest part of the Pennine Way. It is certainly mucky, too often belaboured by rain and wind and frightening in mist.

The rain grew heavier as we climbed into the very mist he was talking about. After an hour or so the sleeves of my plastic mac began to fall off and soon I was left with a long waistcoat. My flimsy overtrousers surrendered to the enemy and split down the middle. We were plunging into an even worse nightmare of peat than the day before.

I had read that the peat on the hill's summit has twice the lead content of the surrounding land; its pools and puddles, of which there are many, have the PH levels of battery acid. As I surveyed the black wasteland that surrounded us I could believe both of those things and imagine far worse. In the morass of mist and peat every pool begins to look the same as its neighbour, and after a while we have little idea of our position on the moor.

In the end we simply head north, following the few footprints we can find. Now and again a forlorn sign appears, leaning at a drunken angle, the peat too insubstantial to support it.

We stop to eat a Mars bar. Mid-munch, Martin stops. "Did you hear that?"

"Hear what?"

So remote is this place I wouldn't be too surprised to hear the howl of the hound of the Baskervilles as Sherlock Holmes did on the Great Grimpen Mire. A moment later I hear an unmistakable call for help.

We abandon the chocolate and head towards the sound. The calling comes from two German hikers, one of whom is waist deep in a pool of slime and stuck fast. I try to grab him and haul him out, but each time I simply sink into the peat while he remains fixed. It's beginning to look as if the peat monster will claim its victim when someone spots an old plank of wood.

I stand on the plank. The ooze beneath my feet quakes and shudders but the plank keeps me out of the jaws of the monster. I heave on the German, who cries out in pain: "My back!"

I hesitate for a moment but decide that he can't stay where he is, so I keep pulling despite his cries of protest. There's a sucking rumbling sort of noise and moments later the German and I are lying in the mud together. Once out, far from being grateful, the German keeps moaning about his back. I'm tempted to stick him back in the hole.

* * *

After several more hours of trudging through the evil peat and dodging the boggy mantraps, we finally descend to the road and stagger to the hostel at Crowden.

It is a blessed relief to get out of our sodden, peat-stained clothes and head for the warmth and bustle of the hostel kitchen where we can cook a meal. The kitchen is full of other walkers jostling for the gas hobs around the room. I am cooking sausages – about the limit of my culinary ability – in a frying pan big enough to feed several Scout groups. They do nothing small in Youth Hostels.

There are signs everywhere: some proclaim where pans are to be stored, others which fridge can be used; yet more indicate where spoons and knives must be placed after use. Over the sink there is one sign larger than all the others. In letters nearly a foot high it declares, 'SAUCEPANS MUST BE WASHED IMMEDIATLEY AFTER COOKING.'

Despite the hubbub one voice, a woman's, rises above all others. This is the hostel warden barking orders at everyone in range. Youth Hostel wardens are a strange breed; they come in all shapes and sizes but are united by two things, a love of regulations and an obsessive desire to exert an iron rule over the hostels in their charge.

Martin takes his courage in both hands and approaches the warden. She is a large, stout woman with blonde hair in braids and the suggestion of a moustache beneath her broad nose.

"Excuse me. That sign, does it mean we have to let our food go cold while we wash the pans?"

The question is innocent enough but the woman fixes him with a glare that would make Medusa proud. She heaves her considerable bosom in outrage and points to the sign, then says, "Immediately!"

"Oh yes," Martin stammers, "immediately means right away then."

"Immediately," her bosom rising and falling with each word, "means, immediately." With that she turns and charges off to seek out some poor unfortunate who has placed a spoon in the wrong drawer. That night we dine on cold sausages.

Later, grateful not to be sleeping in our scanty tent, we climb into bed, happy to be dry and warm. I close my eyes for little more than a moment before I am dragged into instant wakefulness by trumpets and bassoons blasting out inches from my head. For a few seconds my stunned brain can't make sense of what is happening, then I realise the awful sound that has woken me is music and *The Ride of the Valkyries* is issuing forth at ninety decibels from a speaker above my bed.

"Jesus Christ!" I cry out, realising that the whole night has passed and it is morning.

As I cower beneath the sheets, the door bursts open and a pair of bosoms charges into the room closely followed by its owner, the warden. She tears open the curtains and light floods into the room.

"Time to get up!"

With that she and her bosoms are gone, leaving everyone in the room trembling in the aftermath of a Wagnerian nightmare. God knows what would have happened if she had entered the room and found some poor soul enjoying a secret cigarette by the open window. He would have been nailed to the wall of the hostel as a hideous blood eagle warning with, of course, a sign beneath his mangled corpse: 'NO SMOKING MEANS <u>NO SMOKING</u>'.

* * *

The following day, through sheets of torrential rain, we cross Saddleworth Moor and the even boggier White Moss. By the end of the day we're saturated and exhausted but we are beginning to make progress through the landscape. This is the first day we complete our planned route. As we travel further north the treacherous peat gives way to more substantial ground and, most importantly of all, after five days of deluge, it stops raining.

Long distance walking is about rhythm – not only the rhythm of one foot in front of the other but also the rhythm of the land. Hills follow dales, valleys follow summits, descents follow climbs. The days go by and, as the miles drift beneath our boots, we cease to struggle with the country; we learn to be part of it.

There is something unique about taking a linear multi-day journey on foot. The day walker starts and finishes at the same spot – after his walk's end he will return to the familiar, to his routine, to a place where nothing has changed. If you take a longer journey – let's call it a trek – your home comes with you on your back, every day's end is different, and every morning you wake up somewhere else. The routine you follow is decided in a dialogue between you and the land you walk through. The trekker is constantly asking questions. How long will it take to get to the next shelter? Can I make it to that village? Will I run out of food? The answers to those questions decide where the trekker sleeps, the view he sees when he wakes in the morning, what challenges the coming day will bring.

As we move further and further north the character of the land changes. We leave behind the dark cloying peat of the Peak

District, cross wild moorlands with names like Withins Height, Lumbs Tower and even over Wuthering Heights of Brontë fame (or, at least, the places that inspired this fictional location). The day we cross is cold, bleak and windswept. Heathcliffe must have been a pretty hardy soul to live in a place like this. Always heading northwards, we cross the limestone pavements of Malham Cove and head on towards one of the biggest hills on the route, Pen-y-Ghent. Now, even that falls easily beneath our feet.

We arrive in the small village at the foot of the hill too late to catch the only shop, and are compelled to dine on a piece of mouldy cheese I find in the bottom of my rucksack and a couple of packets of peanuts. Such privations are commonplace to us now. One evening we experience the ultimate luxury. In a scene from *The Famous Five Go Mad on the Pennine Way*, we gorge ourselves on sandwiches with lashings of jam provided in the kitchen of a farm where we buy a meal. The farmer's wife keeps bringing us bread and jam while her husband sleeps, oblivious, before the peat fire, his dog at his feet. We eat plate after plateful, miles of walking having given us boundless appetites. Eventually, out of politeness, we decline a fourth plateful and head out into the night to find the local pub. The night is bright with stars. As we swallow pints of the local potent brew, Old Peculier, we relax in the knowledge that the Scottish border is not far away and the end of our quest is drawing near.

I hadn't thought much about gate catches before I walked the Pennine Way. Over the thousands of years gate catches have been in existence, you would think the human race would have agreed upon one design and stuck to it. The opposite appears to be true, however. We encountered hundreds if not thousands of farmer's gates on the Pennine Way, each having a different design of its own, with the result that one meets with an infinite variety of gate fastenings. Martin, who would freely admit he is not the most mechanically minded of people, would constantly struggle with each new device as though confronted with a never-ending series of Gordian knots.

Somehow Martin and I are always late. It takes us longer than we expect to take down our tent. Martin's pack is full to bursting and every morning he battles with straps and zips in a desperate struggle to force his possessions inside. I had purchased the cheapest rucksack I could find for the walk. For no reason I could fathom, it is called a Sky Pack and was probably manufactured by four-year-olds in some terrible Middle Eastern sweatshop. It began to disintegrate on the first day and after a hundred miles it is now held together by string and bits of tape. Unlike Martin I carry practically nothing in it, so I have plenty of space and no packing problems.

On walks like these it's often the unexpected that creates the strongest memories. Six days into the walk we are coming down off the hill. It's late, of course, and below us the village of Mankinholes is settling down for the evening amongst the rolling Yorkshire hills. This is my favourite time of day; I look forward to finding a shop, something to eat and drinking a few pints of local ale while we rest our legs at a village pub.

This evening, we walk weary legged and thirsty into the small village. The stone cottages and tiny pub grow out of the landscape. We'd seen the same stone that built them earlier in the day, breaking through the heather high on the hill; and as we walk lower, in the fading light of evening, we find the stone again in the walls that enclose the sheep-studded fields. Now, in the village itself, the stone reappears in the walls and crooked chimneys of the inns and houses as they follow the contours of the land.

It's so unlike the brick-built housing estates of my suburban Merseyside home, which subsume the landscape. So rigorous are the straight lines of its streets, so uniform the rectangular gardens of the mass-produced semis that little trace can be seen of the land beneath. In my home town, as in most others across Britain, the curves of small valleys have been bulldozed away and the courses of old streams channelled into culverts and buried beneath tarmac and concrete. The houses, pebble dashed or built of anonymous red brick, reflect nothing of the land they occupy – but these Pennine villages, built in odd curves and triangles, are moulded by the countryside in sympathy with it. The villages have an antiquity I have never experienced before. These twisted houses that follow the curving banks of brooks speak of an England long forgotten in urban Britain.

This evening it's so late we forget about food and head straight for the pub. After closing time we look for a campsite and can only find a rather up-market caravan park that has no place for tents. Martin and I stand disconsolately in the driveway and are just about to head away when a portly little man comes running out of the caravan park's bar.

"Have you just come down off the hill?"

"Yes," I answer.

"Well, put your tent up on the lawn. I'll get rid of these caravan chumps in the bar and you can come in for a few pints."

Later, as we relish our pints after closing time, the owner explains that being a walker himself he has no time for the soft van dwellers who provide his income, and prefers the company of true mountain men like ourselves. That night we sleep in luxury on the feather bed of the campsite bar's lawn, cradled in soft grass and illicit beer, sound in the knowledge that we had been admitted to the elite.

* * *

Despite a few luxurious rests, our bodies are beginning to feel the strain. We wake every morning with feet sore, legs aching, feeling the after-effects of the day before and even the days before that. The Way is taking its toll on us. Martin is sitting staring at his left leg, the anaesthetic qualities of last night's cider having worn off.

"I think there's something wrong with my foot." His foot is twice its normal size and so swollen he no longer needs to lace up his shoe.

"You might have broken something," I offer, in a blinding flash of medical insight.

He looks sadly at his Tuff shoes, the cause of the problem. The Tuff shoes look back at him. They have been immersed in peat, pounded across drenched moorland and rock-strewn paths for over a hundred and fifty miles; they don't look so tuff any more.

"I'll just keep going and see how it goes."

I am not convinced it would go at all.

As the Scottish border approaches the land begins to change again. It has a wilder feel than any we have encountered so far, and everything seems to be on a larger scale. Martin's finger follows the thin dashed line as it twists and turns across the map, cutting across contours and over rivers towards the tiny village of Kirk Yetholm, our goal for these past two weeks. He traces the line of the path as it heads over the Cheviot Hills.

"Eighteen, nineteen, twenty," he counts, totting up the miles we have to cover the following day. His fingertip is now descending away from the Cheviot towards our goal. "Twenty-four, twenty-five…" I'm growing increasingly concerned as the length of the journey rises. "Twenty-six, twenty-seven…" Still his index finger is short of our destination, until finally it rests on the village pub in the border village. "Twenty-nine."

"Twenty-nine! Are you sure?" I ask, a little too loudly, causing the regulars in the Byrness Inn to raise their heads from contemplating their ale.

"Twenty-nine."

We sit staring at the map spread out before us, weighted down with cider glasses.

"That's a long way."

Remember my fondness for stating the obvious. We've come a great distance – two hundred and fifty miles to be precise – but the Way has saved its longest and toughest stretch for last. It's like a video game; we have to fight the toughest boss at the end.

"We could camp halfway," I suggest.

Martin looks up from the map and gives me a 'have you taken leave of your senses?' kind of look. Our little shelter, composed of cotton reels and bed sheets, has survived so far – but that has been in the lower campsites of the Yorkshire Dales. This is border country, higher and much less hospitable. In my mind I see a dark, lonely night on the high moors. Rain cascades down in torrents as the wind rampages through the heather like a mad beast. There's a flash of lightning and in the momentary burst of light I see two forlorn, saturated figures clinging, like shipwrecked sailors, to the tattered remains of what used to be a tent.

"We'll just have to set off early and walk it, then."

* * *

Shortly after 8 a.m. Martin and I begin the climb away from the three houses, one pub and a hostel where we spent the night. We are not the two young men who drank tea in the cafe at Edale two weeks ago. The casual observer would notice some obvious differences. Martin is limping, the result of his swollen foot. My Pac-A-Mac now has no sleeves and only one button remains in place to hold it closed. My flimsy waterproof trousers have capitulated completely and split down both legs so that they hang like a nylon skirt from my waistband. The cheap pack I purchased for the trip has burst in a number of places and is only held on to its frame by some orange bailing twine I stole from a farmer's fence. Every step I take is accompanied by a groan from my pack; as the string stretches the load tries to slide sideways and escape. We look, I suppose you would have to say, the worse for wear. That's what you would see on the outside, but inside we are different too. Day after day we have thrust aching legs into filthy, peat-stained jeans, crammed our meagre belongings into disintegrating rucksacks, and walked until we are exhausted.

Today is no different but it is longer. There's no doubt it's going to hurt – it always does – but our concern is just how much pain we'll have to endure before we stagger into Kirk Yetholm and can finally say goodbye to the Way. When we set out we didn't know how far we could walk, how many rolling hills we could climb and if we could carry our rucksacks to the finish 270 miles away. We've learned a thing or two by now. We've learned how to settle in to a steady pace that we can keep going all day, and we've learned how to read the landscape and find the easiest route through bog and over hills. We've also learned to break this big beast down, to set our sights on the top of the next hill, the floor of the next valley. The whole walk is too big to contemplate; let's just make it to that farmhouse, to the next road, across the next field, over the next stile.

We begin to climb out of the valley. The morning breeze tousles the tops of the serried ranks of pine trees in the forestry plantation to the east of the track. The forest is industrial in the symmetrical precision of its planting; each tree is equidistant from its neighbour and the plantation itself sits in an incongruous rectangle stamped on the landscape. Between the rows of trees, corridors of trunks lead to an impenetrable darkness in which nothing but the trees themselves prosper. The scent of pine fills the air as we make our steady progress up the hillside. It is dry here on the lower slopes, but the hillside is shrouded in a grey mist that threatens to return us to the miserable sodden creatures we were in the early days of our walk.

As we climb we both settle in to our own pace. I am learning to listen, to find just the right pace to take me up each hill I encounter. I've learned that every hill is different and that your body changes every day – the trick is to learn to adapt. I listen to my breathing, to the regular creak of the string holding my pack together, to the crunch of the gravel beneath my feet. This will be a long day; I have to find just the right economical pace to carry me over the next twenty-eight miles.

As I find today's pace the mist engulfs us, coating the heather with tiny sparkling droplets of dew and reducing the view to the next hundred yards. A moment or two ago we were walking in the wide expanses of the border country; now our world shrinks to a few yards of dank mist. Closer to the Scottish border the landscape changes. The country grows wilder, the villages fewer and the population sparse. Now we have passed beyond Hadrian's Wall and into the Border country, a place with a long, turbulent history. As we climb towards the hills of the Cheviot the Way takes us over Roman roads where legions once marched. The place feels remote and has probably changed very little since the road was built. I wouldn't be too surprised if a Roman legion marched out of the mist at that very moment. I imagine them standing, wrapped in soaked woollen cloaks, their armour smeared with raindrops, standards leaning sadly to one side, as the fine rain penetrates their tunics. Looking down at the remnants of my Pac-A-Mac I realise we would have had much in common.

Our legs are tired and we are beginning to slow, feeling the weight of the rucksacks, as we head towards the summit of the Cheviot, twenty miles in to our walk. Two weeks ago we wouldn't have been able to walk this distance at all. Now, with miles of hill and bog behind us, our legs are made of sterner stuff.

I wait for Martin to catch me up. "We're going to make it."

Martin grins back. "Aye, looks like it."

He a produces a rain-soaked bar of chocolate and we share a moment of silent celebration, safe in the knowledge that, despite our rickety tent and makeshift equipment, we are about to succeed in our quest.

In between mouthfuls of chocolate I ask, "Shall we do the Cheviot?"

The Way doesn't actually pass over the summit of the hill – it bypasses it by almost a mile – so this will require a detour. It's a testament to the fitness we've gained that we are even considering it.

We dump our packs. As we head into the mist towards the top we meet an old friend. There, waiting for us, is the peat. The slime monster is ready to pounce. A small fence attempts to cling to the perpendicular; the wire, which should be supported by the posts, is supporting them. The only part of the ground that isn't black treacle clings to the base of the posts and I hop from one post to the next until I finally reach a point where even they capitulate and lie, like sunken ships, beached in the mire.

Then the summit of the Cheviot appears briefly through the mist and, for a moment, the weak sun highlights shallow pools in the peat. The landscape appears surreal, prehistoric, with a stark beauty. I'm about to head for the summit when I reflect that my feet are dry right now. The memory of the death bogs of Kinder comes flooding back.

I turn to Martin as he totters precariously on an island of gloop, and deliver my verdict, "Sod this!"

Martin squints through the mist, rainwater trickling down his aquiline features, caught for a second by the lure of the summit at hand. I can see that he wants to carry on but, in his mind, cogs are whirring. Later he tells me that he remembers Kinder and Bleaklow, recalls falling headlong into the black morass of those boot-swallowing hells.

He pauses to wipe a large drop of water that drips from his nose. "Well, I suppose we could always come back another day." I can hear that a part of Martin wants to carry on into the morass and make it to the summit cairn.

"Oh yes, yes," I reply, feigning enthusiasm, "That's what we'll do, come back another day." I'm trying desperately to sound as though I have a burning desire to return for the summit whilst, at the same moment, making a mental vow never to come back to this elevated quagmire. Much to my relief, Martin agrees to leave the summit of the Cheviot for another day. We shoulder our packs and begin the long descent towards Kirk Yetholm.

* * *

As we descend, the open moorland yields to fields of cattle and we leave the mist-shrouded mountains behind to find a gentler climate below. Two miles outside the little border village, our goal for the past two weeks, we meet a middle-aged couple, with neatly creased shorts and clean white hiking socks, out for a stroll. It's the socks I notice. It's been two weeks since I put on a pair of clean socks, so long ago that I've almost forgotten that such unimaginable luxury exists.

The man stops and stares at me and Martin. He steps to the side of the track to let us pass, giving us a much wider berth than necessary. At first I can't understand what it is about us that fascinates him but then I realise what he sees. We are both dripping rainwater, but we're so used to being wet that we no longer notice the rain. Our tattered jeans are blackened with peat to the knees. The fragments of what was once a Pac-A-Mac cling forlornly about my chest, and my pack leans drunkenly from my back; the twine that was holding it together has broken. Martin is limping behind me, lurching under the weight of his rucksack.

"Are you doing the Pennine Way?" the man in clean socks asks. I confirm his suspicions and then he asks, "How far are you walking today?"

"Twenty-eight miles," I intone, unable to take my eyes off his socks.

He shakes his head sadly. "Too far, too far!"

An hour later we are ringing the doorbell of the Kirk Yetholm Youth Hostel, a stone-built place that looks to have been extended in every direction when it was converted from village school to hostel. The warden doesn't ask us if we've just completed the Way. He doesn't need to.

This warden is unique amongst his breed; he has no rules. You are expected to stagger in to the place exhausted, go to the pub to celebrate, come back drunk and sleep in late the following day. Not wanting to disappoint, we cross the grassy village square to the Border Hotel, which is a bizarre mixture of mock-Tudor and stone walls. Martin, clutching his little book full of stamps, heads to the bar.

A film unwinds inside my head while I sit waiting for my free beer. It shows hills and paths, great sweeping tracts of wild places, tiny stone villages, gates, farm yards, streams and villages; two hundred and seventy miles of the English landscape that, for a while, we were part of and now, I realise, have become part of me.

Martin returns from the bar with two pints of beer and Wainwright's guidebook full of stamps. "I had to pay," he announces in dismay. "Apparently Wainwright's fund to buy you a beer after finishing the Way ran out two months ago."

I stir from my musings. "What?"

Martin places the beer before me and we sit in silence for a moment. I take a sip of my beer.

"Wainwright! What a bastard."

4

Three Men in a Tent

It's hot, very hot – in fact it's the hottest summer for two hundred years. I climb slowly, increasingly conscious of the weight of my rucksack. Every breath pulls dry, hot air into my lungs. With each step I take on the path, a drop of sweat falls from my nose and splashes on the parched stones at my feet. I stop briefly, gathering my breath and wiping the sweat from my brow. My eyes wander across the outlines of the hills as they shimmer in the heat haze. This place astounds me. Martin, Joe and I have been walking for three days and, ranged all around us, are green ridges of hills like the waves of a vast sea. Were this the Lake District we would be walking between villages, through farmland, encountering habitation and roads every few miles. But this is our first foray into the wilderness of the Scottish Highlands.

Here, the valleys are empty. The only signs of human life are the occasional Land Rover track or the ruined shell of a crofter's cottage. I am used to paths, signposts, groups of people with dogs and bright orange cagoules. Here, we three denim-clad, long-haired young men meet no one on our journey. We are the only people in this vast landscape. Despite the heat, I revel in this sense of freedom. Best of all there are no signs. Merseyside is full of signs: 'Private. Keep Out', 'No Trespassing', 'Trespassers will be prosecuted'. Worst of all, in driveways, 'No Turning'.

Just how precious do you have to be about the piece of tarmac outside your house to try and forbid the rest of humanity from spending even a few seconds on it?

"There is no law of trespass in Scotland," Martin explained to me in the pub one night before we set off. That concept alone leaves me full of wonder.

"You mean you can go where you want?" I had asked him, astonished by the prospect of such freedom. Now, in this huge, wild place I begin to understand what that freedom means.

"Not too far now," Martin announces as the three of us huddle around his old cloth map. Once we crest the ridge and descend into the valley beyond, there will only be the South Cluanie Ridge to climb up and over before we can walk out to the road and reach civilisation at Shiel Bridge. Already I am dreaming of the cafe there, the delights of the small shop, and – most of all – the little pub Martin promises awaits us there. In our effort to save weight we have rigorously calculated our food rations. On this, the last leg of our three-day walk, the only food that remains between us is three chocolate biscuits. These we have agreed to consume before the last climb out to the road.

Joe's Afro of red hair is overheating in the sun. "Great, I'll be glad to lose this bloody pack."

Ready for the last push over the ridge, I shoulder my pack. Its external aluminium frame takes the opportunity to dig into my flesh as I settle it on my shoulders. Half an hour later I am grateful to feel a cool breeze against my cheek, but even happier because I know that it heralds the summit of the ridge. Images of beer and smiling, friendly women form in my mind. Then it happens. I find myself staring in disbelief. Below us should lie a wide glen with a small river and a short walk to the south side of the ridge between us and Glen Shiel – but what we see is a huge expanse of water. Water that has no right to be there. I look away and turn back in the hope that it's an optical illusion, but the lake refuses to move.

"We've gone the wrong bloody way," I call to Martin and Joe as they catch up with me on the ridge.

"We can't be lost," Martin says, unfolding the old map.

"There's a fucking lake!" I run up and down, perhaps hoping the illusion will be dispelled if I can get a better angle on it.

Martin dumps his pack and stares in disbelief at the expanse of water. "There is no lake," he insists and solemnly hands me the map as though one glance at it will evaporate the thousands of gallons of water barring our way.

Perhaps I should explain. The three of us have developed a couple of navigational mantras forged in the mists of Cumbria. The first is, 'The compass is always right'. We learnt this the hard way after following our instincts on a few occasions when the flickering red needle seemed to be sending us in an absurd direction. When our faith wavered, magnetic north punished us like a vengeful god by revealing, when the mist cleared, that we were miles from our intended destination. We are now high priests in the order of the compass and, whenever one of us dares to doubt the accuracy of the needle, we will chant our compass mantra and follow its lead in silent devotion.

Our second mantra is the one we are resorting to now: 'If it's not on the map it doesn't exist'. Anything that isn't marked on the map has no navigational purpose and therefore can be ignored. Thus we treat new houses, forestry plantations, tracks and fences that were not written in our topographical bible as figments of other people's imagination.

I crouch on all fours, the map spread out before me, consulting the oracle of the compass. No matter how I twist the map the landscape in front of me doesn't fit. The landscape behind me, oddly, fits fine. Slowly an explanation for our plight begins to take shape.

"They've built a bloody reservoir, haven't they?"

"Oh shit!" Joe hurls himself and his pack down on the heather in despair.

'They' made a bloody good job of it too. This isn't a small lake we can walk around in an hour or two – this is an inland ocean that stretches for miles across our path. There will be no beer and smiling girls tonight.

"When was this map printed?" Joe demands, ever practical. Martin is an avid collector of old maps. He spends days in the back of dusty old shops, seeking out ancient relics of the cartographer's art. Many of the maps we have used are printed on cloth, their contours drawn by the hands of long-dead map makers. We've used them happily until now, based on the assumption that mountains don't change.

"Er, 1954," Martin confesses. Neither of us says anything, but we all know that the days of old maps are over.

There is no path around the lochside so we stagger along the boulder-strewn shore, moving constantly in a clockwise direction, our left legs always higher than our right. Martin stumbles on to the rocks and opens a savage cut across his knee. We stop to patch him up with a plaster from one of his numerous plastic bags. Every one of his belongings has its own plastic bag to keep it dry. Packing can take him an eternity – should a bag get lost he has to open every other one to find it. Joe and I each have our possessions in one large plastic bag, but that's too simple for Martin.

For this trip I saved up and now proudly boast an orange Karrimor pack. It has a tubular aluminium frame with shoulder straps attached to it and the sack itself is strapped to the frame. The pack creaks and groans as the weight shifts on each step but it's a massive improvement on the wartime relic I'd used in the Lakes, or the fragile 'Sky Pack' that sacrificed its life on the Pennine Way. I even have a cagoule – well, at least, something that looks like a cagoule: nylon, and as cheap and cheerful as they come, but it's the best I can afford. The cagoule is fine, as long as it doesn't rain, because I doubt it could withstand more than the briefest of showers.

At last we find ourselves where we should have been five hours ago: where the old path emerges from the loch as though from a submerged village. Exhausted by the heat and our interminable diversion around the water, we gratefully erect our tent. It's made from blue, heavy canvas and possesses that ultimate luxury, a sewn-in groundsheet. This tent was never designed for backpacking. You are supposed to drive it around in a car and put it up with folding chairs and a little plastic table somewhere nice near the sea. We are lugging it over the mountains but, despite its weight, once up it is strong and comfortable.

The downside of our enforced camp is that we didn't plan our food to cover it. All we have is the three biscuits I am carrying. Once our sleeping bags are out we settle down for our feast. I fumble in my rucksack and pull out two of the biscuits, then spend a minute or two searching the pockets for the third but come up empty handed.

"I can't find the other one," I explain. This gets Martin and Joe's full attention. When all you have is a handful of biscuits their location assumes immense importance. I tip out my rucksack; spare socks, toothbrush and an assortment of clothes land on the grass, but no third biscuit.

"It's got to be somewhere," Joe says. Frenzied searching ensues. Sleeping bags are shaken out, each rucksack ransacked, but the whereabouts of the biscuit remains a mystery. Now Joe is suspicious. "You sure you don't know where that biscuit went?"

I'm stung by the inference that I might have secretly scoffed it. "No, of course not."

"Well there were three," Martin, the mathematician of our group, interjects.

"I know that. It must have… got lost."

As I say these words I realise they sound like the pleading of a guilty man. Martin and Joe look at me with silent accusations in their eyes. Suspicion clouds the air. That night we each dine on two thirds of a biscuit. We are three men, miles from anywhere, in some of the most magnificent scenery in the world, and the one thought that obsesses all of us is the fate of a Jacob's Club biscuit.

We wake to the mountain breeze tugging at the blue canvas walls of our tent. A few tea bags are found lurking in one of the multitude of plastic bags in Martin's rucksack so breakfast is a cup of black tea. As we make our way towards the ridge we become increasingly obsessed by thoughts of food. The merits of various types of chocolate biscuit are discussed. Joe, it emerges, is an expert in confectionery. Not only does he know which biscuits have the thickest chocolate but he also knows which are real chocolate and which have only fake coverings. A debate over the best type of pork pie lasts half an hour. Joe also has an encyclopaedic knowledge of sausages.

As we progress through the wilderness I realise that I have spent my whole life surrounded by food. I have never been anywhere where the possibility of real hunger exists. We have only missed a couple of meals, yet here, if we want to eat, we must walk. Mountains have a way of reminding you that you can never take even the most basic things for granted.

It's 9 p.m. when we walk in to the bar of the Kintail Lodge Hotel in Shiel Bridge, a white-painted building that was once a small cottage but has been extended over the years in every direction. The bar is heaving with hairy backpackers, climbers, students and young people like us, all in various states of intoxication. Someone is playing a guitar and a sunburned youth is singing a tuneless version of a Pink Floyd song. Huddled in a corner of the bar and drinking with expressions of quiet desperation are a handful of older men. These are locals, forced to sit out this seasonal invasion of walkers, waiting for winter and the chance to drink in peace when the throngs of hill-goers have dwindled away.

Martin is a man with a mission. Joe and I are hungry, but Martin – six feet three inches of gangly eating machine – is close to collapse. Eventually he forces his way to the bar, through the rowdy rabble shouting for beer, and asks for the menu. The large lady behind the bar greets his request with incredulity.

The chef, she points out – as if Martin should have been aware – went home an hour ago. We later discover that getting food in Highland hotels is well-nigh impossible. Bars in the Highlands are for drinking, not eating. As far as I can make out, chefs only work about fifteen minutes a day and then never at meal times.

That night we feast on crisps, Mars bars and peanuts. I drink my body weight in Guinness, telling myself it is as close to being a meal as drink can get. The next morning when I wake, Martin has already left; he is sitting outside the campsite cafe waiting for it to open. When at last the owner arrives and unlocks the door, Martin amazes him by eating four breakfasts in succession.

* * *

This is 1976 and the hottest summer on record. In the south of England it hasn't rained for forty-five days, and Heathrow records sixteen consecutive days over 30°C. The record-breaking drought forces the Government to act. In the hardest-hit areas water rationing and standpipes are introduced. The Government even appoints a Minister for Drought, Dennis Howell, which is like being handed a poison chalice unless you have divine powers and can summon water from the skies. Days after his appointment, the heavens open and there is such a deluge that parts of the country are threatened with flooding. Oddly no one gives Dennis the credit he so obviously deserves; he is cruelly nicknamed 'Minister for Rain', proving that in politics there are no winners.

Britain is also in financial crisis (are we ever not?), and the pound is devalued. Harold Wilson resigns as prime minister and leader of the Labour Party, and James Callaghan replaces him. The Conservative Party elects a woman called Margaret Thatcher to be their leader. My dad, a staunch Tory with an attitude to women that comes out of the Dark Ages, reckons she won't last.

Not much of that worries me. I have just finished my first year studying sociology at Leicester University. My A Level grades were fairly poor, but someone on the admissions panel at Leicester took into account the limited academic support I'd received and let me in. I didn't know what to expect. I was hoping for girls and drugs but I wasn't sure if I'd survive academically or financially. I got close to full grant but, having never lived on my own, I didn't know how far that would stretch. I need not have worried. I coped with the academic work and found that if I worked consistently but not too hard I could get by. Thanks to my student grant, I owned two pairs of jeans, could afford all the beer I needed and even had cash left over at the end of term. I spent the early part of that summer working as a barman in a local Conservative club and saved up so that I could spend two weeks walking in Scotland in September before the university term started again. Martin had already finished his studies and was the only one of us to have a real job, working for the recently established Department of Health and Social Security in Blackpool where he made his home.

A few weeks before the biscuit incident, Martin spreads the map out on the dining room table of Joe's house near Raby Mere on the Wirral. More accurately it is Joe's parents' home, a large detached house called Honister. As teenagers we adopted the place as our HQ. Joe's long-suffering parents tolerate endless cider-drinking parties accompanied by the latest albums from

Pink Floyd.

"We could start here." Martin points to the tiny Highland village of Lochailort on the road to Mallaig. "And then we could walk through here." I'm following his finger as he traces a line through incredibly wild country.

I'm cautious. I've seen that finger before, on the Pennine Way, and I know that finger can cover a lot of ground and get you in deep trouble.

"There's nothing there," I point out as the finger moves northwards from valley to valley across high passes and never meeting a road or any sign of habitation.

"It's certainly remote," Joe says. "Do you think we can carry enough food?"

One of the joys of planning expeditions like this is working out just what might be possible. It's now that the seeds of disaster or success are planted. None of us have seen anywhere even close to this remote. The vastness of the landscape excites us. I've never seen anywhere so devoid of people as this place appears on the map. On the entire landscape there is only one major road and a couple of tiny single-track routes.

"And we could end up here." Martin's finger arrives in Glen Shiel, having covered an impossible distance of nothing. His finger made the journey without any difficulty; I'm not sure I can. "Three days, I think."

Martin is chief mathematician and store master. We plan everything right down to the number of chocolate biscuits required. There are three of us so we need three of everything. We set a date and agree to meet at the village of Glenfinnan. It's my first trip to Scotland.

As we walk up the driveway of the Glenfinnan Hotel we are filled with trepidation. The hotel is an imposing building with battlements, turrets and a cannon. The lawn is immaculately groomed and there are Daimlers parked outside. With our faded flared denims and long hair we are out of place, and having encountered hostility to the walking classes on the Pennine Way we expect to be turned away. An impressive man in full Highland dress guards the entrance, we suspect, to repel 'the likes of us' at the point of the claymore that hangs by his side.

"Can we get a drink here?" I ask tentatively.

Despite his fearsome appearance he greets us like long-lost friends. "Of course, boys, in you go."

It's my first encounter with the Highland term 'boys'. Here it is not a disparaging term, merely an address used for all groups of men. Boys can be in their eighties. Inside, the heads of countless stags stare at us silently from wood-panelled walls, and enormous salmon sit frozen in time. There's a huge redheaded man standing behind the bar. Only his nose and a pair of glaring eyes are visible from behind his wild ginger beard. As I approach the bar he towers over me, great forearms folded across his chest with phrases like 'NO SURRENDER' tattooed in crude blue letters on them. I decide that the important thing at this moment is to show no fear.

"Have you any food?" I ask, hesitantly.

"We've poison bridies," he replies in a broad Glaswegian accent. I wonder if this is some Highland test of manhood. Should I eat the poison bridies and die a horrible death, or refuse and forever be branded a coward? It goes quiet in the bar. If this were a Western it would be the moment in the saloon when the piano player ceases playing and the gunfighters nervously finger the butts of their revolvers.

"Sorry?" I manage, unable to comprehend that any establishment could sell food that is actually toxic.

"We've poison bridies!" he repeats slowly and deliberately, as if talking to a foreigner or an imbecile.

I've never felt more English. It's as if I'm standing before him in a pinstriped suit, with rolled-up umbrella and bowler hat, demanding "I say, do you do scones?"

I feel personally responsible for the Clearances. I want to fall to my knees and say "I'm sorry, it was me who sent your relatives to Canada and replaced them with sheep. I did it! Well not me exactly but my grandfather. We found his diary it said, '*Spent day replacing Scots with sheep. Note to self: buy more sheep, more Scots than expected.*'"

I gather all my courage for one last stand, expecting at any moment for the locals to burn me at the stake in some ancient Highland ritual. "Excuse me, but have you any bridies that aren't poisoned?" I stammer.

The barman glares at me with uncomprehending rage. A bearded young man at the bar is helpless with laughter. He turns to me, laughing, and says, "What he's trying to tell you is, they've *pies and bridies.*"

Language barrier overcome, the three of us sit down in the corner of the hotel bar. None of us had ever heard of bridies, which have never made it south of Hadrian's Wall. It turns out they are a kind of pasty, mainly differentiated from the Cornish variety by the fact that they contain no potatoes, are mostly meat, and are not poisonous at all.

It is Saturday night and the bar is alive with locals. The Daimler owners are downing whisky shoulder to shoulder with fish farm workers and ghillies (Highland gamekeepers). If there is a class barrier here it seems to be forgotten in the bar at weekends, and even we, aliens from the southern world, are welcomed with open arms. As the beer and whisky flow we feel as far from Merseyside as it is possible to get.

Then the room falls silent and, to our amazement, the ginger bear working behind the bar produces a violin and he plays a heart-rending duet with a customer. Well, at least, after several pints it rends my heart.

"That's amazing," Martin says to a tweed-clad and dreamily intoxicated ghillie at the next table.

"Ah well, we've not got the television yet so we have to make our own entertainment."

The concept of somewhere in the British Isles not yet reached by television astounds us. We have stumbled on Brigadoon. Closing time at ten o'clock rapidly approaches, and yet the customary last-minute frenzied drinking does not commence. I wander unsteadily to the bar.

"What time do you close here?" I enquire, hoping we might get a few minutes longer to squeeze in another drink.

The ginger barman looks at me puzzled for a moment, as if he has forgotten that I am a visitor from a distant galaxy. "Ah well," he muses, stroking the great ball of ginger fuzz on his chin, "I suppose we close when everybody leaves."

I have wandered into paradise.

* * *

The following day we catch the train to Lochailort, a place so small I don't think it even qualifies as a village. Here we shoulder our packs, containing everything we will need for the next three days, and head up into the hills. Despite this being the beginning of September the weather is abnormally hot. The map indicates 'Prince Charlie's Cave' somewhere along the route, although we are unable to locate it. From studying the rest of the map it appears that, after landing at Glenfinnan in 1745, Prince Charlie must have been incredibly busy visiting thousands of caves in the area, erecting cairns, building cottages and chip shops. Just about everything you can imagine was, apparently, visited by the pretender to the throne in his ill-fated attempt to overthrow the English king.

We descend into the small glen at the head of Loch Beoraid and from there cross the hills once more, heading for the end of Loch Morar on our route to Glen Shiel. The track winds its way high into the hills in the shimmering heat. Despite the temperature Martin is full of enthusiasm and, a few miles from our intended campground, says he will take the high path that leads over the hills while Joe and I take the direct descent to the shore of the loch.

Joe and I are happy to plod on through the glen. Despite heavy packs, the afternoon passes easily enough for us on the lower route, and a gentle breeze keeps away the worst of the heat. By early evening Joe and I arrive at the camping ground on the shore of Loch Morar and wait for Martin. The dry weather means that the loch is low, and we settle down to wait for our companion on the wide boulder-strewn shore in a place that would be feet under water in normal years. Even in such pleasant weather Loch Morar is dark and forbidding. Although nothing like the size of its big brother, Loch Ness, it is the deepest loch in the British Isles at over a thousand feet deep. Loch Morar has its own tales of a huge mysterious creature lurking in its depths waiting for the unwary traveller. The creature is dubbed Morag by the locals. Loch Ness is surrounded by modern roads and villages, giving one the feeling that even if some ancient dinosaur where to rise from the deep no harm would come to you. But Loch Morar is a different place, wild and lonely. It's easy to imagine being dragged beneath the depths or devoured by Morag in the darkness of the night. While logic tells me monsters are myths, caution repeatedly draws my eyes to the surface of the loch.

Joe and I settle down, expecting to see Martin at any minute, but he does not appear. As the shadows lengthen we grow more concerned. We worry not only for Martin's safety but also for the tent pegs and stove he is carrying. Without these we can't put up the tent or eat a meal; now the wisdom of splitting up our party in such circumstances comes into doubt. As dusk turns to darkness we light a fire from the driftwood at the side of the loch in the hope it will act as a beacon. After what seems like hours we begin to make out the tiny spot of a torch descending the craggy hillside towards us. The pinprick of light stops, presumably at the top of a small cliff, seeking a route between the precipices.

The point of light drops alarmingly, and Joe allows himself a wry chuckle. "Wow, he went down a long way that time!" The light moves, stops, plummets again then moves on.

"Not dead yet," Joe points out with the dark humour common to the outdoor fraternity. Descending broken ground is never easy in the dark; you lose all perspective, and what appear to be short steps can in reality be leg-breaking drops. At last the light begins to home in on our fire and Martin appears, exhausted and wobbling, beneath his pack.

"That was further than I thought," he says, collapsing beside the fire.

Joe and I leap into action. In minutes the tent is up and the meal is being prepared. We are experimenting with various types of dehydrated food, as nothing designed for backpacking has yet been developed. Tonight's meal glories under the name of Textured Vegetable Protein (TVP).

"It'll be fine," Joe insists, always one to explore new technology. "It's made from some sort of fungi. They plan to grow it on Mars." Joe is a science fiction fan. Joe explains that TVP doesn't have a lot of flavour and you have to add it to the mixture, which looks like course gravel. Pans rattle in the semi-darkness of the tent. The flashlight bobs and I hear a stirring sound.

"There, it's ready." Joe hands me a plate. He digs in, coughs, and then there's a choking sound. "I may have overdone the curry powder."

That evening we dine on cardboard mixed with sulphuric acid. "If you ask me, Mars is the best place for this stuff," I mumble when the burning sensation relents enough for me to speak.

That night, as I try to sleep, the logical part of my mind tells me that no monsters lurk in the depths of Highland lochs. But in my imagination I hear Morag coming closer with every rustle of the tent flap.

I wake up in wilderness and, after climbing out of the tent, stand struggling to take in the scale of the landscape. An abandoned cottage is the only sign that a world beyond this place exists. On the Pennine Way we followed a defined track from one village to the next, but this place is trackless and it will be two days before we arrive at anything that could be described as habitation. On every side, steep green hills, raked by cliffs, soar into the sky and then sweep down into the grey depths of the loch. It is difficult to believe that the hillsides I can see, plunging into the water, continue down beneath the surface, unseen, into the dark depths. The surface of the loch is bright in the morning sunshine; strange to think that, beneath the visible, another submerged valley lies, secret and unexplored. The steep-sided glen is broad at our campsite, but to the east, where our route takes us, the glen narrows and fingers of the interlocking ridges close off the outside world. The land is timeless; I feel as though I have been allowed a glimpse into a different world, a place I barely imagined.

Martin climbs out of the tent, dishevelled from sleep, and stands beside me for a moment sharing the awe of the place.

"How did you know it was like this?" I ask him.

"Maps," is his matter-of-fact response.

"It's incredible. It's…" I struggle for words and eventually mange, "huge." Huge is the only word I can find but it is hopelessly inadequate.

"Yes, it is," Martin replies, neither of us able to express how this place makes us feel. For a moment we both stare in silence, lost in the tranquillity of the landscape.

There is a shuffling in the tent behind us.

"Are we having breakfast or what? Why isn't the tea on?" Joe, ever practical, is awake. His stomach, having survived last night's nuclear curry by some fluke, and he is hungry.

That day we wander through the empty landscape, meeting no one, amazed that such empty places can exist in this crowded island. Though we don't know it, we are on course for our encounter with Loch Quoich, the hydroelectric reservoir, that will take us on our hungry diversion. That night, as we pitch camp, I look up and notice a huge shape sweeping through the air parallel to the ridge above us. The great bird covers the ground in enormous, effortless circles. At first I think it is a buzzard but then it vanishes of a summit and it is only then I realise it must have been a golden eagle. There is something special about seeing your first eagle; it is a bird that symbolises of wilderness and remote areas. No matter what else happens in our journey, I'll always be able to say I saw an eagle.

A few days after our encounter with Loch Quoich, we backpack north and make a wild camp beneath the imposing face of Liathach – which, rising some three thousand feet in half a mile from the road, can lay claim to being the steepest mountain in Scotland. We are now in one of the most spectacular areas of the Highlands: Torridon, famed for its towering mountains, its remote corries and (more than anything else) for the ferocity of its midges. We have encountered midges before but here these beasts seem especially ferocious. They bite me and Joe with unbounded enthusiasm but reserve their greatest vitriol for Martin. He, it appears, is a midge delicacy. The savage little beasts are drawn to him from far and wide. We barricade ourselves in the tent but somehow the midges always find a way in, squeezing their tiny bodies into the minutest of holes. We burn incense in the doorway, spray insect repellent, all to no effect.

"We'll have to go to the pub," Martin says.

I don't need much persuasion, but it's only about six in the evening and way before our usual time to be heading for the beer oasis. Our campsite amongst the trees is sheltered from the wind but also happens to be where the midges are at their worst. If we can make it to the road, where there is a slight breeze, we might survive the escape relatively unmolested. Fortunately midges are poor fliers and can't get far in even a moderate breeze.

If you were an interested observer, this is what you would see happening next.

Three young men suddenly burst from a small blue tent, tripping over guy ropes as they exit, arms flailing wildly in the air as they run. Two run for the road, while one – clearly in agony, and battering himself in the face – stays to fasten up the tent. Swearing loudly, the trio run off down the road, pursued by a dark cloud of four million voracious midges.

If you have ever encountered the Highland midge you will know that the above account is no exaggeration. Look in any gift shop and you will find postcards with jokes about midges on them. But these are written by people who have never really encountered midges, because midges are not funny. Midges are a curse. Fortunately, for reasons I've never understood, not only are midges poor fliers but also they don't enter buildings. They will swarm into tents, but houses, shops and (most important of all) public houses are inviolate to them. If it were not for this fact the Highlands would be deserted.

It's still early evening when we arrive at the Ben Damh bar. Typical of many bars in the Highlands, it is the rough-and-ready adjunct to the much smarter Torridon Hotel. This place is intended for the locals whilst the up-market hotel – a mock Victorian castle, like many – hosts well-heeled tourists and, in the stalking season, even better-heeled shooting parties. Like most public bars the Ben Damh is wall-to-wall Formica with an ancient juke box in one corner. The room is thick with smoke and packed with locals forcing alcohol down their throats. There are two kinds of drinking establishments in the Highlands: those that slavishly obey the licensing laws, and those that have never heard of them. The Ben Damh, we discover after a few enquires, is the former. The local folk here have adopted a sort of shift system to cope with this. After work they pour into the bar to begin the early drinking shift, which ends about seven thirty when the place empties out and everyone goes home for tea. The late shift then commences about an hour after that, with frantic alcohol consumption as ten o'clock looms.

We three are happy to join in the revelry. A local piper rises unsteadily to his feet and begins to rend the air with a lively tune. We are keen to hear this example of local culture, and fall into conversation with a grey-bearded ghillie, a sort of Highland game keeper, whose name is Willie – I think all ghillies are called Willie, there must be some law – effusive in his praise for the bagpipe player. But the pipes are deafening and render all conversation (and coherent thought) impossible. After a while

I decide bagpipes are better as outdoor instruments where they can be kept some distance away, preferably a considerable distance.

Willie draws me into a conspiratorial huddle. "Aye, he is a fine piper," he yells down my ear over the din. "At least he was until he went deaf." I can only think deafness must have come as a welcome relief.

Ten o'clock arrives. I expect a polite period for drinking up but instead an alarm bell rings while we fight to consume the last of our pints. Doors are flung open and a blast of cold air clears the bar of accumulated cigarette smokers and drinkers simultaneously. At one minute past ten we are standing outside the pub about to head back towards the midges. Glenfinnan feels a long way away.

I awake the following morning, the tunes of the deaf piper still ringing in my ears. This is our last day before we have to travel back south, back to the sprawling towns and cities of England, back to the 'PRIVATE KEEP OUT' notices, back to normality. We want to make our last day memorable and have decided to traverse Beinn Eighe. This is a giant of a hill – more like a range of hills – dwarfing anything we have seen in the Lake District.

We set off early, a long day ahead of us. The heat still lingers in the glen despite the fact that we are well into September, and in most other years we would be saturated by frequent downpours. The ridge of Beinn Eighe turns at ninety degrees from the road and access to the ridge is gained from a remote coire – or high hanging valley – at its farthest end. The path climbs gently away from Glen Torridon and into the vastness of these hills. The sheer scale overwhelms us. These giant mountains are far from the Lakeland fells we have known.

We step around a corner and a great hidden coire of fierce crags and scree appears, as if summoned into existence by the hand of a magician. Immense cliffs tower over us, split into three vast buttresses. At the foot of the crags nestles a small lochan, its deep green waters clear as crystal. We stop for a few minutes to slake our thirst in the stream that feeds the lochan. The cool water is a delight in the heat and our joy increases when Joe brings out a pack of dehydrated orange juice. The scene holds us in awe; this is Coire Mhic Fhearchair, a secret place, a special place.

Stooping to fill my water bottle from the lochan, I notice a dark shape submerged in the green twilight of the water's depths. It's something mechanical – an aircraft wheel, I realise. Refreshed by the cooling water, we head on past the loch towards the ridge and here we discover a piece of engine, then a shattered section of fuselage and other aircraft parts too mangled and twisted to identify. The steel parts we find are corroded with age and only the aluminium sections have defied the elements to retain their original form. It is clear that, whatever catastrophe occurred here, it must have taken place many years ago.

* * *

Later, I asked the barman in the Ben Damh if he knew what had happened. He produced from behind the bar a battered old copy of the Scot's Magazine that he kept for such enquiries. On the 13th of March 1951 Flight Lieutenant Harry Smith Reid, DFC, was piloting a converted Lancaster bomber home from a reconnaissance mission over Rockall. On their return to RAF Kinloss they encountered freezing conditions and a strong north-easterly wind. What Reid and his seven-man crew did not know was that strong winds had pushed them far west of their intended course and that they were flying towards the towering peaks of Torridon. In darkness and with poor visibility they were on a collision course with disaster and, some time around midnight, their aircraft flew into the triple buttresses of Coire Mhic Fhearchair. They struck the buttress around fifteen feet from the summit in an area that is now known as Fuselage Gully.

When they failed to return to Kinloss a search was mounted. For two days rescue teams scoured the Northern Highlands for the crashed aircraft. With little information to go on, the search teams had an almost impossible task; they were searching a huge area and it is not surprising that they were unable to locate the aircraft. But on hearing about the missing plane a young boy from Torridon village recalled seeing a glow high on Beinn Eighe. Armed with this information, rescue teams soon located the crashed bomber high on the Triple Buttresses. The impact of the collision had driven the aircraft into the gully and wedged the fuselage deep into the mountainside.

At that time RAF rescue teams lacked the skills to reach such an inaccessible site, and offers of assistance from local mountaineers were rejected. In atrocious weather the RAF rescue team made a number of futile attempts to reach the stranded aircraft. It was not until a week later, when the services of two Royal Marine commandos were enlisted, that the crash site was finally reached. Sadly, all the crew were dead when the commandos made their grim search. It seems highly likely that the eight men, mostly in their early twenties, were killed on impact. I hope that they were spared the fate of a lonely, lingering death in such a remote place. On the positive side, the crash led to the establishment of specialised RAF Mountain Rescue teams who are now the most skilled people in the field of search and rescue, and have been responsible for saving numerous lives on the mountains of Britain.

* * *

High on the ridge we climb into cloud. An eerie silence descends on the mountain. The long ridge has short sections with exposed pinnacles, but the mist deprives us of any views and so we scramble on, oblivious to the drop beneath our feet. For hours we walk in the cloud, isolated in a silent white world where only the next few feet of rock are visible. At last we descend out of the mist and back to the tarmac road and the joys of the Ben Damh bar.

On the train home I feel as though I had travelled a new and different world. My mind keeps taking me back to Knoydart, to the vast lochs and sweeping ridges, to a place of adventure and magic. One day, I vow, I will return to the green lochan beneath the towering cliffs. Perhaps I will camp there and sleep in that special coire. To wake there and see the dawn break on the mountains of Torridon is something to dream of.

* * *

1977 is a pivotal year in my life. It's my final year at Leicester University and I am finishing my degree in Sociology. University life has pushed the hills into the background over the last couple of years. Martin, Joe and I travelled north for one summer trek but, unfortunately, the Highland weather was as brutal towards us as it had been kind on our previous visit. Not much was achieved apart from a lot of drinking and muddy walks from the tent (which was wet on the outside) to the bar (where we got wet on the inside).

The music of my life has changed forever. For all my teenage years the gods of Progressive Rock reigned supreme. Their high priests played in mega bands and lorded it over us mere mortals, travelling to stadium gigs in helicopters and earning unheard-of sums of money. But in the late seventies all that changed. Far from the multi-million-pound psychedelic studios of the super groups, young men with no money and sometimes even less musical ability began making records. While the elite sang about topographical oceans and the trials of the super-rich, the garage bands sang about unemployment, their lack of a future and sometimes nothing at all. The garage bands came screaming onto the stage, full of anger, pain and spit. In a few short months Punk Rock had displaced the old super groups. The sordid bedsits of Leicester, where most of my friends and I lived, throbbed to the sounds of bands like The Clash and the Sex Pistols.

When I finished my degree, I volunteered for Camp America and spent the summer looking after eleven-year-olds at a Jewish camp near Detroit. The camp was little more than a collection of wooden huts in the forest outside the motor city. There I met a climber called Jon, short and powerfully built. He suggested that, after the camp finished, we head for the Rocky Mountains where we might be able to do a climb or two.

* * *

The drop below me snaps at my boots like an angry terrier. If I sit still on the sloping ledge of wet gravel, I start to slide off into space. I have to keep moving, shuffling on my backside away from the void. In this way I can stop myself sliding by keeping up a crab-like reverse crawl, pushing the gravel away. I keep wondering what will happen when all the gravel is gone. A couple of feet away, Jon sits, water dripping onto his helmet, watching my struggle with grim fascination. He abseiled down first on to the ledge and has wedged his short, stocky body into the only semi-secure position. Jon didn't think to bring any equipment down with him so couldn't set up a belay and is left clinging to the rock. I came down second, and even if I'd had any nuts or slings I wouldn't have known what to do with them. So here we both sit, waiting for the third climber, David, to bring us some equipment. A full-blooded Rocky Mountains thunderstorm shakes debris from the cliffs around us and static electricity sparks off the rocks.

Jon turns to me, the grim light of terror in his eyes, water droplets gleaming in his ginger beard.

"See, if you fall off?" he says.

"Yes?"

"Don't grab me, will you?"

"No." I have no plan that includes what I'll do if I fall. Not falling is my only aim right now. I shuffle back on the rain-soaked ledge one more time.

"You gonna pray to your god now, Limey?" he says in his

Midwest American drawl. Assured of his own safety, Jon is becoming philosophical.

"Nah, too late now." I may have laughed or it might have been a sob. We both lapse into silence waiting for David to arrive. Three days ago we had arrived in the Rocky Mountains.

* * *

It's 3 a.m. when Jon finally steers his ancient car down the main road of Silverton, Colorado, a little mining town. We have just driven for twenty-four hours through the endless rolling farmland of America's Midwest. On the way here, in the middle of the night, there was a sickening thump below the vehicle as we drove over an unidentified animal, and the sump has been leaking oil ever since. The town's single street looks to have changed little since the gold rush days. The shops have garish painted signs and names like Mad Mama's Pies, the Grand Imperial Hotel and the Empire Bunkhouse.

Standing in the street I feel as if Rooster Cogburn might walk straight out of *True Grit* at any moment and greet me with a casual, "How's it goin', pilgrim?" Even worse, I might suddenly be challenged to a gunfight when I don't own and have never even held a gun.

The streets and bars are full of drunken miners, men who look like they move earth with their bare hands and might rip the head off a grizzly just to pass the time. Numerous pickup trucks, each displaying a rifle in its back window, are parked outside saloon fronts. Huge bored dogs are tied up outside the bars, most of them dozing the night away, waiting for their owners to drink their fill. I have stumbled on the American version of Glenfinnan. Like everything in America, it is louder and bigger, but it has the same feeling of a place apart.

The following day, together with David, Jon's climbing partner, we backpack in to the mountains. Jon revels in this place, and as we climb higher all three of us are excited by the freedom this wilderness offers us. As we cross a high pass Jon turns to me.

"Bet you got nothin' like this in Britain, Limey?" he asks.

"Well, Scotland is fairly close, but not as high."

In truth, the mountains around Silverton remind me very much of the Highlands. Despite the difference in height, the hills are similar – but the Rockies are more arid. Conifers ring the lower slopes of the mountains, whilst the high slopes are draped in loose scree up to the easy walking of the summit ridges. Jon is amazed to hear that Scotland has hills and is disparaging of the rest of the world's mountains.

"Why," he declares expansively, "the Rocky Mountains is the marrow of the world. Sense tells me the Andes is foothills and the Alps is for children to climb!" Here he is quoting Robert Redford playing mountain man Jeramiah Johnson in the film that was produced in 1972.

That night we camp high in the mountains beside a small green lake at the foot of a towering rock face.

The following morning dawns bright and clear. Jon, David and I pack rucksacks full of bits of wire, loops of nylon webbing, and all kinds of bizarre equipment whose purpose is a complete mystery to me. Then we head for the rock face. Jon and David decide we will climb a shallow 1,000ft gully, but I have never climbed on rock before and the sudden verticality of it unnerves me. Somehow I had expected huge holds and ladder-like footholds, but the delicate slab underfoot has no such easy aids. At first I am reduced to a gibbering wreck but gradually gain confidence and we begin to make progress.

A few pitches from the top we hear a distant rumble, and not far away lightning spouts from an ominous black cloud. We start to climb as fast as we can and hope that it will pass us by. But the cloud, it seems, has spotted us, and is coming in our direction with an uncanny accuracy. Within moments we are sitting in a deluge, our ropes coiled beneath us, while the mountain gods play with an electric light show and sparks crackle off the rocks. At first we try to sit it out, thinking that it might pass over in half an hour or so. Then the shallow gully we have been climbing turns into a waterfall. There is a terrifying roar as a huge rockfall sweeps the face only a few feet from where we are crouched.

"We can't stay here!" Jon shouts.

Despite my inexperience, I've already worked that out. We begin climbing again, only now we are battling through a vertical waterfall. Fortunately the summit is only two rope lengths away. The summit turns out to be a rock-strewn plateau, surrounded by cliffs.

Jon turns to me, rain bouncing off his helmet. "Have you ever rappelled?"

"Is that like abseiling?"

"Yes." He grins enthusiastically, glad that I have some previous experience.

"Then no."

David locates an anchor and Jon sets off down the rope

as rain lashes the summit of the mountain. After listening to David's brief instructions on how to abseil, I follow. It's now that I find myself sitting on the sloping ledge with no anchor, sliding into oblivion. After ten minutes teetering on the edge David arrives with some gear and, to my enormous relief, I am once more attached to the rock face. Another short descent and we are safely at the base of the cliff.

"I didn't like to tell you at the time," David says, "but you know when you were abseiling down?"

I nod. Those few minutes of terror stand out with blinding clarity in my mind.

"Well, the boulder I had the rope anchored to started to move. I had to sit on it."

"Oh shit." I visualise looking up and seeing that boulder, the size of a phone box, hurtling towards me. Sometimes it's best not to know how close you come to death.

* * *

Back in Silverton we down copious amounts of beer and discuss what to do next. Jon says he's always wanted to see the Grand Canyon and, since all of us are a little chastened by our climbing experience, we decide to head south.

We have been driving for hours. Despite having all the windows rolled down, the heat of the desert in southern Colorado is oppressive. The desert scares me. Mile after mile of arid land pass by the windows of Jon's old car. It's like travelling through a gigantic box of cat litter. In the mountains I have some idea of how to survive, but here, in the heat and without water, I am in a hostile landscape. The colours of this land fascinate me.

Here and there, wind-blasted spires and dunes rise from the flat earth tinged with an infinite variety of russet browns, golden yellows and the deeper reds of sandstone. Harsh as the desert environment is, it has a unique captivating beauty.

Jon's old car rattles on through this empty landscape devoid of human habitation, past the rusted wrecks of cars washed up on the shores of the desert. At last we come to a solitary shack with a sign swinging in the wind that simply says 'GAS'. This is part of an Indian reservation and the old man who sits behind the dilapidated desk is a Native American. Jon asks for the toilet, and the old man, his face a map of ancient wrinkles, gestures towards a free-standing cubicle outside. Jon heads out but returns a moment later requesting toilet paper.

The old man looks up slowly and takes us all in. He sees three young, privileged white men, and in his heavy-lidded eyes I see the memory of three hundred years of oppression. He remembers Wounded Knee, the Night of the Long Knives; he remembers Custer and the pounding hooves of the 7th Cavalry. Silently he reaches below the desk and produces a roll of toilet paper which he places reverentially on the table top as if it were a precious artefact. Then, deliberately and with great care, he takes one sheet, tears along the perforations and hands it to Jon. At that moment, if you listen very carefully, not far away, you can hear the drums of an Apache war dance. Somewhere Sitting Bull is smiling.

That night we camp under the stars on a rocky rib overlooking the Grand Canyon. As the sun goes down the desert comes alive with changing colours. The walls of the canyon are striped with multi-coloured layers of sandstone in a painting that has taken tens of thousands of years to complete. As the sky turns pink the walls of the canyon respond with deep reds, chocolate browns and golden yellows. Sunset in the desert has a beauty beyond description. The canyon is so big it is impossible to comprehend its scale. I try to compare it with other things I have seen, but the canyon is over a mile deep and 277 miles long – by coincidence, almost exactly the length of the Pennine Way. What fascinates me about America is its sheer size and diversity. With one tank of 'gas' you can drive to deserts, jungles, vast open plains or high snow-peaked mountains.

Jon warns me not to turn over boulders. "That's where rattlesnakes live," he says with a grin.

Not everything in this place is benign. As I stand looking at the view I suddenly become aware of something moving inside my underpants. Scrambling to remove whatever it is, I feel a stinging bite to my scrotum and realise it must be a red ant. They're famous for the size and sharpness of their pincers. Trousers half down, I leap about wildly in the desert in a desperate attempt to dislodge the intruder from my underwear – and it is at that moment I think I invented break dancing.

* * *

When I return to my Merseyside home in the autumn of 77, Liverpool has become a ghost town. In the city centre most of the shops are closed and boarded up. Those still trading are surrounded by fortifications of steel shutters and barbed wire, so great is their fear of crime. So severe is the slump in the economy it feels like the place has fallen to its knees, never to rise again.

Everywhere there are grey-faced people. Many Liverpudlians cling to football as though it were religion; the city football club's success in the European Cup is the only glimmer of hope in these bleak times. Norman Tebbit, the Tory minister, urges the nation to get on its bike and look for work. I do just that and spend days cycling between the factory gates of the Wirral. Everywhere I am turned away by bored security men guarding run-down factories. Despite the economic slump I am comfortable enough, back home with my parents; my meals are provided and the only work I do is signing on once a fortnight. Uncertain of what I want to do for a career, I start applying for social work posts, but even they seem thin on the ground. Joe is unemployed too. Martin is the only one of us with a real job, working for the Department of Health and Social Security Blackpool, where he spends his days ordering artificial limbs.

* * *

I spend the days filling in application forms, watching dull TV, standing in line at the Labour Exchange or walking my dog through the streets and parks of suburban Merseyside. I am absorbed by the mundane trivia of life, carried along by the current of day-to-day living, yet there are moments when the mountains return to me. Times when I remember the endless jagged horizon of the Rockies and I feel the breeze from across Loch Morar against my cheek.

I'm sitting drinking cider with Joe in his father's house at Raby Mere. Three years have passed since I was last here and it feels like I've come full circle.

"I've had an idea," I say to Joe over the blare of Pink Floyd on his stereo.

Joe looks up, curious, suspicious. He knows I've had ideas before, not always good ones.

"We could go to the Lakes for a few weekends this winter," I explain.

"Yes." As Joe turns the idea over in his mind, I can see he's not convinced. "I suppose we could," he adds reluctantly.

Both of us know we have no experience in winter. I imagine ice-blasted summits, endless snows and bitter cold.

"We haven't any gear," Joe points out, being practical again. What he doesn't need to add is that we don't have any money to buy equipment with either.

"Well, maybe we could try." The urge to head for the hills won't leave me alone.

Walking into Ellis Brigham's shop in Liverpool is like entering an Aladdin's cave of climbing equipment. There are ice axes, crampons and framed rucksacks hanging everywhere. By pulling together all my Christmas money I have saved up enough to buy a better sleeping bag. Practically any sleeping bag would be better than the rose-covered one that I bought second hand and shivered in on the Pennine Way. The best sleeping bags are filled with down – light and warm but way beyond anything we can afford. Joe and I look at them as though they are religious artefacts, treasures beyond our imagination. We stroke them, feel their softness; we can't afford them but we can touch them.

There is, however, another rail with bags made of a revolutionary new fibre, Hollofil. Its makers boast it is warm when wet, an advantage in our climate, and it's much cheaper than down. There are two or three bags Joe and I might actually be able to afford. We spend hours debating them. In the end I settle on a Mountain Equipment Fitzroy, a three-season bag (and therefore marginal for winter), but the best I can manage. Joe, who has just got a job on a car production line and has a little disposable cash, goes for the luxury of a four-season Cerro Torre. At last we have our first pieces of custom-made mountaineering equipment. We might not be ready for Everest but maybe we can manage Grasmere.

* * *

The old maroon bus – the same one that carried me and Martin on our summer adventures five years earlier – rattles its way up Great Langdale, finally depositing me and Joe outside the Old Dungeon Ghyll Hotel. As soon as we get off the bus the cold air hits us. This is early January. The road has a dusting of snow, frost hangs in the air, and there is a powerful smell of snow, heather and sheep mingled together: the smell of winter. Gone are the hordes of caravans, the cyclists, the grannies, the armies of wailing kids and fine-weather hillwalkers. In winter the roads are clear and the campsites mostly empty. It's almost dark but we can see the snow-covered hills outlined against the clear winter sky. The sight fills us with excitement.

Upon pushing open the wooden pub door we are greeted by a scene from Middle Earth. The low, smoky room is filled to capacity with stocky men sporting huge beards and scruffy pullovers. There are men swigging beer from great two-pint pewter tankards. Battered and scarred from nights of drinking, many pots hang above the bar awaiting their owners like trophies of ale-filled nights. Some tankards sport three handles so no matter how inebriated the drinker one handle was always points towards them, bringing the foaming brew within easy reach. These huge tankards are filled with Old Peculier, a dark, potent beer brewed in Masham by Theakston. The corporate stamp of the massive breweries is everywhere, and small, independent breweries have almost died out. Mass-produced brews made in sterile faceless factories, and injected with gas from pressurised cylinders, have almost annihilated the small breweries that once populated England. Here, in deepest Langdale, real ale is making a stand. Theakston's dark beer symbolises our escape into a world far from the grim reality of Merseyside with its dying city centre and mass unemployment.

In one corner there is someone banging out a song on a guitar, competing against two or three other singers in different parts of the room. A few young girls are trying to find the space to dance. Joe and I are in awe of the denizens of this dark lair. These are true mountain men, seasoned in the pursuit of ice and snow. Escapees from urban sprawl, refugees from Manchester, Preston and Liverpool; they have established a kingdom apart here in Langdale. That night we stagger back to our tent expectant of adventures to come.

I spend the night shivering in my new bag. Mountain Equipment had only boasted that this sleeping bag is adequate for three seasons but the ice inside the tent tells me it is definitely the fourth. With all my clothes on I'm just about warm enough to sleep, but only if I keep my legs straight. If I bend my knees a cold spot appears where the insulation is compressed.

Eventually a weak sun begins to find its way into our tent

and I drag my frozen body out of the sleeping bag. The morning is cold and still. Around us is a cluster of tents where last night's hairy bar dwellers still slumber. Only a few folk are stirring, and I realise that most of the people we met last night have no intention of braving the snow-covered hills – a far cry from the iron-hard mountain men we imagined. As I shiver beside the tent I pull on multiple pullovers and top the ensemble with my old oiled cotton fishing jacket. Joe and I set off up a route called the Band, an easy-angled ridge that runs parallel to Langdale. At first we are walking on frost-hardened ground, but higher on the ridge we step on to snow. Now it feels like we are on a mountain – uncharted waters for us both. The snow is soft and we can follow the footsteps of previous parties. Barely equipped, and even less experienced, we finally find our way to the summit of Bowfell. The cloud has descended high above the snowline and there is only an eerie white. But we don't care about the lack of view; we have climbed our first winter peak. This may be an easy snow-covered hill in the Lake District, but Joe and I feel like we have conquered Everest.

A couple of weeks later I return to the Lakes with Martin. Joe can't make this weekend – he has just started a new job working in the same factory as his father at Vauxhall's, assembling car gearboxes. The money is good, but he has to work two twelve-hour days followed by two twelve-hour nights followed by four days off. It's a system designed by someone who knows all about how cars work and nothing about how people function, and as a result Joe's body clock is constantly set to the wrong time zone. Martin has managed to save up enough money to become the proud owner of a pair of crampons. These are unfamiliar. We spend hours examining the spikes and straps, trying to decide how they are supposed to work. The campsite at the little village of Braithwaite is deserted and officially closed, but no one cares about two foolish young men who want to spend a night out in the cold, so we pitch our tent there and no one bothers us.

After another shivering night, Martin and I set off to climb Skiddaw. This is a big hill by Lake District standards, characterised by great sweeping ridges that are exposed to the wind. In summer it is a huge mound of scree but in winter its size gives it a degree of seriousness other Cumbrian fells lack. With the conquest of Bowfell behind me, I am confident Skiddaw will present us no real problems. The frozen earth quickly gives way to soft snow and the higher we climb the harder it becomes. Then the cold takes us by surprise. Despite my multiple pullovers, ice is beginning to coat the outer layers of my clothing. My ears, nose and fingers are growing numb. The cloud descends, obscuring the view, but occasionally it lifts and offers us tantalising glimpses of the Cumbrian countryside far below. Then we enter the world of the ice god.

Weird sculptures begin to appear, coating every upright surface. Rocks, fence posts and old gateways are festooned with delicate structures of beautiful hoar frost. The white landscape takes on a surreal aspect unlike anything we have seen before. So great is the transformation it's hard to believe that we are amongst the same hills we walked a few years ago on our school trip. We are alone in the landscape and meet no other travellers in the ice world.

Wind has compacted snow on the summit ridge and turned it to solid ice. Martin struggles to fix his new crampons to his boots. I stand watching him, shivering in the cold as he fiddles with a tangle of unfamiliar straps and buckles.

"I'll never get used to the gravity on this planet," he says, wryly, as the crampons fall from his feet for the third time.

At last, after managing to get the crampons to stay on, we set off up the hill. The thought of Martin with spikes on his feet makes me nervous. As we head higher up the ridge the value of the crampons becomes increasingly evident – my boots constantly lose traction, and I'm forced to perform wild gyrations just to stay upright. As the ridge narrows close to the summit, a long drop opens beneath my boots. If I slip here I might not stop until I reach the valley floor.

"I'll have to hang on to you," I tell Martin. So, he climbs on with me clinging to his rucksack straps like the blind mole in the *Deputy Dawg* cartoons I watched when I was five. Sylvester, the mole, would cling to the tail of his muskrat friend while they tried to steal eggs from Deputy Dawg's hen house.

"What's happ'nin'? What's happ'nin'?" Sylvester would cry, unable to see what was going on. That's exactly where I am now.

"Where are we? Where are we?" I ask Martin constantly, unable to see past his six-foot frame. I wonder if Chris Bonington was ever led to a summit clinging to his mate for grim death.

Finally we make it to the summit cairn, an ice-rimed pillar rising from an arctic landscape.

I cling to the triangulation pillar. "It's incredible up here. My god it's cold."

Since Martin's woollen balaclava is frozen solid I can assume he's noticed that it's cold, but somehow I feel the need to point it out.

Martin breaks a piece of hoar frost from his hat. "It's like the North Pole. That wind is going right through my jeans."

I let go of the pillar and try to take an unsupported step, which results in a few penguin-like gyrations. Moments later I'm face down on the ice. Martin takes hold of my rucksack and helps me up, and then we set off down, Martin leading, me clinging to his rucksack.

"Where are we?" I ask at intervals on the long descent.

* * *

Our trip up Skiddaw has brought home to me that, if I'm going to venture onto the hills in winter, I'd better get some proper gear or my career is likely to be short. There are a handful of mountaineering shops around but most of the specialist equipment they sell is way beyond our pockets. Here World War II comes to our rescue. Although the war ended over thirty years ago it is still possible to find a lot of army surplus kit around.

My uncle Alan gives me his pair of RAF trousers. They fit me perfectly, are made of wool and have a high waist, forties style. The trousers boast a razor-sharp crease and easily outsmart my faded denims. I am very proud of my World War II kit; there is something comforting in knowing that your trousers played a part in the downfall of Hitler.

I send my mother to jumble sales in search of ex-army long johns and, the greatest prize of all, a long-sleeved woollen vest. The great property of wool is that it remains warm when wet, and we're frequently wet – in fact, it would be more accurate to say we're rarely dry. The woollen underwear itches ferociously, and when I first put it on I find myself twitching as though suffering from a terrible nervous affliction. Fortunately, after a little while, I begin to get used to the itch and the twitching subsides.

Joe's dad gives him a beaten-up old minibus which he struggles manfully to keep on the road. It is the first time any of us has had transport and the set of wheels gives us a new freedom. We are no longer tied to train and bus schedules, and it also means that we were not restricted to what we can carry on our backs. We borrow a heavy canvas tent, which has the luxury – not only of being 'full length' and thus able to accommodate Martin's feet – but also having a sewn-in groundsheet (not quite as luxurious as we'd imagined). I begin work as a trainee social worker, and so have some funds, although the pay is meagre.

Today you can walk into an outdoor shop, of which there are many, and walk out with a better sleeping bag than we could afford in the seventies for less than the price of a tank of petrol. In our early climbing days, equipment that would keep you warm could only be dreamt of, or perhaps fondled longingly in the climbing shops that were then beginning to pop up all over the Lake District. This meant that, if I slept in my long johns, Bomber Command trousers, gloves, hat and two pullovers it was possible to sleep through the cold Lakeland nights, provided you drank enough Old Peculier. In fact, it is possible to sleep anywhere if you drink enough Old Peculier.

After our trip to Skiddaw it's obvious that sharing one pair of crampons between two won't get us very far, so in our first winter season I manage to save up enough money to buy an ice axe. I choose a long wooden-shafted walking axe – designed for less vertical hillwalking and mountaineering – despite the shop assistant's attempts to persuade me to buy a more expensive type of axe that might allow me to climb a bit.

"I don't want to climb," I tell him. "I just need a walking axe."

I'm incredibly excited by my purchase of the ice axe. I don't know anyone else who owns such an implement, and I was certainly the only person travelling on the train through the tunnel back to my home in Merseyside carrying one. Now I have an ice axe I am free to explore the Lake District in winter. I dream of adventures in the ice-covered mountains, of travelling to places where few bold wanderers could venture. I am becoming a mountaineer.

5

The Hidden World

It's April and I am walking though the ice-frosted streets of Sheffield in the early evening looking for the Youth Hostel. A young woman totters out of the shadows on high heels, her skirt incongruously short for such a cold night. She smiles at me and, as I pass by, I realise that she is older than she at first appeared, her face a mask of thick make-up. I don't smile back. I spent my student days in the red-light district of Leicester and know instinctively that if this woman knew how little money I had she wouldn't give me a second glance.

The hostel is a cold, austere building. As I slide beneath the sheets on the squeaking iron bed frame I wonder who comes to this place on holiday. The old steel town has an air of decay, only slightly less severe than my home town. Somehow I feel at home here.

Tomorrow, I have a job interview for a trainee social worker in the nearby town of Barnsley. Unused to such things, I am unaware that one is not supposed to have to seek out the cheapest possible accommodation and that a hotel would have been perfectly acceptable place to stay, so here I am in the hostel. Besides, I've never stayed in a hotel; I wouldn't know what to do.

Last week I travelled to the urban sprawl of Tower Hamlets. A dowdy council official led me down the endless Town Hall corridors into some sort of underground complex. I was then interviewed by a small panel of officials led by a large, chain-smoking middle-aged woman who exuded an air of theatrical decay.

"And finally, John, I have one last question." She paused and flicked her cigarette into an ornate silver ashtray. "Have you ever committed a criminal offence?"

"Well, I've never been caught," I replied, in a last-ditch attempt to inject some humour into a tedious interview.

The woman froze, cigarette halfway to her mouth, staring at me in horror. Then it dawned on her that I was joking. Suddenly she and the interview panel convulsed in laugher. The woman coughed out cigarette smoke and wiped tears from her eyes. They laughed for a long time and I decided it must have been a while since someone cracked a joke in Tower Hamlets. A few days later a brown envelope with a Tower Hamlets logo dropped onto the mat of my parents' home. Inside there is a job offer. I can't afford to turn it down but I've seen enough of the place to know that working there will be a question of survival.

Fortunately, the interview in Barnsley also results in an offer of a post as a trainee social worker so I choose to work in the small Yorkshire town. Sheffield seems to offer a more attractive place to live. I already have a few friends in the city and I know it has access to the Peak District.

I find a dingy little flat in the city's leafy Nether Edge area. The flat is a rundown bedsit with a small kitchen, a shared bathroom and toilet filled with fag ash. I rarely see the other residents apart from one cheery little middle-aged man who is completely toothless. Chatting to him outside the communal bathroom he explains that he works at Bassett's sweet factory in the city. He cheerfully tells me that he works in an atmosphere permanently thick with sugar dust – he and his workmates have accepted the inevitability of rotting teeth. I'm appalled by this information but he just laughs it off as an occupational hazard.

I begin working in a small mining village just outside Barnsley. The people are immensely warm towards me and the only real problem I have to face is the language barrier. I can decipher the broad Yorkshire accent easily enough, but in these tightly knit mining communities they use words that have different meanings even a few miles away.

For example:

"He's fast on." Meaning: "He's fast asleep."

"At top o'note." Meaning: "Income after tax."

"Ave us snap." Meaning: "Have our lunch."

"Wait while." Meaning: "Wait until."

Yorkshire folk are fanatical about their slice of England. My colleague, Ian, often goes into raptures about his Yorkshire home.

"That's Yorkshire tea you're drinking, brewed from Yorkshire water in a pot made in Yorkshire," he would constantly point out. Eventually, I could stand it no longer.

"So I suppose this cup is made in Yorkshire. And these tea leaves that make the tea they come from, India actually. I know everything comes from Yorkshire. I'm in bloody Yorkshire!"

In my days off I begin to explore the Peak District, which is only half an hour's drive from my flat. The area does not have the fine ridges of the Lake District or Wales; instead it has great expanses of rolling moorland that have a remote charm all of their own. On misty days – and there are many of these – the world retreats until I find myself alone in a haze-filled world. Ian is a marathon runner and keeps trying to persuade me that I could run a marathon. I've always run a few miles a week, but the idea of running twenty-six miles is something I never thought I'd be capable of.

If he can do it, I suppose I can, I think.

I spend the next few months pounding the streets of the city. Gradually I get fitter and leaner until, eventually, I can run out into the Derbyshire countryside. One day I head to the Derwent reservoir a few miles from the city. This is a long chain of reservoirs set in a deep valley; here the Dambusters squadron practised for dropping Barnes Wallace's bouncing bomb during WWII.

It's misty on the day I set off for my run. I run beside the shore of the reservoir in that eerie silence that only ever seems to accompany mist. Running is easy in the cool air, and now and again the towers of the enormous dams emerge from the mist – the towers the Dambusters used as targets. I'm fairly fit by this stage but, after fifteen miles, I'm still glad to see my car waiting for me.

The day of the race arrives and I'm pretty nervous. I'm not going to compete to win; it's the challenge of running the full marathon distance that inspires me. I set off amongst a few hundred other runners. The first half of the race goes well but during the second half I'm plunged into my own private hell; looking around me, I can see everyone else is suffering in the same way. Around twenty miles is the crunch point for most marathon runners. You've just run the first twenty miles when the depressing thought enters your mind that you have another six to go. It's at this point, with a talent for planning I can only marvel at, the race organisers put an enormous hill in the way. Halfway up the hill, my mind fogged by pain, I'm wondering if I can fake a broken leg and get airlifted out when I hear someone calling at me.

"Go on, flower. You can do it." The words call me back from my personal hell.

They come from an eighteen-stone miner who is standing, solid as a slag heap, watching me run past. The miner has an evil-looking ferret in a cage in one hand and the hand of his young son in the other. Barnsley folk glory in being known as 'strong in't arm, thick in't head' but they also have immense compassion. The miner's words spur me into action and, at least for a mile or so, I forget the pain in my legs. Perhaps only in Barnsley would a man who must live a gruelling life stop to encourage a flagging runner – and definitely only there would he call him 'flower'.

If the twentieth mile is the hardest psychological moment for a marathon runner then, oddly, the twenty-third is the easiest. I pass twenty-three miles and realise that I have only three miles left. Three miles is nothing to a marathon runner. I cruise home, but I would never have made it if it weren't for the miner's kindness; I had learnt how important a few words of encouragement can be.

Despite managing to get around the arduous course of the Barnsley marathon in a little over three hours I know that marathon running is not for me. I lack the discipline to put in tedious hours of training to achieve good time, and even maintaining my running fitness isn't something I want to do.

Once more I am drawn back to the mountains.

Despite the trauma of my first encounter with rock climbing, it's something I want to develop as it will allow me to explore the more inaccessible parts of the hills. In my Peak District wanderings I come across long, low cliffs – or 'edges' as they are known locally. These are the playgrounds for thousands of local climbers. Sheffield, I soon discover, is the ideal place to learn to climb. The city is the UK's climbing capital and the home of people like Paul Nunn, a Himalayan veteran and president of the British Mountaineering Council. Leading climbers such as Rab Carrington and Alan Rouse drink in the pub around the corner from me. Climbing, though, seems a bit of a closed society, and I begin to realise that climbers are weary of non-climbers. This is a brotherhood and there's no gaining admittance to the doors of the temple without some experience.

It's Thursday night and I've heard a rumour that the climbing club meets in a room behind a pub called the Rising Sun, somewhere on the outskirts of the city. When I walk into the pub things don't look right. The place is crowded with middle-class women dripping gold jewellery and drinking red wine. The men are expensively dressed. Displaying material possessions isn't done in the outdoor community, so I know for certain these folk are not climbers.

I leave through the doors at the back of the pub and am about to head home when I notice a stone-built outbuilding. I enter hesitantly, unsure if this is the right place – or, if it is, whether I will be accepted. Inside are a dozen or so men and women. Everyone is wearing jeans and scruffy clothing. The men look lean and fit and the women don't wear gold. This is the place. I approach a group of the bearded heroes and they point me towards the club's meets organiser, who explains about weekends away and summertime crag climbing.

There are no organised courses, and you can't learn to climb from a book, so I need the club to introduce me to the world of ropes and rock faces. Climbing is different from other sports. You can play table tennis by picking up a bat, you can cycle by jumping on a bike, and anyone can delude themselves they can play football. If you get any of these sports wrong the worst you'll get is a grazed knee. If you get climbing wrong, there's a good chance you die. There is also the fear – the kind of fear that leaves you sweating and trembling with your stomach in knots. These climbers know they can cope with that kind of fear, but I don't know if I can.

A week later I'm out on the club's evening meet at one of the local edges, desperately scrabbling upwards on the rock. Around Sheffield the short rock cliffs are formed from gritstone, a kind of hard sandstone. I call it gripstone.

"Have you got me?" I call up. I'm not a natural climber.

"I could hold an elephant." Andy's voice is calm. His job in the club is to literally teach novices the ropes. Andy has recently retired and is now able to indulge his love of climbing as often as he likes.

More scrabbling. I'm at least ten feet off the ground now and the rope above me is so tight if you had a violin bow you could play it.

"You're sure you've got me?"

I manage to move up, and for a few moments there are at least four inches of slack in the rope.

"Definitely."

I cling desperately to the rounded holds of the cliff. The fear has made the palms of my hands sweat and they keep sliding off the rock. This is an incredibly bad design fault in the human body – the one time you don't want your hands to sweat is when you are clinging, scared shitless, to a rock face. It's a kind of vicious cycle: you get scared, your hands sweat and start sliding off the rock, this frightens you more and your hands sweat more, making them increasingly slippery. Clearly, evolution cocked that one up. A few moments later I emerge over the edge of the cliff, gasping for breath, legs shaking and eyes bulging. I cling to a boulder, waiting for the earth to stop spinning.

"You'll get used to it," Andy reassures me. Over the next few weeks he teaches me how to belay, and how to put gear – odd wedges attached to wires – into the rock cracks so I don't get killed.

"You have to put a little twist into the rope as you coil it, so it doesn't kink," Andy says as he meticulously coils the climbing rope at his feet.

"Like this?" It's my turn. I put a little twist in the rope and it kinks twice as much.

Andy looks sadly at the mass of knots and tangles I have managed to create in only a few moments with the rope. Coiling a climbing rope so it doesn't tangle is a dark art – it takes practice, I discover. Even when you have mastered the technique I find that climbing ropes are not to be trusted. They lie there perfectly coiled and untangled, but if you turn your back on them they twist themselves into a Gordian knot.

Afterwards, Andy teaches me to abseil. He does this safely,

with a backup rope, so that if I faint with terror on the way down I won't die. This, I realise, is how you are supposed to learn to abseil, and not hanging off a cliff in the pouring rain in the Rocky Mountains anchored to an unstable boulder.

Now that I know a little more about climbing I begin to realise that my American climbing partners were to safety what icebergs were to the Titanic. Survival had been a matter of luck; leaving me perched on a wet sloping ledge with nothing to prevent a fall was mind-blowingly incompetent. I could easily have taken what climbers describe as a Desmond. This is rhyming slang for a Desmond Dekker which means falling off and hitting the ground, as in the deck. Desmond Dekker is a popular reggae singer. I have learnt a valuable lesson in climbing – be careful who you trust.

I now face the next challenge: getting some equipment of my own. Joe and I buy a climbing rope between us. In the garden of a friend's house we uncoil the new rope to its full length. With Joe at one end and me at the other, I can't help noticing how far you'd fall if you went the full 150ft. I make a mental note to avoid this. A few of the club members give me old bits of kit they don't need – odd-shaped nuts for inserting into cracks, a few wires. I buy some rock-climbing shoes called EBs, French in origin. Buying the EBs feels like a rite of passage: in purchasing these I am leaving the ground where I was a walker and taking to the cliffs where I will become a climber.

In Blacks mountaineering shop the assistant places the rubber-soled shoes on the counter with reverence, aware of the significance of the purchase in my life. "Now then, you want to get these shoes as tight as you can stand them and then go down a size. That's what all the really hard climbers do."

I follow his advice, and I must be a really hard climber because my EBs are so tight I can't bear to wear them for more than twenty minutes the pain is so excruciating. Go to any crag and you can see climbers sitting in their socks easing the pain of over-tight climbing shoes; the tighter the shoes, the harder the climber.

* * *

I am not a natural rock climber, but slowly, by climbing at weekends and in the light evenings, I gain some competence. With the summer approaching, Martin, Joe and I begin to plan our next expedition. Having walked through the glens of Knoydart the logical next step seems to be to walk across the summits. There is one problem – in order to do that we have to reduce the weight of our backpacks.

The most important item we need is a lightweight tent. This is difficult; there are lots of two-man tents on the market, and a few four-man tents, but ones designed for three are rare. Here we encounter one of the myths of tent manufacturers. They seem to design tents for a specific breed of dwarfs who only exist in the outdoors. Two-man tents are designed for two childlike creatures who never move. Try cooking or moving around in any of them and you'll find yourself in a contorted heap with your travelling companions.

The three of us spend long afternoons poring over a glossy copy of Field and Trek's catalogue with all the ardour of adolescent boys peering at a girly mag. Lightweight tents are in their infancy and the range is limited. In the end, we choose a High Country, made by Ultimate, one of the few tents on the market designed for three people. It's a traditional design with two uprights and a ridge pole – a palace, with space for all three of us plus our gear. Most important of all, it is far lighter than the canvas monster we lugged across Knoydart the previous summer.

Knoydart inspired us with its rugged terrain and sense of remoteness. Now, equipped with our new lightweight tent, we looked to Scotland again to provide us with a new challenge. Our Knoydart walk had largely taken us through the glens, occasionally crossing high ridges as the route demanded. Now we wanted to explore the high tops themselves, remaining at height for as long as we could. That summer we choose the ridge that runs between Glen Cannich and Glen Affric, rising to the summit of Carn Eige at 1,183m. It ends with a hill called Sgurr nan Ceathreamhnan (which would have the distinction of being the hill with the longest name we'd ever climbed). The ridge runs through some of the finest mountain scenery in Britain – rewarding enough, although the physical challenge is daunting.

In July 1978 we climb aboard a rattling old bus in Inverness, which eventually deposits us in the Highland village of Cannich. We proudly erect our new three-man tent and learn a new rule about camping. Once you take a tent out of its bag you can throw the bag away. This is because, unless you happen to have a PhD in origami, you will never be able to fold the tent up into a small enough bundle to go back into the bag. Tents are packed by an elite group of super folders in a trade whose secrets are passed down from generation to generation. Somehow they can get all the air out of the tent as they roll it up. As we pack there is always a small pocket of air somewhere in the fabric that moves around like a trapped hamster. You can chase it all you like, but it's always there; the tent has no chance of ever going back in.

That night, after a session of darts and beer in the Glen Affric Hotel, I learn another secret rule of camping. Whenever you get comfortable in a tent, just as your sleeping bag gets warm and cosy, the bladder demon comes to life. At first you try and ignore him but the bladder demon never goes away.

I'll just go back to sleep. I don't really need to pee, I tell myself.

All is quiet for a few minutes but then the demon returns. This time he is more insistent, the pressure in my bladder greater. In the end, I slide out of my bag. Now I face another challenge: getting out of the tent. I fumble in the dark for the zips, trying not to step on my companions sleeping beside me. The number of zips on the inside of the tent has multiplied overnight. I pull one; it's the wrong way, nothing happens. I pull the zip the other way and that is somehow wrong too. I manage to get one a few inches open and it jams in the darkness. By now the bladder demon is screaming at me, repressed for so long there is every danger I'll shower the inside of the tent with urine. I'm blindly pulling every zip I can find in every direction I can think of when one finally moves and I break out through the door. My trials are not over, I'm not out of the tent yet, I've merely made it into the porch between the inner and the flysheet.

"Mind the water bucket," Joe, ever practical even in his sleep, murmurs from the depths of his sleeping bag.

Crouched in the darkness I remember that, lurking somewhere in the tent porch, there is a bizarre creature. This is the folding canvas water bucket Joe has borrowed from his father's stock of ancient caravanning equipment. It is a canvas box, open at the top, that stays upright when full of water and folds away when empty. I know it's somewhere in the porch but I can't see it. If I overturn it, I'll flood the tent. Crouching under the flysheet, I decide where I think it is and edge carefully away. Suddenly my backside turns icy cold.

"Oh shit!"

"What's happened?" Joe replies.

"I've sat in the bloody water bucket."

"Wouldn't you be warmer in your sleeping bag?"

Oh the joys of camping.

* * *

Our plan for the following day is to start as low as we can on the ridge, effectively in the foothills. We do this because we want to be able to say we have completed the whole ridge and we can only say that if we start at its foot. Unfortunately, as we break off the road and try to find a way through the forest on to the ridge, it begins to rain. This is the worst kind of rain for walkers – fine, warm rain, the sort of devious rain that gets you wet without telling you. You are standing there, trying to decide if it's wet enough to put your waterproofs on and, while you're thinking about it, the rain sneaks up behind you and soaks you to the skin. That's not fair. Honest rain doesn't do that.

Honest rain comes up to you and says, "Good afternoon. I'll be falling for a while now, so if I were you I'd put my waterproofs on." That's reasonable.

This rain says, "Me, raining? Oh no, not at all. I'm only a

thick mist. Why I wouldn't bother putting your waterproofs on. You're not even damp." All the while, pouring several gallons of water down your neck.

I pull on my newly acquired Henri Lloyd regulation orange nylon waterproofs only to realise I'm soaked before I put them on. My cagoule is heavy and high-vis orange. If you go out in the Lake District on a wet day, the hills are full of bright orange blobs in a chain visible from space. I soon discover that although the jacket is completely waterproof the bright orange dye isn't and everywhere I go I leave a trail of little orange droplets. Soon everything I possess has an orange tinge.

Climbing up through the forestry, waist deep in heather, is slow and exhausting. At last we break through the tree line and on to the open hillside.

"Oh God, I'm soaked," Joe declares, throwing down his pack in disgust.

"Me too." Opening my cagoule, I survey the rivers of condensation running down the inside of my jacket. Martin arrives and stands, disconsolate, surveying the rolling bog we now have to cross. He too is saturated. We are the brotherhood of the soggy.

Although we have not covered many miles, we have established ourselves on the ridge and, perhaps more importantly, above the tree line. We make camp, unfolding our pristine tent on top of the bog. It is now we learn the next law of camping: no matter how hard you try the water always gets in. Martin is meticulous. All his possessions are protected by individual plastic bags which he carefully folds up and stores in other plastic bags. We leave our boots in the porch, take off our waterproofs and fold them inside out, wet surfaces together. All these precautions against the ingress of the wet are futile. Somehow, inevitably, inexorably, the damp always gets in – and you and everything you own become moist.

After a warm, wet night we set off again along the ridge. At first we are dodging between bogs but, as we climb higher, the ridge narrows and the ground becomes drier and more solid. Now the showers thin out. By the time we reach the first true summit, Toll Creagach, we see glimpses through breaks in the cloud of the endless ridge running away to the west. We encounter no one. We are alone in this huge mountain landscape.

"There's no paths!" I exclaim in astonishment.

The three of us stand surveying the way ahead, swaying under our packs. Curtains of rainclouds part to reveal wave after wave of undulating ridges. I can see no paths or houses for miles in any direction – no trace of humanity whatsoever – and ask Joe if he can see anything.

"No, nothing at all."

Everywhere I have ever been in my life there have been paths. Merseyside is full of them, waymarked, signposted and fenced. In the Lake District, wide, well-maintained motorways guide the walker from one junction to the next. The Pennine Way is, by definition, a great long path. The discovery that there are places in Britain where so few people walk that they leave no mark on the landscape is a revelation. In the Highlands we have found a huge place to explore, a lifetime of possibilities.

We walk on for hours, following narrow ridges and climbing up and over a series of summits with long descents between each top. We haven't covered many miles after a hard day's walk, but much ascent and descent, and grow weary as we search for somewhere to camp for the night. There's no water on the ridge so we have to drop down to find somewhere to camp. Our legs rebel on the steep descent into a sheltered corrie that, even this late in the year, holds a patch of snow the size of a football ground. Even here we search in vain for a flat space and find none. In the end we have to settle for camping on the snow – the only level area around. We savour a drop of Glenmorangie, our favourite malt, which Joe carries in a small flask. The corrie below the summit of An Socach – Gaelic for 'the snout' – is our highest camp ever, and as the shadows lengthen it feels as though we have travelled to a different world.

That night I suddenly wake unable to breathe. Sleeping with the top closed on my mummy sleeping bag, I have rolled away from the opening and my face is now pressed hard against the fabric. This may sound inconsequential but I'm filled with blind panic. I locate the opening of the bag and fight the urge to tear it open. This won't work – the cord is well beyond my ability to break – but I'm filled with a claustrophobic fear so strong it blocks out rational though. Sweating and gasping for air, I finally manage to find the little toggle fastener that closes the bag. The damn thing is always fiddly to open but eventually it yields and I can breathe again. I lie in the tent gasping and sweating. How strange that such a small thing can cause so much terror.

The following day we strike the tent and pick up any litter, taking pleasure in the fact that the only traces of our visit are a few peg holes in the snow. As I climb out of the corrie and back towards the ridge I try to convince myself that, as we've consumed most of the food, the pack has grown lighter. This is what my mind says; my legs, however, are unconvinced. This time we have up-to-date maps. We don't want to be ambushed by some thug of a hydroelectric dam waiting to dump a lake in front of us. We have learned from Knoydart. On our third day, we finally climb the last few feet on to the pointed summit of Sgurr nan Ceathreamhnan. This magnificent mountain is one of the remotest hills in Scotland. Its top marks the point at which a series of fine ridges meet, and its name means 'the hill of the quarters' – a reference to how the ridges of the mountain divide the land.

We find a jam jar buried in the summit cairn, and inside it a notebook signed by other visitors to this remote place. After scrawling our own names, we begin the long descent into the glen. By the time we plod down to the main path that runs from Glen Affric, past the remote Youth Hostel at Alltbeithe, and on through the high-sided glen over the Bealach an Sgairne to finally bring us to the campsite at Morvich, it's raining heavily. The walk has taken us three days through some of the most spectacular scenery in Britain and in all that time we have not seen another person. We have come a long way from our crowded Merseyside home. That night we celebrate in our favourite Highland haunt, the Shiel Bridge hotel, its bar packed to the rafters with young hikers.

The following day we attempt The Saddle, a big hill with fine long ridges that towers over Shiel Bridge. But the weather is getting worse; after a thousand feet of climbing, it begins to rain heavily and Joe discovers that he has left his cagoule in the tent. Armed with an excuse to retreat, we scuttle back to an afternoon session in the hotel. Martin, who is rarely to be seen more than a few feet from a railway or ferry timetable, suggests we travel to Kyle and take a cruise on a small boat to discover the coastline. Our legs, still recovering from three days on the ridge, heartily agree with this suggestion. In Kyle we feast on apples, relishing fresh fruit after days on fake mountain food.

A local was so surprised to see anyone eating an apple he stopped to comment as we sat on the steps outside the grocer's crunching through our Cox's Orange Pippins, "Ah, you like good food then, boys!"

It has to be remembered that fruit was only classified as a food in Scotland in 1976. Even today, after many failed attempts to deep fry them, apples are regarded with suspicion by most people north of the border. We share the small ferry with American tourists and a bus tour from Bolton. The boat holds about fifty people and smells of diesel and Brasso. Someone has clearly made a big effort – all the brass fitments are polished bright with pride. The boat is named the *Vital Spark* in a flagrant attempt to ride on the coat-tails of the Para Handy stories. This humble vessel makes two sailings a day to Toscaig, near Applecross, carrying mail, locals and tourists. As we take our little cruise we are witnessing the end of an era. For thousands of years the most efficient way of travelling around the Highlands of Scotland has been by boat. The road network is still developing, and even as we board the ferry many A roads remain single track. In the winter they are frequently blocked by snow or washed away in heavy rain. This small boat is much more than a tourist cruiser – until only a year before it was a vital lifeline for small communities dotted along the edge of the

Applecross peninsula. A new road was only opened the previous year taking the coastal route in the north from Torridon. Prior to its existence, the only way to these small communities was the formidable hill road over the Bealach na Bà ('pass of the cattle' in Gaelic). The road rises over two thousand feet from the foot of the pass at sea level to its summit and takes a series of hairpin bends that have been the undoing of many an unwary motorist.

Near the end of our holiday, the weather turns and provides us with a couple of fine days. We backpack over to Torridon and camp amongst the midge-infested trees once more. This time we climb the imposing Liathach, perhaps the steepest hill in Britain, rising some three thousand feet in little more than half a mile and with the added excitement of a series of pinnacles running along its crest. I lead our little party as we climb towards the ridge, weaving our way up between the short cliffs and terraces of this Torridonian giant.

The day is warm and dry, and we have left our rucksacks, with their loads of sleeping bags and camping gear, far below in the glen. The climb feels easy and relaxed without our burdens. We gain height quickly, and soon the vast landscape of Torridon is revealed below us, like nothing we have seen before. There is something prehistoric about this place. It is a landscape of steep, rugged mountains, russet-brown cliffs and horizontal grass-green terraces. To the east Beinn Eighe rises, a complex giant of a mountain, with its hidden corries and multiple summits linked by sweeping scree-clad ridges. To the west the great pyramid of Beinn Alligin towers above the coast, its ridges sweeping down into the sea. Beneath this mountain is the tiny village of Torridon, a settlement so small it would barely register as anywhere at all in our Merseyside home. There is a shop that doubles as a post office, its shelves crowded with everything from light bulbs to tinned food – everything needed to support this isolated community. A ribbon of twenty-odd white-painted houses runs along the shoreline, picked out between the green of the hillside and the blue of the sea. Standing on the mountainside this July morning in 1978, cooled by the heather-soaked breeze, I see a place where the hand of man has had little influence. If I were standing here a hundred years ago, or perhaps a thousand, the view would be little different.

We climb higher. I try to read the terrain ahead of me, to find a way through the rocks, short cliffs and impenetrable heather. I am learning to listen to the mountain, to move in sympathy with it, to follow where the hill leads and let it show me the easiest way up. Many hill-goers don't possess this ability. They seem to blunder into the hill before them, to assault it head on, to lack sympathy with the land. There are old ways through these hills. There are stalkers' tracks, used for over a hundred years to bring the carcasses of deer down the mountains. Older than these are shepherds' routes, followed by people, dogs and sheep for generations. Older still are the ancient routes between communities now long forgotten, paths made by people whose homes exist only in the stone outlines of houses swallowed by heather and in the memory of these hills.

Freed from our packs for the day, the ascent feels easy; and once the traverse of the ridge is complete, we relax and look out across the immense vista. The Torridonian hills are unique in the British Isles. Torridonian sandstone is one of the oldest rock types in Britain, characterised by steep terraced faces consisting of terraces broken by short cliffs. These terraces can be a nightmare if you are trying to descend them in mist or failing light. Finding a safe way through the maze of short vertical cliffs can be a long and nerve-wracking process.

"I wonder what this place is like in winter," Joe murmurs to himself as we stand looking up at the towering bulk of Liathach.

"Yes," I reply, "I wonder." Our next challenge has been set.

* * *

Six months later we are driving through the night on our way to our first Highland winter. It's 4.00 a.m. and I'm dozing on the back seat of my Morris Marina (the first vehicle I have ever owned). Joe is driving, and the car sways gently as we head north through the darkness up the A74. It's a few days before Christmas and the possibility of our first Highland winter fills us all with excitement. I slip in and out of consciousness, dreaming of white virgin snows and catching odd snatches of conversation.

"It's too long." Joe's voice. He's arguing with Martin about something and I can tell he's not winning.

Martin is adamant. "No it isn't, 65cm is perfect for my height, six foot three.'"

"But you don't need that length and then there's the weight."

"The weight helps drive it into the snow."

Joe has lost the argument and there is silence for a while as I drift towards sleep.

I am dozing, dreaming of snow covered hills, and am only roused when Martin starts rummaging on the back seat for a can of Coke and sandwiches he stashed when we stopped for petrol on the M6. A constant supply of food is required to maintain Martin's fuel supply. I hear the *shfffut* of the Coke can being opened, followed by the rattle of the sandwiches being unwrapped. A moment later the car gives an odd lurch.

"Shit!" Joe shouts.

Then there is a strange sensation, as if the car is floating. Now the car shudders and I hear the unmistakable sound of one of the rear tyres blowing out. The car feels normal for a few seconds, but then it begins to spin gently.

"Oh shit, I've lost it!"

I cower on the back seat, curling myself into a foetal position as the spinning accelerates with hands folded behind my neck braced for impact. The lights of the dual carriageway spin past the windows – once, twice, three times. The car begins to slow.

Maybe we will get away with this.

Something explodes into the side of the car. Broken glass showers across the back seat as the vehicle writhes like a beast in pain. Everything stops and there is a moment of frozen silence.

I sit up, dazed, worrying about the possibility of fire. "Is everyone okay? Get out, get out quick!"

Moments later we are all standing under the street lights staring at the car. A wall stopped our spin. The car's final 360° took it into the entrance of a petrol station and onto its low perimeter wall. The car now has a wall implanted in the front passenger door.

Martin is standing, crushed drinks can in one hand, dripping with Coca Cola, the remains of a cheese sandwich in the other. Joe is shaking his head in disbelief.

"I just don't know what happened," he intones over and over again.

I know what happened. The Morris Marina has a reputation for having zero road holding. These cars are simple in their construction and have a deceptively powerful engine. The Marina is capable of 'doing the ton', as it is affectionately known, but it can only do that in a straight line. Any attempt to turn the vehicle will almost inevitably result in a skid. The Morris Marina is the ballet dancer of cars in the 1970s – at any moment, and with no warning, your car will suddenly begin performing Swan Lake.

"Oh look, a sparrow has crapped on the road," the car says. "I'll just do a few pirouettes." Joe braked on a corner and that was enough of an excuse for the Marina to go into its dance routine. In incidents like these life always hangs on the merest fragment of chance. If we had spun on past the garage we might, at worst, have lost a wheel; a few yards earlier and we might have entered the garage forecourt, taken out the petrol pumps and turned the place into a fireball.

The car now has a massive hole in the front passenger door and it looks like the frame is buckled too. Basically, the car is bent. Like most outdoor folk I'm not too attached to material things. To me a car is a box for going climbing in, not 'my pride and joy' as some people regard these machines. We are all uninjured, so I don't worry too much. A siren wails and a police car pulls up. Two bored-looking officers take a look at the car and then at me. As soon as it's clear we are sober they lose what little interest they had, but they ask for the car's MOT, which I don't have.

"Why have you no got the MOT?"

"I sent it off to get the tax disc renewed." I indicate the tax disc, which is a couple of weeks out of date.

The officer scratches his arse, clearly wishing he was in bed. Eventually the police, too bored to try and charge us with anything, head back to the station for cocoa.

We replace the tyre and limp back to the Lake District,. Martin has to hold the door shut, bent and windowless. It's a long, cold, defeated journey.

I never thought I'd spend Christmas wild camping at the head of Langdale but you don't always end up where you think you will. The highlight of Christmas dinner is a packet of dehydrated custard as we listen to the rain bounce off the tent's flysheet. Joe produces some whisky and we manage some cheer, but the premature demise of our 'Highland winter' leaves us all deflated – although in considerably better shape than my Marina.

6
Winter in Langdale

When I limp back to Sheffield, new year celebrations behind us, winter arrives with a vengeance – the coldest winter since 1963. The streets are buried in two feet of snow and a glaze of ice. With industrial unrest wracking the nation, the winter of 78/79 has been dubbed the Winter of Discontent. Prime Minister James Callaghan introduces legislation to curb pay rises in an effort to contain growing inflation. This sparks strikes across Britain, with lorry drivers and public service workers downing tools. Before long, many cities have rubbish piled up on the streets; in some places the dead remain unburied. The Government declares a state of emergency.

When the men who drive the gritting lorries turn off their engines in defiance of the Government, Sheffield grinds to a halt. Devoid of cars, the streets take on an eerie silence as winter conditions I have only previously seen in the mountains grip the towns of South Yorkshire. As travel breaks down, the gritter drivers become objects of venom to many in the city for going on strike when they are needed most.

To be fair, if you drive a gritter there is not much point in going on strike in July, is there? Picture yourself sitting in the garden with the sun beating down, sipping a cold beer when your wife appears, distraught, from the kitchen.

"Darling, terrible news: the gritters have gone on strike."

"Bugger 'em, we'll starve them out."

The streets turn into ice rinks. Soon, the few cars bold enough to venture out are bouncing off each other with gay abandon. After only a couple of weeks every body shop in the city is full of injured cars, their bodywork bent and buckled as if from some huge battle. My Marina languishes for weeks in a jammed automobile casualty ward.

For mountaineers, a bad winter is good news. In late January, with my car still out of action, Martin and I catch a train to snow-bound Windermere. We are hopeful of returning to Angle Tarn now it is firmly in the grip of winter. But due to the snow, the train is late and we miss the last bus down Langdale to the hiker's bar of the Old Dungeon Ghyll. It's ten o'clock in the evening and the price of a taxi is well beyond our means so we decide to spend the night at the station.

The waiting room is warm and snug and a fine place to shelter from the frosty night air. It even has a coal fire, its embers dying as we settle down on the wooden benches in our sleeping bags. I'm just sliding off in a warm, dreamy sleep when the waiting room door creaks open. The station master, a small, stout man in a tight-fitting uniform, double takes when he sees our somnolent forms recumbent on British Rail property.

"You'se can't sleep here!"

The cheery station master depicted in *The Railway Children* would have turned a blind eye to two hill-goers down on their luck, but this gentleman is the real thing – and any kindness he might once have possessed has long been supplanted by railway regulations. Blustering at our audacity, he ejects us into the frosty night air just as a few flakes of snow are beginning to drift from the heavens.

"Where we going to sleep now?" Martin asks.

"Here," I reply indignantly.

Martin looks down in puzzlement at the station steps. A smile creeps over his face. "They can't stop us sleeping outside the station, can they?"

In mute protest, we unroll our sleeping mats on the concrete steps right outside the locked doors of the station, pull the tent flysheet over us, and try to sleep.

It feels like only a few moments later when I become aware of people stepping over us. Pulling back the flysheet, I find that it is Saturday morning and early day-tripping shoppers are flooding into the station before heading off to hunt for bargains in Liverpool's Marks & Spencer. Mums and their daughters regard us with thinly veiled disgust, but despite an inch of snow having fallen Martin and I spent a remarkably comfortable night on the steps of Windermere station. Part of me would have delighted at the station master finding two frozen corpses on the steps in the morning. I would like to think that finding us dead might cause him to reflect on his inhumanity, but I suspect he would simply have sighed, opened his book of railway regulations, and turned to:

Para 4 (b) What to do when you find young men frozen solid outside the station.

We are down and out in Windermere.

Martin examines his watch. "The bus for Langdale leaves from here in ten minutes!"

"Best get packed up, then." I leap out of my sleeping bag, fortunately fully dressed.

"We'll never make it!"

Martin's equipment has a habit of expanding during the night and being impossible to pack in the morning. Ten minutes is nothing like enough time for him to prepare for departure.

I point to the bus stop only feet away. "Of course we'll be ready. It's only over there."

"Can't be done," he repeats.

Much grunting and frantic packing follows. The bus arrives and I leap on, followed by Martin with most of his belongings bundled under an arm and bootlaces untied. The bus driver looks at us with disbelief.

"You want to go to Langdale? In this weather?"

"Yes!" I respond enthusiastically.

"With all this snow, road's probably blocked." He pauses for dramatic effect. "Foolhardy, I'd call it. What with all this snow."

I thrust money towards him and he looks sceptically at the crumpled notes.

"I don't think I should sell you a ticket right now. We might not get there, and then where would we be?"

An answer leaps into my mind: *presumably not in Langdale.* I think it, but leave it unsaid; the driver looks even more disconsolate and I don't want to risk deepening his despair with an attempt at humour. He draws me towards him into a conspiratorial huddle, his thin fingers clutching my rucksack strap.

"See, I told them. Only a fool would want to go down Langdale in this weather. But me boss wouldn't listen, said I had to take the bus out. There'll be no passengers I told him but here you are. Two of you!" He cast a baleful look towards Martin, who has just dropped his spare socks on the step of the bus. "Foolhardy."

Eventually, shaking his head and muttering, the bus driver agrees to attempt the suicidal. We set off for Langdale. The snow is piled up in the fields as the ancient bus creaks its way up the valley, and the dry-stone walls are capped with two feet of snow, bringing them up to the height of the bus windows. Martin and I watch in fascination as a transformed landscape passes by. Twenty minutes behind schedule, the bus forces its way through the snow drifts and into the car park of the Old Dungeon Ghyll Hotel. I pause by the driver's window and proffer the crumpled notes once more.

"Well, I've been thinking." He sighs, eyeing the notes with deep suspicion. "If I sell you tickets you'll have been passengers and, like I told the boss, there'll be no passengers today. So if I sell you tickets he'll say there was passengers, and I'll have to come back in case there's more, and that would be…" His voice trails off as he searches for the word.

"Foolhardy?"

"Exactly. Foolhardy." Now he has some agreement, he warms to his task. "So if I don't sell you any tickets there won't have been any passengers – and I won't have to come back. I'm sure you can see the sense in that?"

I grin at the prospect of a free bus ride. "Of course!"

Martin and I step off the bus into the snowy wastes of Cumbria, content in the knowledge that the impeccable logic of the nation's transport staff has been preserved once more.

It's early afternoon when we arrive at Dungeon Ghyll. Martin wants to camp beside Angle Tarn but, it being my birthday the following day, I am glowing with the prospect of foaming pints amongst the cheery cave dwellers within. I explain this to Martin.

"The pub'll be the death of you," he growls, and marches off towards Angle Tarn. I follow with reluctance, thigh deep in the snow, looking longingly at the inn as we pass by.

Langdale climbs gently for the first few miles and it is only when the path reaches the base of Rossett Pike that a short, steep climb begins. Burdened by camping equipment, in deep snow and – at least as far as I am concerned – going in the wrong direction, we climb in silence until we reach the amphitheatre that encloses the little lake. The friendly Angle Tarn I walked beside a few summers ago is gone. In its place is a frozen, hostile wilderness. The sparkling water of the summer is stilled to a hard, brittle silence by the cold. With the fading of the light, the oncoming darkness brings a deep, profound stillness. Nothing moves here now. The snowflakes that drifted through the air as we climbed to the side of the tarn lie still. No wind moves the drifting crystals. This is January and winter has cast its spell.

As the night sky clears, a million stars appear and the Milky Way becomes a great sparkling band across the sky. We erect the tent and can feel the temperature falling rapidly. By the time darkness comes we are already burrowed into our sleeping bags, fully clothed, in an attempt to armour ourselves against the cold – but our three-season bags are way out of their depth. I feel the frost seeping in through the bag's insulation, past my uncle Alan's RAF trousers and my WWII regulation long johns. My trousers might have defeated Hitler's air force, but they are no match for a Cumbrian winter.

"I could be drinking Old Peculier in the bar of the Old Dungeon Ghyll right now," I point out to Martin, my breath freezing in the torch light inches from my face.

"It'll be better in the morning," Martin claims with no particular logic I can understand. "Let's get some sleep."

I switch off the torch and try to convince my toes they are warm and comfortable. My toes, however, are having none of it and I'm forced to wriggle them constantly to get some warmth into them. If we sleep at all it is fitfully. A couple of hours pass, or it might be ten minutes.

"Martin, are you awake?"

"Yes," he responds instantly.

I switch on the torch and we find our tent transformed. Our frozen breath hangs in delicate fronds of ice from the fabric above us. Every time we make the slightest movement, fragments of ice detach themselves and fall on to our sleeping bags, where they melt. Not only are we cold but now we are damp. We light the stove and get a little warmth before attempting to sleep again.

I wake in the cold darkness. Somehow I've managed to get warm enough to sleep in our ice-wreathed tent. It's then it happens – I am betrayed by my own bladder. I'm going to have to pee. The bladder monster has returned. I ignore the urge for a while, hoping that by willpower alone I will be able to suppress it; but slowly, irresistibly, the urge grows. I fumble with the sleeping bag fastening and wriggle free into the tent. I have to thaw the zips with my fingers. After thrusting feet into boots I step out into the night, leaving behind my cagoule – I'll only be out for a moment. There is almost enough moonlight to see, so I plod a few feet away and enjoy a moment of blessed relief.

In that moment, clouds obscure the moon and the blizzard recommences. Turning back, I can't see the tent.

No problem. I'll just follow my footprints back. I follow the footprints through the gloom and the fast-falling snow but there is no tent at the end of them.

It must be this way. Still no tent. I zigzag, realising with growing panic that I'm lost. I'm cold now. The wind is driving snow through my pullover.

"Martin! Martin!" I call into the darkness. There is no reply. The wind is rising and, if I'm not close enough to the tent, he won't hear me. As the snow in my pullover starts to melt, I start to shiver uncontrollably.

"Martin! Martin!"

No response. The white world engulfs me and I fall face forward into a drift, unable to tell where I'm stepping.

I've got to find that bloody tent. Time rushes past; every step takes me further from survival.

"Martin!"

"What?"

He sounds close, but I can't tell which direction his voice is coming from.

"Put the bloody light on," I yell at him.

Suddenly a mound of snow a few feet to my left emits a dim glow. I plunge through the frozen tent flaps, trembling as much from fear as cold.

By morning the storm has abated and we emerge stiff-limbed from our long night. Despite the deep snow surrounding us we decide to head for Scafell Pike, the highest mountain in England. The hill is close and we are already high up – it should be easy pickings. We break trail in the fresh snow with no sign of other walkers. In this severe weather, there's no one else up here but us.

As soon as we pass over Esk Hause, a place where many routes meet, the spaghetti junction of the Lake District, the weather again deteriorates. I stand for a moment surveying the blizzard-torn landscape.

"My god, look at it!"

This is what we have come for. Now we are in the midst of real mountains. No longer are these gentle hills – this place is both remote and wild, scary and exhilarating. Neither of us has experienced anything like this before. A heady mixture of fear and excitement fills us. If we can cope with this extreme weather, we will have won our spurs as winter mountaineers.

But the blizzard grows more ferocious with every foot we climb. A few hundred feet from the summit of the mountain, I stop and turn to Martin.

"What do you think?" I yell above the wind.

"I think," Martin says from deep inside his balaclava, "that this is far enough."

I am not about to argue. It is becoming difficult to stand as the wind whips snow across the landscape. We have made our point – as has the weather. It's time to go down. I expect the weather to improve as we lose height but it actually gets worse. Soon all we can see is a few yards in the whiteness. We look for Esk Hause to materialise below us, but the landscape looks unfamiliar, transformed by the snow and wind. Our tracks are obliterated moments after we make them so we cannot follow our route. The wind tries to tear the map from our icy gloves as we attempt again and again to make some sense of where we are in this huge, white ocean.

We can't linger for long in this weather.

"We'll have to abandon the tent," I point out.

Close by is shelter, warmth and food. We are near to survival but we have to find it first. Abandoning our precious tent is the last resort but it is rapidly beginning to look as though we will have no other option. From our location we should be able to descend to Eskdale, a long way from where we want to be – but at least out of the blizzard. I look again at the map, trying to pinpoint our position. My mental map of the place twists and turns but I can't get it to agree with the compass or the terrain.

If we can't find the path junction at Esk Hause, we'll never find the tent – and wandering lost in this weather could be fatal. Reluctantly, we head for Eskdale, defeated but alive. I turn one last time to look at the ravaged landscape and suddenly something clicks, the map inside my head lines up with the mountain, and the compass falls into place.

"There's Esk Hause." I point wildly to the small plateau a few hundred yards away. It's a place we have been crossing and recrossing numerous times over the last hour or so.

"Are you sure?"

To me it is as if there's a neon sign above the place, but Martin's unconvinced. He follows, less than persuaded I'm not following some frozen mirage.

"Here we are!" I declare in triumph upon reaching the small area of level ground.

"We can't be. Where's the shelter?"

Martin is referring to a little cross-shaped stone shelter of four intersecting walls that sits at the path junction. He is right: the shelter is gone, yet I know we are in the right place. I'm pacing about looking for it when I stub my foot against something hard in the snow. I hop around on one leg swearing. Martin prods the offending object with his ice axe and then begins to dig.

"Aha!" he declares in triumph, like Sherlock Holmes solving a case, and pulls his long ice axe out of the snow. "Here it is."

"What have you found? Excalibur?"

At his feet is a cross of stones. This is the shelter, completely buried in snow, and the reason we couldn't find the path junction is clear. We were already there but couldn't see it.

The wind abates slightly as we descend to the tarn, crampons biting into hard snow. I turn to Martin, delighted that we have escaped the trap.

"Almost there."

"What's the matter with your face?" he responds. Touching my cheek, I find it numb and coated in ice; I'm close to frostbite. I scrape off the ice and warm my cheek with my hand. Sensation painfully returns.

"We better get down."

Half an hour later I arrive back at the tent to find it completely buried in snow. Martin arrives moments after me.

"Where's the tent?" he demands.

"You're standing on it!"

We look down to where his crampons have neatly punctured the flysheet. Neither of us wants another night in the fridge, and this time, when I suggest we head for the pub, Martin doesn't argue.

Back in the bar of the Old Dungeon Ghyll, Old Peculier in

hand, I hold forth to the small group of climbers and recount our day's adventures. That night, too tired to walk to the campsite, we camp in two feet of snow in the pub car park. As we settle down in a fog of beer-induced comfort, Martin switches on the light.

"Oh, by the way. Happy birthday." In the excitement, the milestone has slipped my mind.

I am twenty-four.

7

The White Giant

Four months after our frozen epic by Angle Tarn, I am with Joe in the Alpine town of Chamonix. It's late morning in Snell's Field, the little campsite at the foot of Mont Blanc. Hung-over climbers emerge from their tents, shivering in the chill at the start of the day. The air is full of languid chatter and the roar of Primus stoves and the campsite is a sordid jumble of tents and improvised plastic shelters; ropes, carabineers, boots and ice axes litter the ground. Last night's campfires send wisps of smoke curling into the still air as they smoulder and die. The sun has not yet reached the campsite. Mont Blanc looms over the little community of climbers and casts a long shadow across the valley of Chamonix far below its stark, ice-white summit.

I'm squatting over my pan, gently poking a teabag around in the hot water. As I watch the liquid turn brown, a police car pulls up on the dirt road – one of those fragile 2CVs that look as though they are made of egg boxes and corrugated cardboard. A tall, young police officer steps out. With meticulous care he straightens his cap, incongruously smart amongst the chaos of the climbers' camp. Slowly he walks across the field cluttered with tents, stopping here and there to question the bleary-eyed tent dwellers. His footsteps are measured, gaze steady, expression sombre as he moves methodically from one tent to another. He is looking for someone.

Stillness follows him as he passes the sleepy climbers; gradually the whole place falls silent and every eye turns to watch the tall blue figure's deliberate progress. He stops at one tent, and the occupant stands, nods and then points. The gendarme follows his gaze to where a young girl waits. She is in her early twenties, in blue jeans and a scruffy pullover; blonde hair, an unkempt mass, hides her face. I notice she is trembling as the policeman walks towards her, and looks like she might turn and run. Instead she waits, motionless. He comes close to her and whispers a question. She nods. The gendarme talks to her quietly for moment, then the girl's knees buckle and she is falling. The young police officer has been expecting this; he catches her shoulders and steadies her.

Together they walk towards his car: the gendarme, erect and smart in his blue uniform; the girl, scruffy in her jeans and wild hair, sobbing quietly. I watch, mute with horror, as they drive away down the dusty road in the policeman's rattling car. Once the car passes from sight the camp becomes alive with rumours of rockfall, avalanche and tragedy.

It's only than that I realise who he is, that tall young man in the blue uniform. He is the angel of death.

* * *

Let's rewind to the previous winter.

There are different kinds of blizzards. Some arrive like a trainload of football hooligans, full of bluster and bravado, knocking down anything that gets in their way. Others, like the blizzard we are in now, sneak up on you, soft footed. Martin, Joe and I have been climbing slowly towards the summit of Ben

More above the village of Crianlarich for a couple of hours now. Last night we camped, in a foot of snow, in the goods yard of the village's Victorian station. That's one of the nice things about snow; it changes all the rules. Had we camped there in summer we would have roused yet another station master's fury, but now, with winter in control, no one cares. Snow puts things in perspective. Station staff stay indoors with hot chocolate, warming their feet before coal fires. If you are crazy enough to sleep in the snow, they leave you alone.

As we climb up the ridge, following the footprints of a large party, it begins snowing. At first it's a matter-of-fact kind of snow; a little flurry here and there, just a dusting, nothing too serious. It must have sneaked up on us because the world is being gradually obliterated by falling white. We are in the midst of a no-nonsense, road-blocking blizzard, and even the sounds of our voices are deadened.

"This is getting deep," Joe says, prodding a snowdrift with his ice axe.

"We've not got much time either," Martin adds, aware that our train north to Fort William is due in a few short hours.

Our resolve to reach the summit is weakening and the truth is that, in this weather, even if we get to the top, we'll simply swap one patch of white for another. We turn and head for the valley. With little wind the blizzard holds us in a cocoon-like embrace. Our world shrinks to the few feet we can see around us. I feel almost comfortable here. It's not even that cold, but I know this place has a hidden hostility.

We find the top of the ridge unusually icy as we start the descent, so decide to stop and put on our crampons. I've only worn mine on a few occasions. For the uninitiated, crampons are spikes you strap on your feet so you can walk on slippery ice. That sounds simple enough but crampons are uniquely tricky customers. I struggle with a spider's web of straps that slide and tangle in my gloved hands. My crampons won't cooperate. They were quite happy in my rucksack and don't like being out here in the cold. They fight back. Halfway through putting them on I realise that I've got them on the wrong feet and have to start again. Once I have them strapped on my boots I face the ultimate challenge: tightening the straps in a blizzard with thick gloves on. Eventually I take a few tentative steps. But the battle is not over – walking about with spikes on your feet is tricky. The crampons know this and do their best to trip me up with every step.

Joe, practical as ever, gets his crampons on with little difficulty, but Martin's crampons are possessed by the devil. His crampons were, of course, packed in a plastic bag which is now doing its best to use what little wind there is to escape. Martin frantically pursues the bag, swearing as he wrestles with straps and metal while Joe and I stand resigned to watch the battle.

"Right then." Martin rises, victorious at last, lethal spikes on his feet. "Let's get going."

My crampons crunch into the ice and I have to learn a new way of walking. I no longer avoid the icy sections where I would have slipped without crampons; now I seek out the slippery places and drive the metal teeth into the ice where they bite securely. Difficult as they are to fit, once you get them on your feet there is a new freedom. You can step anywhere you like, knowing that you won't fall. I step forward with increasing confidence. All is well for a few moments until the spikes of my right foot catch the straps of my left and I plunge forward into the snow like Buster Keaton on a banana skin.

"You all right?" Joe asks.

"Yes, I think so." I get to my feet awkwardly and stand brushing the snow from my body. I shake myself; everything works, only my ego has been bruised.

"Did you hear that?" Martin is a few paces from us, motionless, listening.

"Hear what?"

"I'm not sure. There was something." We listen. There is nothing but the sound of the softly falling snow. "Maybe nothing," Martin concedes and we turn to head down the ridge again. Then, from somewhere out in the sea of white, there is a cry. It's faint but defiantly human in this isolated place. The snow distorts sound and in the stillness it appears to come from several places at once.

"Hello!" I yell. The response is instant.

* * *

As the train heads north through the rolling hills of the Borders the landscape grows increasingly wintry. The dusting of snow that was present as we passed by Cumbria has given way to sweeping snowfields in a Narnian landscape. All three of us watch the snowscape drift past the window with growing excitement. This time it looks as though we are going to make it. We are, at last, about to experience a Highland winter. A year ago, when my Marina spun us into a wall, we didn't even get this far. The train, we decide, is more reliable and definitely safer.

Martin looks anxiously at his watch. "It's going to be close."

"What is?" I reply, tearing my eyes from the arctic scenery.

"We are running late and have to get across to Glasgow Queen Street to make the connection. We won't have a lot of time. If we miss it, we won't get to Fort William tonight."

The thought of losing a whole day of our precious holiday in the north, because of one missed train, fills us with despair.

I set off down the platform at Glasgow's Central Station at full tilt, my backpack bouncing as I run. Ice axe, crampons, spoon, mug, cooking pots all rattle in a musical jingle as my boots hit the floor. We sprint past startled shoppers and commuters in a desperate race to make the train north. A ticket collector at the end of the platform watches us charging towards his gate with obvious alarm. All six foot three of Martin, his huge rucksack complete with giant Excalibur ice axe waving in the air, is bearing down on him. The ticket collector retreats inside his little box and waves us on without any attempt to take our tickets. At last we've got the better of a British Rail official. Once out in the street I accelerate away.

"Left!" Martin yells. Now I'm running up Renfield Street, dodging on and off the pavement to avoid the startled shoppers trudging home.

"Right!" Martin yells. We charge down West George Street, past shops and offices, pubs and hotels and out into George Square; now I can see Queen Street station.

"Platform three." Martin's voice is more distant now. He and Joe are about a hundred yards behind me.

I head through the station, and to my delight there standing at platform three is our train. We've made it! Then, to my horror, the train begins to move. I'm close enough to leap on but Martin and Joe are still coming through the turnstiles. Then I remember that there is a rule: if I can get the door open the train has to stop.

I sprint the last few yards and hurl open the door. The train gathers speed. The guard should be looking down the platform but he isn't. He is somewhere up the front of the train with his nose buried in *The Sun*, content in the knowledge that all his train doors are closed. Martin and Joe are gaining on the train but still too far away. I can't leap on – I'd arrive in Fort William with only half a tent and no way of contacting the rest of the crew. The platform attendant has joined in now, a little plump man waving a red flag and blowing a whistle, but despite all this the train gains speed. I'm having to run full tilt to keep up with it. Martin and Joe are still too far away so I concede defeat and slam the train door shut.

The platform attendant comes up puffing and we stand together watching the train recede into the distance.

"You got the door open!" the attendant declares, outraged. "He should have stopped!"

"He didn't see me," I explain to the red-faced guard.

The little man stamps his feet in fury. "I waved my flag!" he says, waving the flag. "Blew my whistle." He mimes blowing the whistle, furious that his authority has been flouted.

Martin and Joe arrive.

"What now?" I ask, dejected. Once more it looks like we have failed to make it to the Highlands in winter.

Martin is deep in thought. "There is an alternative. We could get the Oban train and stop in Crianlarich."

"What's there?" I've never heard of the place.

"There's Ben More, we could climb that."

* * *

So it's thanks to an accident of rail timetables that we are here, high on Ben More, in a blizzard, listening as voices are carried to us through the snow. Had the train guard on the 6.45 northbound train from Glasgow Queen Street been paying attention, we would now be in Lochaber. I call again and the cries are more insistent this time. We move towards the sound and after only a few paces stumble over a group of three folk, two men and a woman, huddled together in the snow.

"Hello, can you help us?" asks a large bearded man with a thick Dutch accent. "I have hurt my back. I cannot go down."

A woman who might be in her thirties, muffled in yards of woollen scarf, explains. "He fell." Then she asks an odd question: "Are you experienced?"

Joe, Martin and I look at each other. In many ways we are still novices, but compared to the folk sitting in front of us I suppose we are experienced. Given the obvious distress of the people we were talking to, I decide that this is not the time for modesty.

"Yes," I reply, trying to sound every inch an Everest veteran. "We are experienced." Fortunately, they didn't see me falling over my crampons only minutes ago.

It emerges that the party had been with a large Holiday Fellowship group. We had been following their footsteps in the snow. On reaching the higher section of the mountain, having no crampons, they had decided to descend – but had encountered difficulties on the icy section of the ridge. The leader of the party has made the elementary mistake of splitting up his group. Ice is always more difficult to descend. It is much easier to fall and gain momentum on the way down, so what the party managed climb up they are unable to reverse.

The Dutchman tells us that he hurt his back in the fall and he is moving stiffly. How to get them all down safely is the issue. They have been huddled together on the mountainside for a while and are all very cold, so we must get them moving quickly.

I make the only suggestion I can think of. "There's three of us and three of you, so why don't we take one each and help you down?"

As no one can think of a better suggestion I team up with the Dutchman who is the heaviest of the three. He probably outweighs me by a couple of stone, but I hope that the time I have spent in the gym has given me the strength to cope with his weight. The Dutchman is wearing a suit of orange neoprene – which is one of the slipperiest substances known to man. Should he fall, he will set off down the mountainside like an orange torpedo. I stick as close to him as I can as we head slowly down.

At first the going is easy and, although the party is slow, we make reasonable progress down the mountain, each of us leading one of the other group. After a few hundred feet, the ridge steepens and the snow gives way to hard packed ice, without crampons, the Fellowship group are struggling dangerously, barely able to keep their feet.

"Martin, pass me Excalibur."

Martin hands me the huge ice axe. I swing it in a great arc

into the ice at my feet and, as it strikes, it chops holes big enough to step into. The massive ice axe is perfect for cutting steps. I've only read about this technique in books. Before crampons were invented, the old pioneers – with ice axes like Martin's – would cut steps into the ice to allow them to cross steep slopes. My neoprene-clad charge is obviously unused to the mountains and steps awkwardly into each footing. I know if he falls his only defence will be to use his ice axe as a break.

"Has anyone told you how to use these ice axes?" I ask.

"No," they chorus back.

Joe catches my eye and we share a moment of despair. Back in the Lake District, all three of us spent days acquiring the skills to use our ice axes. We found a steep slope with a soft landing at the bottom and hurled ourselves down it from every conceivable position. We slid down sideways, rolled over on it, jumped off backwards all to ensure that we could halt any fall from any angle. There are several tricks you need to know when using an ice axe. The first is that if you are falling you need to drive the pick into the ice slowly. If you panic and ram it in fast the pick will bite into the ice so hard it will tear the axe from your hand. The second skill, and probably the most important, is not to stab yourself with the damn thing. Falling down a mountain comes fairly high on the list of 'things to be avoided in life'. But if you happen to be in exactly that situation, taking with you a lethal weapon that is basically a stick with three sharp points on it only adds to the seriousness of falling. An ice axe is perfectly capable of disembowelling you should the mood take it. Injuries from practising ice axe falls are not uncommon. Carrying an ice axe on the hills in winter is not enough – you have to know how to use it.

I look out into the sea of white that surrounds us. The snow is falling so thickly I can only see a few yards, but I know from the map that not far below us are steep cliffs. Our little procession moves on slowly, Joe and I cutting steps while guiding our charges one step at a time. Step cutting is tiring and slow but gradually we are making our way down the ice and closer to safety.

There is an awkward steep section. I try to cut bigger steps than usual. As he steps down, the Dutchman slips and falls heavily, dropping his ice axe, and begins to slide away face down on the ice. I have to stop him. I wonder if I can brake for both of us. I leap on to his back and drive my axe into the ice. We both gather speed as the axe rips through the ice, and for a few seconds I don't think I can hold us – but then the axe bites deeper and we begin to slow. A few feet more and we stop. My mind is focused on the drop below. An image of the Dutchman vanishing down the slope and over the cliffs flashes through my mind.

Before you think you are reading about a hero, I want to assure you of one thing: if my two-man ice axe braking idea hadn't worked, and we had continued plummeting towards the cliffs, I was planning to jump off his back and leave him to his fate. I have no intention of going to hell riding a Dutchman.

After a few hundred feet, the slope eases and the hard ice gives way to softer snow. We no longer have to cut steps but progress is still painstaking, and the fall has robbed our party of what little confidence it had. By now the blizzard is even worse and the light is beginning to fade as the short winter day comes to a close. Every now and again the neoprene-clad plummet monkey I am supporting stops and stares out into the white wall of the blizzard that engulfs the mountain.

"What are you looking at?" I ask him, as I can see nothing but a wall of falling snow.

"The view."

Now I know we're in trouble – there is no view. He is looking at a view that only he can see. I read somewhere that bizarre behaviour is a symptom of exposure, and seeing a view no one else can see is definitely weird.

I wonder if there is any way to get some heat into him. "Do you have anything hot you can drink?"

"Oh sure." He rummages in his bag, produces a flask, pours a cup of black tea and offers it to me.

I push it back to him. "No, no, not for me, for you." He's been carrying a flask of hot tea all this time and it never occurred to him to drink it. It is going to be a long night.

* * *

An hour later the blizzard begins to subside. We are only a few hundred feet from the valley floor when Joe spots a pinprick of light advancing towards us.

"There's another." Joe points to a second light and then a third.

"It must be the Holiday Fellowship crew looking for their mates," I call to him. There is a line of lights below us now. I take out my whistle and blow three blasts.

"The distress signal is six blasts," Martin points out, always conscious of rail timetables and the correct number for everything.

"We're not in distress are we?"

"Er, well no," he concedes.

I blow again and one of the pinpricks of light heads towards us.

* * *

At last we make it to the road and are surrounded by Holiday Fellowshippers, or whatever the collective noun for them is.

The Dutchman turns to me, almost in tears. "Without you we would have died."

I do that typically English thing of modestly rebutting all praise. "Oh no, I'm sure you'd have made it down."

Actually, I'm not too sure at all. He thrusts a bundle of five and ten-pound notes towards me. I know one thing – heroes don't take money, and politely, if reluctantly, refuse.

* * *

That night in the pub in Fort William, aglow with the satisfaction that we might have saved lives today, we mull over the events.

"That was dodgy, leaving some of the party without crampons to descend alone," Joe murmurs over his pint of Newcastle Brown.

I think for a minute. "I can understand it in a way. They just weren't experienced enough to know that climbing up ice is easier than going down."

"Maybe, but I'm not sure they should have set out to look for them themselves."

"Yeah, they must have been tired and they were probably not

that experienced either," I concede.

"Hardly a rescue team, were they?"

"No." I take a sip of my beer. "I can understand them going looking for their mates but that put the whole party at risk."

"Well if that train guard had been doing his job we would never have been there," Martin states from across his cider, and we all lapse into silence.

Whether the three people we helped down would have survived without our intervention I will never know, but one thing is certain: if we weren't experienced before we certainly are now. Next time we are in the Old Dungeon Ghyll, downing our Old Peculier, we'll have our own story to tell. I might see if I can get one of those three-handled tankards.

We've made it to our first Highland winter and, so far, this one hasn't disappointed. There is snow a foot deep in Fort William and the following morning it's still falling. We gather supplies and take the small rattling bus round to Glen Coe. The little bus comes to a halt and sits, its engine throbbing, filling the air with diesel fumes, waiting to disgorge us on to the frozen tarmac. I heave my rucksack down the steps of the bus and step out into the frigid air of the glen.

I've been here once before in summer, but now, in winter, the place they call 'The Coe' is transformed. In summer the long glen is overshadowed by towering rock faces with peaks crowding in on all sides like playground bullies. Glen Coe is a spectacular but sometimes dark place. The sight that greets me now halts me in my tracks, for sheathed in snow the glen is magnified. Sparkling ice covers the grey rocks of summer and the deep snow catches the sunlight making the place alpine in scale. Excitement runs through us. We have come a long way from the Lakeland fells that once filled me with awe but now feel tame by comparison. These are not the gentle hills of the Pennines or even the high fells of Cumbria; this is winter in the Highlands, and these are mountains that will challenge us on a whole new level.

That night we drink in the Clachaig Inn, the cradle of Scottish mountaineering: a white-walled building dwarfed by the peaks around it. The bar is crowded with a rabble of assorted walkers and climbers hurling foul fizzy Scottish beer down their throats. Every now and again the barman chucks a log onto the open fire. Despite all his efforts, and the mass of hairy, wool-clad bodies thronging the place, the temperature struggles to rise above zero.

The three of us huddle together trying to make ourselves enjoy what the Scots call 'Export'. Real ale is virtually extinct north of the border, so there is nothing else to drink apart from the delightful Glenmorangie malt whisky we treat ourselves to late in the evening. The bare whitewashed walls drip with moisture and we watch our breath condense in the fetid air of the bar. Fortunately the desperate days of 10 o'clock closing are now behind us and we can enjoy an extra half hour's drinking than we could if we were in England, where closing time is still 10.30. None of the occupants of the Clachaig seem to care as they become slowly intoxicated in a bar festooned with old climbing gear and photos of Hamish MacInnes, the patron saint of Glen Coe.

The following day we plough our way up Sgurr nam Fiannaidh, the western peak of the Aonach Eagach ridge, which stands immediately above the Clachaig Inn. It is a long and unrelenting slog up to our thighs in three feet of powder snow. After five gruelling hours, we collapse exhausted on the summit. Two guys catch up with us there. They look remarkably fresh.

"How long did it take you?" Martin asks, his obsession with numbers kicking in again.

"Two hours," one of them tells us cheerfully. That's the difference between breaking a trail in deep snow and following one. I make a mental note to avoid being the first through such deep snow again. If someone needs a snow plough it's not going to be me.

* * *

The next day, New Year's Eve, we head to Fort William to make our first attempt on Ben Nevis the following day. The little Highland town is thronged with shoppers when we arrive. Huge queues emerge from every shop that's selling alcohol. People are emerging with armfuls of beer and boxes packed with whisky.

We stand, amazed, in the street.

"What's happening? Are they introducing prohibition?" I ask my mates.

Martin shrugs. We fight our way through the queues and buy some beer to see in the New Year. By the time we set up camp, temperatures are falling rapidly and it is already -10°C.

Martin is shivering in his bag. "Let's go to the pub," he suggests.

The twin draws of warmth and alcohol are impossible to resist.

* * *

To our surprise the little hotel bar is quiet. Martin goes to the bar to bring us a round of drinks and returns in a solemn mood.

"The barman says they close at ten tonight."

"Ten!" I reply in disbelief, mortified at the idea that our meagre supply of beer will have to last two hours. But Martin hasn't finished.

"Yes, the barman says they close at ten, but for three days."

"What? They close for three days!" I greet the news with more dismay. At least the pubs give us some respite from the freezing temperatures.

"Oh well," I say, resigned. "We'll just have to go somewhere else."

Martin shakes his head slowly. "There isn't anywhere else. Everywhere is shut."

Suddenly the reason for the panic buying of drink becomes clear. This is Hogmanay in Scotland and everything stops. Only in Scotland would they close the pubs so everyone can get drunk.

* * *

We trudge back though the snow to our little tent, uncertain how we will survive in the arctic waste for three whole days without at least being able to spend a few hours in the warmth of a hotel bar. Back at the tent, we discover there's no point in waiting up to celebrate New Year – our beer is frozen solid. It's so cold our little gas stove can barely function and trying to thaw the cans only results in a few mouthfuls of flat, ice-cold liquid. I settle down in my sleeping bag. I'm wearing everything

I have and the tent is caked in ice. From outside I can hear people cheering from the warmth of their homes and realise it must be midnight. The three of us lie shivering in our sleeping bags, and that night, camped in the snow at the dawn of the new decade, the eighties, we can't think of anything to cheer about.

The following day we emerge from the tent stiff and aching from the cold night. We haven't managed to sleep much. At least the weak sun boosts the temperature a few degrees and, as we move around, we begin to feel a little warmth in our bodies. We decide to climb Ben Nevis via the tourist route, reasoning that it is unlikely to be any colder at 4,406 feet than it had been in our tent last night. I try to force my feet into frozen boots and we head off up the mountain.

I have since learned to love Ben Nevis, but the tourist route is possibly one of the most tedious climbs in Britain. Martin and I had never been on the Ben in winter, so that much at least is a novelty – but it is sad that one of Britain's finest mountains is such a dreary ascent for the thousands who climb it each year. The tourist track is raced over and jogged up, and innumerable people, with names like Farquhar and Penelope who have never been up a hill in their lives, get sponsored to climb it. People even haul pianos up there. These folk are all shepherded up the route by mountain guides and members of local rescue teams for whom it is a nice little earner, thank you very much.

Such a shame that, despite being a long slog, the tourist route on the mountain is so easy. It is also an unspectacular climb, having none of the grandeur of the North Face. What a pity Ben

Nevis is not a couple of thousand feet higher – then we would be treated to permanent snow cover and a couple of glaciers, and the mountain would be spared the indignity of being climbed by folk dressed as vicars and tarts (excluding people who actually are vicars or tarts, of course, which is perfectly acceptable).

On that morning, the first of January 1980, Martin and I try to coax our tired, semi-frozen limbs up the tourist track. Most of the folk we meet look to be in much worse shape than we are, having been celebrating into the small hours. Fortunately, the route has had some traffic, so there's a path broken through the unconsolidated snow. But it takes until around 2,000 feet for my boots to thaw out, by which time their frozen rigidity has torn holes in the back of my heels. Martin's having a similar struggle with his gloves, which froze shut in the campsite and refused to yield to his cold hands as he tried to force them inside. By the time we reach the summit, we're considerably warmer than we had been in our sleeping bags the night before, and are at last rewarded with a spectacular glimpse of the snow-covered Highlands before the inevitable cloud sweeps in.

After another long night in the icy tent we can only manage a short walk up towards the North Face of Ben Nevis in the morning. We had heard great tales of this iconic mountain wall, but again the cloud prevents us from seeing anything; we return to our tent, with its dwindling food supply, increasingly tired. We haven't slept much for three nights now and our bodies are drained from fighting the endless cold. The temperature rises a few degrees the following morning and it is possible to sleep. No one suggests leaving the tent and so we simply remain snoozing all day, enjoying the sensation of being slightly warmer than before.

I wake about 7 p.m. and realise that the pubs must be open.

Heavy with sleep, I try to raise my two comatose friends. "Joe, Martin, the bar's open!"

I get only murmurings in response and I'm so tired the prospect of climbing out of my sleeping bag, fighting to get my semi-frozen boots on and struggling through the snow to the bar feels insurmountable. I lapse back into sleep and am woken, hours later, by Martin's alarm clock. Our train home leaves in two hours. Yesterday's brief respite from the cold has gone and our small world is once more gripped by ice. We remove the poles supporting our tent and it remains rigid, frozen in place.

Once on board the southbound train, the heat on the British Rail carriage feels like a luxurious warm bath. For the first time in three days I can take my gloves off. A frozen wasteland cruises by the window as the train begins its voyage, and our first Highland winter recedes into memory.

"Well, that was some adventure," Martin says, grinning across the table.

"It certainly was," Joe agrees.

Minutes later we are all sound asleep.

* * *

After our snowy trip to the Highlands has had time to sink in, we feel a growing sense of achievement. Now we have climbed our first Scottish winter hills and we even have a rescue of sorts under our belts. We have faced a new level of challenge and the possibility of climbing ice is beginning to stir in my brain.

We've certainly moved on from our training ground in the Lake District, and new possibilities for adventure beckon in the snow-covered Highland hills.

This is 1980 and the beginning of a new decade. Two things happen in this year that, for me, change the world forever. That summer I'm back at Leicester University studying for my Social Work qualification. As part of the course I have to spend three months working in a Social Work team. One morning, as I settle down at my desk in the crowded town centre office, a colleague makes a casual remark.

"That's awful, you know, John Lennon being killed, isn't it?"

I don't know and the shock hits me like a physical blow. In my Merseyside home, everyone feels a connection with the Beatles, as though they are somehow part of our family. The first album I ever bought was Lennon's *Imagine*. Up until that point I had believed that certain things in my life were constant: my parents, giants like Lennon and McCartney, Pink Floyd and everything else that made up the fabric of life. Now, I realise that everything is tenuous and that all things eventually crumble.

Lennon was an iconic figure to everyone I know, a rebel, a genius, a poet. He and three other lads from just across the river had taken the music world by storm. In Merseyside everyone knew the Beatles personally. Everyone had a story to tell about meeting Lennon or McCartney at a party. Well, in fact, these stories were mainly about *almost* meeting them.

"I went to this party and Paul McCartney was there. Well, he wasn't actually there, but he was going to come but he didn't. Mike McGear, his brother, was there and I'd have met him if he hadn't left before I arrived."

Close but no cigar. Lennon and McCartney almost went to a hell of a lot of parties in Merseyside.

Nature too makes a statement in 1980 as Mount St. Helens erupts in the USA. The explosion blasts away one side of the mountain, and the subsequent lava flow destroys 47 bridges and 15 miles of rail track.

* * *

Sometimes I get ideas. I'll be casually staring out of the window, not thinking of anything much, when a notion will pop into my head. I've no idea where they come from; all I know is that I seem to get more than most other folk. They are not always good ideas but they usually manage to make life interesting.

I'm sitting in the Old Dungeon Ghyll, my legs aching from a long plod up a snow-covered Great Gable. My uncle's RAF trousers valiantly fought off a blizzard earlier in the day, and are steaming quietly to themselves, shedding moisture in the warm pub air. With luck, by the time we have to leave the pub and head out to our frozen tent, my trousers will be dry. Joe is elbowing his way through the throng of bearded trolls at the bar to get our second – or perhaps third or even fourth – pint of Old Peculier. Several guitar players all equidistant from my head are playing different tunes. They play with equal enthusiasm but with varying levels of skill and intoxication. I look up just in time to see Joe squirming his way back towards me, foaming pewter tankards held high, when it happens – an idea forms in my mind. It's vague at first but by the time Joe is sitting beside me it's almost fully formed.

"I've had an idea," I announce as Joe sets the beer down.

Joe looks at me dubiously. He's heard some of my ideas before.

"Let's climb Mont Blanc," I yell in his ear, struggling to be heard over the applause as one of the guitar players overbalances and hits the floor.

"Oh Christ, you're not serious!"

"I'm sure we could do it, it's just a big snow climb. We can do that."

I'm trying to remember a conversation I had with one of the bar trolls. If I'm right, he had not actually climbed the thing but, of course, knew someone who had and declared it easy.

"That bloody thing's huge," Joe says. "It's the highest mountain in Europe and we've never even been there. I'm not doing it. It's madness."

Part of me knows Joe is right, but I am full of Old Peculier and, after all, it's only five times the hill we climbed today. I pour some more beer down Joe and the idea becomes a plan. That's probably how Scott decided to go to the Pole, or Columbus to circumnavigate the Earth. These aren't things the rational mind would agree to but in the pub it all seems perfectly reasonable.

Next morning, I awake in the cold light of a Lake District dawn and try to piece together last night's conversation. I instantly understand two things: one is that I have committed to climb the highest mountain in Europe and the second is that my trousers are damp. I wonder if the two are connected.

First we need gear. So far we have survived on World War II relics and the few bits and pieces of real gear we can afford, like the tent and cheap sleeping bags. By the summer of 1980 I graduate as a social worker and begin to earn something that is recognisable as a salary. It's not enough to buy everything we need but it allows me to get the one thing that can provide me with the basic requirements for my Alpine adventure: my first credit card. With it I buy my first long-dreamed-of possession, a down bag. It costs almost as much as a second-hand car but the Canadian-made Caravan Deluxe promises to have me slumbering comfortably in the kind of temperatures only experienced on the far side of Uranus. I buy a book, Yvon Chouinard's *Climbing Ice*. The book is already dated but is the only guide to ice climbing techniques I can find. One thing Chouinard says resonates with me.

Real adventure is defined best as a journey from which you may not come back alive, and certainly not as the same person.

Chouinard also talks with great authority about two essentials for the aspiring ice climber. 'If you want to dance on ice you must have rigid boots,' he insists. By this he means that I need to replace the soft-soled hiking boots I have been using so far with a much heavier boot that will not bend and will remain firm on steep ground under the stress of hammering crampon points into solid ice. The credit card takes another big hit. This time I walk away from the local climbing shop with a pair of Alpine monsters under my arm. These boots have rigid soles, plastic toe caps and soles that look as though they could crush a mountain. These are Galibier Super Pro. I think that any boot combining the words 'Super' and 'Pro' in its title must be the business. There is only one problem – when I am wearing them my feet feel weighed down by concrete.

Chouinard also advocates the purchase of his own design of ice axe, the vicious Zero, a beast with curved pick and savage-looking teeth. When that arrives in the post, all polished wood and gleaming chrome, I know things have changed forever. I am now a climber.

I approach this climb as I have approached all others: I buy a map. Joe and I spread it out on the kitchen table of the house I share in Sheffield. It doesn't look like any map we've ever seen.

"Shit, look at all that ice," Joe exclaims, running his finger down something called the Mer de Glace.

"That means 'Sea of Ice.'" Finally the smattering of French I gained at night school is becoming useful.

"Really? I wonder why they called it that?" We both share a laugh.

Gradually I start to make sense of the contours, and the shape of this mountain begins to appear before me. I can see long sharp ridges leading in elegant sweeps to the ice-bound summit. But this isn't a British Ordnance Survey map like I'm used to, and the severity of the terrain isn't obvious.

"Here." I begin to follow a likely line up the mountain with my finger. "This looks possible." I can see what looks like a route up from the valley of Chamonix to the snow ridge named the Gouter, and on to the summit.

"Well, we could always buy a guidebook," Joe says with a sigh, for some reason unwilling to follow my finger.

The thought of getting a guidebook had never occurred to me. A quick excursion to Sheffield's Ellis Brigham and we return to pore over the little plastic-backed book.

"Look, I was right." By some miracle it seems that I had found the easiest route to the summit.

"What do you think it means by 'Facile'?"

"It says it's easy."

"Easy compared to what?" Joe poses the question neither of us can answer.

The problem is that we have nothing to compare it with. Will we find it easy, or will this giant beast spit us out and leave us crushed in one of its great glaciers like a couple of pieces of human flotsam?

P.G. Wodehouse's Bertie Wooster once described the First World War as 'that bit of unpleasantness in France', in a masterful piece of understatement. Perhaps the guidebook is his equal. We decide to take the whole thing slowly.

A few weeks later we are walking through the village of Chamonix. It's early, and the place is still waking up. Shops are pulling up their shutters and the air is full of the scent of Gauloise cigarette and freshly baked French bread. We are heading up on to a little ridge to try and get a feel for the terrain – and to get a better view of Mont Blanc itself. The early morning sun rises over Chamonix while we climb through serried ranks of trees, the air full of the scent of the pines. As the village below rubs the sleep from its eyes and welcomes the day with innumerable coffee pots, we climb higher into Alpine meadows filled with flowers and the sound of tinkling cow bells.

Higher still the meadows give way to scree and then rock. We have climbed a few thousand feet, perhaps the height of a Scottish mountain, and can see the beast we have come to climb. Mont Blanc still towers over us; a few hours' climbing have done little to diminish its bulk. From our viewpoint on the crest of the ridge the mountain is a colossus, its summit gleaming a peerless white in the late-morning sun. My eyes follow the great ridges that sweep down from the summit to the ragged glaciers thousands of feet below. The jumbles of enormous ice blocks that cascade from the foot of the mountain fill us with awe. We have seen nothing like them before, and their presence confirms what we know already: this is a serious mountain. Above the rivers of ice are the rock spires of incredibly steep ridges, and even a tower of aluminium atop the Aiguille du Midi, perched incongruously like a rocket awaiting launch. A cable travels all the way to this space vehicle, allowing tourists spectacular views of the mountain.

Joe and I sit on the summit of this tiny ridge, smoking cheap French cigarettes and gazing up at the enormity of our task.

"Big, isn't it?" My ability to state the obvious remains undiminished.

"Yes, it certainly is," Joe replies.

Something in his voice suggests we could both go home now and everything would be okay. I follow the line of our route up on to the huge shoulder of the mountain and then upwards, over the dome of snow the French call the Dôme du Gouter. My gaze crosses its bulging white crest and on to the summit of the mountain. I'm stunned by the scale of this place.

"Jesus, it looks a long way. Do you think this thing is too much for us?" We've climbed some snow-covered Scottish hills, scrabbled up some easy rock climbs, but does that really make us capable of climbing the highest mountain in Europe?

Joe doesn't get the chance to answer. We hear a cry from on the ice cliff below us.

"What was that?" Joe asks, jumping to his feet.

The cry comes again. Neither of us can understand what's

being said but there is no mistaking the distress in its tone. We run to the edge of a corniced cliff and there, about thirty feet below, is a young man climbing steep, hard ice.

"He's only got one axe," I observe. He is swinging one long ice axe on a face so steep that even Mr Chouinard would concede he should have two. A rope would be handy in a place like that as well.

"He's either bloody good or in deep shit."

It's very clear that if the young man falls from where he is he will go several hundred feet down into the cirque below.

There are two young women above him looking anxiously down.

"Oh succors!" one yells. This stretches my night school French to its limits but it doesn't take a genius to work out she's calling for help. I remember the rope coiled in my pack.

"I am a rope!" I call back in French.

The young woman exchanges a puzzled look with her friend, who says, "Ah, Anglais." What she actually means is: only an Englishman could speak French as badly as that.

"Can you 'elp us?" she yells. The language barrier is turning the whole desperate situation into a scene from *Allo Allo*.

"Tell him to stay where he is," I shout helpfully.

It doesn't occur to me that right now his whole being might be focused on exactly that. Frantically I scrabble in my rucksack for the rope. It hasn't been uncoiled since Joe and I travelled for seventeen hours across France in the back of a converted cattle truck in 30°C heat. For those unfamiliar with the nature of climbing ropes let me inform you that they are not to be trusted. Unless you constantly coil and uncoil them, the things take on a mind of their own. Turn your back for a moment and they will instantly twist themselves into a tangled heap. The rope I pulled from my bag had been mortally offended by the train journey and, in a gesture of revenge, had tied itself into the Gordian knot.

Swearing and sweating, I manage to free enough rope to reach the climber, and begin searching for something to anchor it to. The surface of the ridge proves to consist of thousands of small pebbles frozen into four inches of ice. No boulders or cracks break the surface. There's only one thing I can do: I lift my gleaming Zero ice axe over my head and drive it into the icy ground with all my might. The axe sinks its teeth into the mountain with all the tenacity of an Aberdonian snatching at a falling fiver.

Joe ties a loop in the end of the rope, hurls it to the young man, and signals to him to put his body through the loop. I pull, hoping the Zero won't let go of the ice, and feel the rope go tight as the Frenchman starts to climb. All I can see is the rope disappearing over the edge of the cliff. I have to feel what is happening on the other end. The rope stops moving and I sense that he must be just below the overhanging lip of ice at the very top of the cliff. Even for an experienced climber this would be a formidable obstacle. Feeling him move again, I take in a few feet of rope, keeping it as tight as I can.

Suddenly there's a pull and I can hear the fibres creaking under the strain as the rope stretches, absorbing some of the shock. It's now or never – I have to be able to pull him up and over the cornice. A tremendous weight comes on the rope. He must be swinging below the cornice. I pull with all my strength but can't shift him. The rope is biting into my shoulders.

I bend my knees, summon one last effort and use my legs to pull. At the cliff edge there's a sudden crunch and the head of the Frenchman pops through the cornice. He blinks the snow from his eyes like a sleepy mole peering out of its burrow to check the weather. The two girls cry out with relief and run to help him over the lip. Joe, realising that stepping on to the fragile cornice could spell disaster, abandons any attempt to communicate verbally and resorts to waving his arms like an air traffic controller. The Frenchman flops over the cornice and collapses. He staggers to his feet and heads towards me with hand outstretched.

"Merci, merci, merci," he says, grinning.

"I think he's thanking you," Joe says to me, no doubt pleased that he is finally beginning to grasp the French language.

I collapse at this point, gasping in lungfuls of air, and spend the next ten minutes trying to persuade my brute of an ice axe to relinquish its hold on the mountain. I discover that the Zero has one major drawback: once embedded deep in the ice it never lets go.

Back in Chamonix, Joe and I stroll past the white-painted bars and shops, enjoying cheap Gauloise cigarettes. We sit outside a bar and allow ourselves the luxury of an ice-cold lager while basking in the satisfaction of having pulled off another minor rescue.

"We'll have something to tell them back in the Old Dungeon Ghyll now," Joe says with a laugh.

"Yes I suppose we will." A thought passes through my mind. "Only if we make it back there."

My mind races to a scene in the future. I'm in the Old Dungeon Ghyll, it's December, and outside the snow is falling thick and fast. Inside I'm sitting by the glowing fire, pint of Old Peculier in hand, relating my tale of how we rescued a Frenchman from certain death in the Alps. Amongst climbers such tales – or epics, are they are known – are the food and drink of pub evenings. Such stories form the legends and folk tales that bind together this small group of outsiders. Doubtless I will exaggerate a little, perhaps even lie; but none of that matters. It's the tale that is told that counts.

Twenty thousand years ago men hunched around fires, pinpricks of light in the primeval darkness. They chewed roots and fungi that slewed their thoughts and sent their minds into intoxicated delusions. Their tales were of charging rhinos, ferocious sabre-toothed tigers, close shaves with dangerous beasts. Our tales are of rotten ice, desperate struggles in a vertical world, fingers slipping from tiny ledges. On the surface they are different but underneath they are all the same – they are tales of life and death. They talk of what it is to be human in a hostile world. I just hope I'm going to live to tell this one.

As Joe blows cigarette smoke into the air, my gaze alights on the massive jumble of ice that is the Bossons Glacier, and then wanders on up to the summit. I can't help thinking how far away it looks.

* * *

A few days later, after playing at ice climbing on one of the mountain's glaciers, we decide that there is nothing for it but to take on the beast itself. We approach the mountain as we have all others, with the view that we have to climb it from the bottom to the top. There will be no cheating by using cable cars to get out of the valley. Joe and I hike directly up from the village.

It will be a three-day climb. On the first day, we will climb up through the forest and establish ourselves beside where the little mountain railway ends. On the second day we will have to make it the Refuge du Gouter, a climbers' shelter perched high on the mountain within striking distance of its summit. On the third we shall climb to the summit of the mountain and return to the valley.

On the first day, after hours of toil up from the valley floor, Joe and I settle in to our tent a thousand feet below the snowline. We're camped in an Alpine meadow of close-cropped grass. The climb out of the deep valley and on to the shoulder of the mountain has exhausted us, and we fall into a dreamless sleep.

I wake suddenly. There's something moving outside the tent – something big, sniffing and grunting.

"What the hell's that?" Joe whispers.

There's another snuffle and something prods the tent. The hair on the back of my neck stands up and I begin to sweat with terror.

"It's a bear!"

"They don't have bears in the Alps!" I declare between clenched teeth.

"You sure?"

I'm an avid watcher of wildlife documentaries. My mind races through all the ones I've seen on bears and mountain habitats. Images of bears tearing big holes in flimsy tents flash through my mind. Black bears and grizzly bears live in North

America – at least that's where Yogi Bear came from, but that's about all I'm sure of right now. Where is David Attenborough when you need him? I'm beginning to doubt my credentials as a naturalist when something furry brushes against the tent and I realise that there's at least two or three creatures out there.

"There's a few of them. It's okay, bears don't hunt in packs," I inform Joe as if I'm passing on the best news he'll ever hear.

"Are you sure?" he whispers, hunting in the darkness for his torch.

"Yes, I'm sure." I'm just beginning to relax as my confidence grows until another thought punctures my world. "Wolves! Wolves hunt in packs."

"Shit." Joe's face is suddenly illuminated in torchlight. Cautiously he begins to pull down the door zip to look outside. He only gets the zip a few inches down when a black nose juts through the opening. We both howl in terror. A pinks tongue follows the nose and gives Joe's face an enormous, affectionate lick.

I collapse back on my sleeping bag howling with laughter. "It's the dogs from the farmhouse we passed a while ago."

"I nearly pissed myself." Joe takes a little longer to see the funny side.

The following morning we begin the climb in earnest. Once above the snowline the intensity of the Alpine sunlight takes us by surprise. The air is so clear that the sun has little to filter its rays, and light bounces back off the snow with amazing power. We are heading up to where the Gouter hut sits perched, incredibly, on the massive shoulder of the mountain. We will spend the night there and set off before dawn the following morning, if we can get there that is. We are crossing a huge snowfield leading to a rocky ridge that seems to climb into the sky. On a massive glacier below us, huge blocks of ice glisten in the sun, each capable of crushing a house with ease.

At last we reach the base of the rock ridge that leads up to the hut. The hut is a strange, alien structure, all gleaming aluminium, as though some Martian space traveller has carelessly abandoned it high on the mountain. The ridge is broken rock and snow, relatively easy climbing but very exposed. Here and there are brass crosses that have been driven into the rock, recording the names of climbers who have fallen to their deaths. Joe and I rope up and climb the ridge slowly and carefully. The crosses come in handy for belays.

Oddly, amongst all this ice and snow, it's the heat that gets to us. The sun is unrelenting and we sip on our meagre rations of water. Joe has a rather snazzy pair of mirrored sunglasses to protect his eyes from the glare. I couldn't afford such luxury and am wearing what appear to be welder's goggles, giving me the appearance of a startled frog. I've smeared white glacier cream – a sort of barrier cream made from lard – all over my face and am gently frying. We have been climbing the ridge for over two hours but the gleaming hut appears no closer than when we began.

"Christ, how far is it?" Joe asks.

"It can't be far now." It's more of a plea than an answer.

It seems an age before I finally grasp the metal steps that lead to the veranda of the hut and haul myself on to the balcony. The wooden boards feel good beneath the soles of my heavy Alpine climbing boots. By now it is 3.00 p.m. and the sun has been on the steep slopes of the mountain for several hours. 3.00 p.m., it turns out, is avalanche time. We watch, spellbound, as the slopes below us crack open and spew thousands of tons of snow down on to the glacier with a sound like thunder. With each new explosion, the metal hut vibrates.

This is my first visit to an Alpine refuge and I'm struck by the odd assortment of humanity that joins us on the terrace to watch the power of nature unfold. There are groups of Japanese climbers, small and wiry, looking incredibly tough beneath their brightly coloured bandanas. They look as though nothing could scare them. I wonder if they don't fear death in the same way I do. I've heard that in Japan there are brass plaques at the foot of some climbs, welded to the rock. When a climber falls to his death off that particular route they simply engrave another name on the plaque and the faller is remembered for his glorious end. I think I'll try and keep my name off brass plaques; I want to die an inglorious death, preferably in bed at a ripe old age.

There are middle-aged Germans too. All of them seem to carry prodigious beer guts held in check by specially designed German drinking trousers constructed with extra-strong braces and belts. How they managed to get their bulk up to the hut at all is beyond me.

That night the hut is bursting at the seams. The guardian allocates me and Joe floor space underneath a table, but in truth, sleeping in the hut is an academic pursuit at best. The whole hut wakes at 2.00 a.m. and bursts into a frenzy as over a hundred semi-conscious people fight for the room to down something that might be described as breakfast. I spend the night tossing and turning, worrying about the coming climb. As the hut wakes I'm sitting at the end of a table – which is occupied by huge farting Germans – trying to force some black tea down my throat. Joe, who has the ability to sleep pretty well anywhere, is still fast asleep while the Germans on the table above force huge cold sausages down their throats with enviable gusto.

"Joe, Joe!" I yell, shaking him. "We have to go."

* * *

My brain struggles to grasp what is happening. The voice in my head is saying: It's 2 a.m.; we should be asleep. We are on a mountain! What the hell's going on?

All I can see is a few feet of snowy trench illuminated by my head torch. Around me and Joe, in the blackness, strange alien voices whisper to each other. Someone coughs, a head torch flickers on and there is the metallic chink of karabiners. Soon we are plodding forward, part of a long crocodile of climbers. The snow creaks beneath our boots. We walk onward for a few paces and then the line of humanity stops and we wait, like in some strange theatre queue. After a few minutes of this I grow frustrated. I wonder what will happen if I step out of the trench – instant death perhaps?

Full of trepidation, I step into the soft snow beside the trench and we leapfrog a few groups before falling back in line in the darkness. Everyone else is roped together, despite the fact that there is no conceivable chance of falling anywhere on this broad section of the mountain. Joe and I move unroped and soon discover that we can outpace everyone. I read somewhere that only ten per cent of the folk who leave the Gouter hut make it to the summit. Now I can see why.

I worry that we are moving too fast. Perhaps the other climbers move at a more pedestrian pace for a reason – maybe I'm going to run out of strength. In the darkness, we plod on, blindly following the trench. Slowly the darkness yields to a faint blue light as dawn approaches. Gradually figures become visible as the sun rises. We are going well. In my home in Sheffield I studied the maps of Mont Blanc over and over again, so I know where we are with every step. Soon a great snow dome rises before us: the Dôme du Gouter. Once over this mushroom-shaped mass of snow I know that the ridge will narrow before it finally turns in a graceful arc to reach the summit.

I'm feeling increasingly confident. So far the ascent is a cruise.

I turn to Joe. "This is easy!"

A few hundred feet higher and we hit the altitude. Now I am plunged into a lung-bursting world where even the smallest activity leaves us gasping for breath. I count steps; I can take ten before I have to stop for a few moments, hunched over my ice axe, gasping for breath. My head is splitting with pain and I can feel my heart racing in my chest. As the ridge narrows, perhaps a thousand feet from the summit, our progress has turned to a crawl. It is no longer easy.

This is a strange kind of fatigue. I stop to catch my breath, but when I move on my lungs suck in the thin, oxygen-starved air and in two or three steps I am exhausted again. The ridge narrows now. We are walking a tightrope with France on one side and Italy on the left. The Italian side of the mountain is much steeper; a fall to our right would easily carry us several thousand feet.

"I think we should put the rope on," Joe suggests, conscious of the exposure.

But I feel secure. "Ah, it's okay," I reply casually.

"Well, I think we should put it on here."

"Nah, we won't come off," I reply with a confidence born more of lack of oxygen than ability.

"I want the bloody rope on!"

The insistence in his voice reminds me that the decision to rope up is not mine alone to make. My oxygen-starved brain makes me clumsy and I take a couple of minutes to tie us in. We move on, climbing higher into thinner air.

"The ridge is beginning to turn!" I yell to Joe.

He looks puzzled. "What?"

"We are close to the summit, almost there."

I've spent so long studying the route, dreaming of this moment, the map is fixed in my mind. At last we pull up on to the snowy top. Chamonix looks tiny, almost a mile below. Light aircraft fly beneath us. I've never been anywhere so high. Great mountains sweep away in all directions, huge glaciers roll towards the valley, and towering rock pinnacles rise from mountain ridges like cathedral spires pointing to heaven. Far below us, insignificant now, is the small hill where, only a few days ago, I stood staring at this summit and wondering if I would ever make it. I'm elated at what is a huge triumph for us and tears fill my eyes as I revel in the moment.

"My feet!" Joe's voice cuts through my rapture. "My bloody feet."

"What about your feet?"

Joe, ever practical, stamps on the hard snow. "They're freezing. Let's get out of here." My joy is short lived.

* * *

We descend the narrow summit ridge cautiously, conscious of the vast drops on either side. Below that, the ridge broadens and soon we are running down whooping with delight, no longer hampered by the energy-sapping thin air. We have become gods – we have become alpinists. On the way down the mountain we take the cable car. Gods don't have to walk to the valley.

The following morning I'm lounging outside the tent, luxuriating in the afterglow of our success and hungover from our celebratory binge on cheap wine, when the blonde girl who left with the policeman walks back into the campsite. As she picks her way through the tents the campsite falls silent, just as it did when she left. The girl looks tired but the look of despair, which I saw in her face a few days ago, has gone.

We gather round her in a small huddle and, hesitantly, as though trying to recall a nightmare she barely believes took place, she tells her story. The morning after her boyfriend Chris and his climbing companion had left for their climb, she had a premonition of disaster. When the little police car had rumbled down the dirt track into the campsite she had known instinctively that the young police officer had come for her.

She tells us how kind he had been, how gentle with his words. He had told her there had been an accident and drove her to the hospital where Chris lay unconscious, his head bandaged and a machine breathing for him. As she recounts this her eyes fill with tears and her voice crumbles. A red-haired young woman hugs her until she is able to speak again.

She talks of the hospital doctors telling her how bad things were, that she needed to be strong, when she felt so weak. She tells us about phoning Chris's mother and of the awful silence at the other end of the phone when she had broken the news. She tells us how she sat beside his bed for two days, of how helpless she felt, of how still he was.

Suddenly her eyes brighten and she babbles uncontrollably. "His eyes opened and he said something. I couldn't believe it. He's off the machine. He's okay!"

Chris and his companion had been high on a climb when blocks of rock had detached from the face and come crashing down upon them. They had been lucky; the largest debris had missed them, but Chris had been knocked unconscious. It had been three hours before one of the rescue helicopters had been able to pull them off the face. Chris had been saved by his climbing helmet. I'm glad to hear he had the same helmet I wear, a Joe Brown Super, which has a reputation amongst the climbing community for being the toughest on the market. I'm not sure if it's the toughest but, from personal experience, I can testify to it being the heaviest – my neck muscles are left in agony after a day of wearing it.

I am so glad to hear that the young woman's story has a good ending, although I will never forget the horror in her eyes as she was led away by the young gendarme.

8

North and South

In early January, darkness descends at speed in the Scottish mountains.

Tonight, as clouds block the waning moon and obliterate the stars, the lightless void consumes us. In this blackness Joe and I inch our way along the narrow ridge of Stob Coire Sgreamhach, occasionally glimpsing the ghostly white outlines of the hills around us. We have just completed our first winter climb and are both exhilarated by the achievement but humbled by the realisation of our incompetence. We should have been back in the Red Squirrel Bunkhouse hours ago, eaten a meal, got out of our hill clothes and be thinking of heading for that Mecca of Scottish climbing, the Clachaig Inn.

The valley of Glen Coe, however, remains a long way below us as we follow the bobbing lights of our head torches, their beams throwing patches of light onto the snow in an ocean of darkness. With the climb behind us, the descent should be easy, even if it will be a long plod in soft snow.

Joe is muffled in a balaclava beneath his climbing helmet. From a few yards behind me he calls, "Did you hear that?"

"Hear what?" I turn and blind him with my head lamp.

Joe casts about the hillside. His meagre torch beam fades away in the darkness after less than twenty feet.

"There was a cry," he insists, but I can hear nothing.

Moments later three pinpricks of light appear from the gloom. Two men and a young woman come hurrying down the slope towards us.

"Is this the way down?" one of the young men asks in a brown-sauce-and-pickled-eggs Brummy accent.

"Yes, this is it," I confirm, confident I know our position. Joe and I turn to head off down to where my old Marina van is waiting by the side of the A82.

The young man consults the rest of his party for a moment, and then calls after us, "Can we come down with you?"

Instantly, I realise what has happened. Our climbing helmets, ice gear and rope create the illusion that we are more competent than we actually are. They think that we are experts. I'm fairly certain we know little more than they do, possibly less. It occurs to me, however, that explaining this to them right now, high on a mountainside in the pitch dark, is probably not too wise.

I respond with a nonchalant shrug. "Yes, of course, no problem."

Secretly I'm rather pleased that they are with us; a party of five is a lot more secure than a party of two. As we head down towards the glen the wind picks up and snow begins to fall. Higher, the slope was icy and our crampons were an advantage, but as the hillside becomes covered in soft snow the spikes on our feet begin to trap the snow and become less effective. When the snow is not compacted crampons collect huge snowballs, known as 'balling up' in the trade, and quickly become useless.

"I think we should take our crampons off," I suggest. Everyone agrees, so we divest ourselves of the ironmongery.

The slope steepens five hundred yards below, and here the

wind has stripped the snow leaving a few yards of bare ice. The night reveals a vast, black chasm beneath. I decide to risk crossing the slope without spikes and try to kick my boots into the iron-hard surface. I manage a few steps before my feet fly from under me; moments later I'm hurtling down the slope towards the ravine. More from instinct than skill I force the pick of the axe into the snow. The axe bites deep, showering me with fragments of ice as it gouges a groove but I don't stop. I lift the shaft of the axe to drive the pick deeper. I'm no longer accelerating but neither am I stopping. The ravine gapes below me.

"Come on! Come on!" I yell at the axe, urging it to stop me, knowing if I hit the steeper ground below even the Zero might not be able to save me.

"Come on! Come on!" I bring my weight higher on the axe, forcing the pick deeper with my body weight. There's a wrench as the Zero sinks its steel fangs into the mountain and I come to an abrupt halt. I lie for a moment gasping with relief, clinging to the axe.

A light appears above me. "What the hell are you doing?" Joe calls down.

"Falling off."

Joe hacks his way across the slope above me. "Oh. I don't think you should be doing that here."

Gingerly, I make my way across to softer snow where Joe is smoking a cigarette as if waiting for a bus.

"That would have been easy if we'd kept our crampons on," he thinks aloud, handing me a cigarette. He knows I'll need one to calm my nerves after the near disaster.

The three following us huddle together for a short conversation, trying to make a plan for crossing the ice. After a few minutes, they decide to follow us across the treacherous slope. The young woman leads. She steps on to the ice, instantly slips and cries out as she falls heavily. She hits the ground hard and drops her ice axe which skitters away into the night. Without the tool she cannot stop her fall. The four of us can only watch, in helpless terror, as she vanishes down the mountain into the yawning darkness.

* * *

It's been raining for three days. In that time we have barely left the tent, and now we watch as the rainwater begins to seep in. There is an immutable law in camping: any tent can only resist a downpour for a limited time until, eventually, the water always gets in. Always – there are no exceptions – if it rains long enough, no matter how good your tent, you get wet. At first you bring the rain in yourself every time you enter with wet rain gear. You only bring in a little each time, but once in, that water never dries and slowly it begins to build. Gradually the damp patches on the tent join up until every time you touch the walls you get a little damper. After a while, you and everything you own become get increasingly soggy. It's then that the rain uses its secret weapon. It knows you can resist it falling from above so it decides to tunnel underneath.

Martin pokes the groundsheet with his long, pianist's fingers. The groundsheet ripples away.

Joe looks at the tiny waves in despair. "Oh God, we're floating."

This is the beginning of the end. A small pool has formed outside the tent, held back by the groundsheet's vertical side wall, but now the water has found its way underneath and nothing will stop it. We know what happens next from bitter experience. First, small pools will form at the seams; then, once the water becomes bold enough, it will start to pass through the material itself. Then we, our sleeping bags and everything else we own will dissolve into a soggy mass. Sleeping in a wet tent in winter is a bit like watching an endless Des O'Connor show – you're still alive but death is preferable.

For weeks, Joe, Martin and I have been looking forward to spending New Year in the Highlands. We dreamt of ice-covered summits, vast snowscapes and adventures amongst the hills of Torridon. Instead we are slowly dissolving in the Highland rain. There is no alternative – we'll have to surrender.

"I wonder if we can get in the hostel," Martin muses, referring to the SYHA at the far end of the glen.

Joe is unimpressed. "Oh God, no drink, in bed by ten. It'll be like being back in school."

He's right but the alternative is miserable.

"It's Hogmanay. The place'll be stowed out. It's a waste of time," I suggest.

Martin prods the sodden groundsheet once more and the three of us watch in silence as it ripples away towards the rear of the tent, giving ample evidence of the rising water level beneath.

"Oh well. Okay, it's worth a try I suppose."

Images of the Viking warrior wardens of our Pennine trek flash through my mind. I'll be dragooned into cleaning pots and castigated for coming in drunk. Our Highland holiday is going from bad to worse.

* * *

The hostel looks incongruously modern as Joe's ancient Saab carries its soggy triumvirate into the car park. The hostel – a child of the sixties, when everything anyone constructed was a box – is an angular, white building with a sloping aluminium roof. It's about as sympathetic with its surroundings as if you'd landed the starship Enterprise in the glen. It nestles at the foot of Liathach. We had hoped to see it snow covered but today its summit is shrouded in cloud and its gullies and streams spout endless rain.

The three of us stand, nervous and forlorn, at the reception desk, expecting to be hurled back out into the rain at any moment. Martin rings the bell on the desk and we wait. It takes three rings before we hear movement in the office beyond. Eventually a cheerful little man emerges, in his mid-forties and wearing his pullover inside out.

"There's three of you, you say? Yes, yes, yes, we've beds."

He leads us off down a long corridor and flings open the door of a bedroom. The room is in darkness and a chorus of grunts and swearing greets the warden's entrance.

"It's not this one," he announces and leads us off down another corridor. Three rooms later he finds the empty one.

We have to sign a book. Martin scribbles his name and then asks, "What time do we have to be in by?"

"In by?" The warden sways slightly, unable to grasp the question.

Martin tries a different tack. "I take it there's no alcohol?"

"No alcohol!" The startled – and slightly dishevelled – custodian produces a can of lager from behind the counter and takes a sip as if to steady himself. "Do you not drink then, boys?"

"Oh yes," I explain, "it's just we thought there would be rules, like in England."

The warden chortles to himself as he plods away from the desk, shaking his head. "Ha ha, like in England. Rules indeed."

This is a very different hostel than the ones we have experienced in the past.

The Ben Damh bar, at the only hotel in the glen a few miles away, closes at ten so the real party can begin. Only in the Highlands do they shut the pubs so that everyone can get drunk. Villagers poor into the hostel carrying whisky, beer and wine. It's a raggle-taggle mixture of folk who throng the hostel lounge. There are climbers and walkers, mainly distinguished by the fibre pile they wear which, over the past few years, has displaced the tattered woolly jumpers that used to be the uniform of the outdoor community. There are ruddy-faced estate workers, weather beaten from lives spent in the harsh Highland weather, dressed in ancient tweed jackets, veterans of a thousand shooting parties. Students are here, home from university, mingling with middle-aged men who wear dark business suits, their hair plastered with Brylcreem, like 1950s throwbacks. These suits are the only smart clothes they possess, and serve for church on Sunday, weddings, funerals and drunken celebrations alike.

At midnight, to the accompaniment of an unsteady bagpiper, the warden's wife emerges with what looks like a long pie. This, she explains, is a Black Bun: a Highland tradition, and something like a Christmas cake wrapped in pastry.

"It's to soak the alcohol up," she explains.

It'll need to be a damn sight bigger than that, I think.

Overnight gatherings merge into early-morning parties and continue into the next evening. Some parties never end as revellers ebb and flow, some taking a few hours' respite only to rise and take up where they left off hours later. This is another world, far from our Merseyside home, a place where the rules no longer apply.

* * *

The following morning, as 1981 dawns, the three of us somehow find our way to bed. Joe, hungover and drowsy, peers through the bedroom curtains.

"My God! Look at this, it's snowing," he calls, standing in his underwear by the window.

"What! It can't be." I leap out of bed, forgetting in my haste I'm in the top bunk, and land in a heap at Joe's feet.

Joe laughs, looking down at me. "Careful – you'll hurt yourself."

Our prayers have been answered. The rain has turned to snow and the temperature has plummeted. This is what we travelled north for. Soon the snow is over a foot deep in the glen and falling so fast it looks like it will never end. Roads close in and out of the village and the place becomes marooned – not that anyone is worried in the slightest, but no one is going anywhere. This is Hogmanay in the Highlands and time no longer has any meaning. By the second of January the blizzard eases and Martin stands contemplating the vast whiteness as we finish our breakfasts.

"There must be somewhere we could walk to."

Days confined to the tent, the endless New Year celebrations, and then further days snowed in are beginning to make us restless.

"Maybe we could make it into Coire Mhic Fhearchair?" I suggest – the magical place we visited a few summers ago, when we traversed Beinn Eighe in the heat of a July day.

Joe drops his toast, suddenly coming alive, inspired by the thought of returning to the coire. "I bet it looks fantastic right now."

* * *

The old Saab fights its way through the snow and pulls up at the car park between the brooding giants of Liathach and Beinn Eighe. They dwarf me as I step into the snow. In summer Scotland has hills; in winter she has mountains.

Joe's experience of cold feet on Mont Blanc had a profound effect on him and he decided, once back in Chamonix, that he would never again suffer the indignity of cold toes. He scoured the little Alpine town's climbing shops until he found the warmest pair of climbing boots imaginable. They are sheepskin-lined double boots with massive soles.

"Jesus," I tease him, "you could take those to the North Pole."

"I'm not getting cold feet again," he says emphatically. I don't doubt him.

Having put on our boots, snow gaiters and jackets, Joe and I resign ourselves to the next fifteen minutes which, we have learned from long experience, will be waiting for Martin as he struggles with his equipment. Joe and I watch in silence as Martin searches through his plastic bags for his snow gaiters, at last finding them in a forgotten pocket. He then spends an age struggling with zips and buckles, cursing as they refuse to cooperate. Joe and I used to get frustrated by this, but now we simply watch, with a Zen-like acceptance, until finally Martin has got all his bits of kit in more or less the right place. Twenty minutes after Joe and I were ready, we head up the steep-sided glen towards the coire.

The blizzard begins again as we climb and we are forced to fight our way, painfully slowly, through feet of driven snow. One of the things I love about Coire Mhic Fhearchair is the way it surprises you. The coire sits at the far end of the mountain from the road and is hidden from view for most of the approach, but then, as you turn into the coire, it suddenly reveals itself. Today the great ice-sheathed cliffs rear up beyond the lochan with a startling suddenness, and the wind drives us to take cover behind a boulder. This is one of the things that fascinates me about the Scottish hills – their moods are ever changing and dramatic in their contrasts. The silent coire we sat beside on that hot July day, with its placid green lochan, has vanished. Now it is replaced by a huge rock cauldron where the forces of nature rage against each other as wind-driven snow batters against the cliffs. In the once tranquil lochan, icebergs four feet across bob and dance in the wind, colliding and groaning as if fighting for control of the water. So fierce is the wind that, despite the sub-zero temperatures, the small lake has been unable to freeze solid and has been forced into a jumble of broken ice. We could just as easily be in the Arctic as Northern Scotland.

As we crouch out of the wind behind the boulder I turn to Joe. "Are your feet warm then?"

"Nice and toasty."

"Thank God for that," I reply and we share the joke whilst shovelling jam sandwiches and snow into our mouths.

Looking up at the tall cliffs, I reflect that it must have been on a day like this that the Lancaster bomber hit the crags in the fifties. In my mind I hear the roar of the engines, feel the ground shake with the impact, and see the explosive flash of burning fuel. All that must have happened in an instant before silence returned to this high, lonely place, a silence that has reigned here for thousands of years and will stand for thousands more.

"Wouldn't it be amazing to camp here in winter?"

Martin laughs and shakes his head at the folly of such a plan.

Joe considers it more seriously. "Maybe, but you might want to wait for better weather than this."

* * *

On the way back down to the hostel the Saab's petrol warning light comes on. The little petrol station in Torridon is closed until the end of the Hogmanay festivities which, as far as we can see, is some indeterminate point in the future.

Joe looks disconsolately at the petrol gauge. "Damn, I should have got petrol in Inverness. We're stuck here now."

"Maybe we can get some in Achnasheen," Martin suggests. Achnasheen is almost twenty miles away up a steep single-track road now closed by snow.

"We'll never get there. Bugger."

Joe is annoyed at himself – for once he didn't plan ahead.

At this moment two young men stroll past our parked car and, for no apparent reason, one of them collapses. We rush out to help only to find his companion leaning against a wall having a cigarette while the other man lies unconscious at his feet.

"What's the matter with him?" Joe demands anxiously.

"Oh nothing," the casualty's companion replies. "I think it might have been the wine he drank."

"Really?" Joe stares incredulously at the motionless figure in the snow.

"You sure he's not drunk?" I ask. At this point, the fallen one emits a loud burp and begins snoring.

"Well, he might be a bit I suppose," his companion reluctantly concedes.

Together we hoist the unconscious individual into the car. On the way to the village we explain our petrol predicament to the young man.

"Ah, it's Hamish you'll be needing," he tells us.

"Oh great," Joe says. "Where can we find him?"

The young man sighs. "Well, he can't be far away, I suppose."

I leave Martin and Joe at the hostel and trudge down the shoreline road, kicking my way through the snow, as an icy wind tugs at my shirt collar.

"I'll be back in half an hour," I tell them as I leave. "This shouldn't take long."

Torridon village is little more than a road with a row of houses on one side and the sea loch on the other; surely it won't take long to find a man like Hamish? I knock on the door of the first likely looking house. A large middle-aged woman wearing a tatty jumper opens the door. No, Hamish isn't there. I turn to walk away.

"Will you not have a dram?" she asks.

"Oh, no thanks I…"

"Och come on just a wee one. It's New Year!" she says, pushing the door wider.

"Oh no, well, I really…" But the expression of outrage on her face stops me dead. At Hogmanay, I realise, it's rude beyond imagining to refuse a dram.

"Just a small one then."

She smiles. It turns out there are more houses in Torridon than I anticipated, although after an hour and a half of going from door to door the drams start to take effect and I'm beginning to wonder if I may have visited the same house more than once.

Eventually I'm directed to the postmistress's house near the end of the village. As I wobble up the path I hear the sound of merriment and fiddle music. Inside, the house is a confusion of bodies, bottles, dogs and half-eaten meals. I step over a couple of sleeping sheepdogs. Everyone tells me Hamish is here but no one is sure where. At last I find Hamish and the postmistress entwined together in the cupboard under the stairs.

"We've no petrol…" I begin to explain, but before I can finish Hamish pulls a set of keys from his pocket and hurls them at me, returning his attentions to the postmistress.

* * *

"Where the hell have you been?" Joe asks, standing in the snow at the hostel door as I plod unsteadily up the path.

"I was invited in," I stammer. "Well, I didn't want to be rude."

Martin looks at me disdainfully. "He's drunk!"

"I only had one or two," I retort, outraged at the suggestion. At this point the ground beneath my feet gives way and I am pitched into the snow. Dignity in tatters, I concede. "Well maybe three or four."

"The petrol, what about the petrol?" Joe demands.

"What petrol?" I can't recall anything about petrol.

"You went to get petrol!"

Triumphant, I produce the keys from my pocket. "Here, I've got the whole bloody petrol station."

We fill up the car and leave the keys and the money on the petrol station counter. On the fourth of January we have to drive home. As we head away from the village Hogmanay shows no sign of ending. We had travelled to another world, one we all know will call us back again and again.

* * *

New Year in Scotland has now become a ritual. For us, the Highlands are the only place to be as the old year passes and the new one begins. Each year we escape from family Christmases and head north on our annual journey into the fickle Highland weather. New Year is the only time that work and family commitments give us enough space to spend a few precious days north of the border in the winter. We never know what we'll meet on these trips – sometimes torrential rain, sometimes snow and bitter cold. No matter what happens, there will always be nights in the pub surrounded by the climbing brotherhood and, somehow, always adventure. Soon Joe and I begin to look towards winter climbing while Martin remains firmly a walker with his newly acquired (and diminutive) girlfriend, Jennifer.

The Lake District, where we first set foot in winter snow, is becoming increasingly crowded. In past years the crowds had fled the Lakes with the onset of winter and, on a snowy day high on a Lakeland hill, it was still possible to walk in solitude across the unbroken surface of fresh snow. By the early eighties all this had changed. One Sunday in January I made my way to the summit of Blencathra, a little gem of a hill in the north Lakes with fine little corries and sharp ridges, but not as sexy as Helvellyn or Skiddaw. I expected a quiet day. That Sunday I found over thirty folk eating sandwiches, drinking tea from flasks and taking photos on the icy summit.

In a handful of years, from when we began to explore the Lakes in the early seventies, there has been an explosion in outdoor pursuits. Hillwalking has grown from a pastime of hairy outcasts to a mainstream activity. Every year there are more and more folk on the hills. Campsites are more crowded and local pubs overflow with walkers and climbers.

Something else changes too. Not long ago the outdoor fraternity were a raggle-taggle army, distinguished by their threadbare trousers and ancient pullovers, treated with suspicion by the respectable community. By now things are different. Roused by thousands of tramping boots, the marketing men have woken up. Fibre pile, a lighter and warmer version of the old woolly jumper, is being mass produced in regulation navy blue. For the first time clothing specifically designed for outdoor use is becoming accessible to the average man or woman on the hill.

In 1981, after months of waiting, the time for our New Year

pilgrimage to the Highlands arrives. This year we decide that instead of heading for Torridon we'll go south to Glen Coe: it will offer me and Joe lower-grade climbs to try, and Martin and Jennifer ample hillwalking. Looking for accommodation, we arrive at the Red Squirrel Bunkhouse which was really a converted cottage and an old barn.

I pull up in the farmyard in my old Marina van and we step out into the cold night air. The night is cold and crisp and hoar frost sparkles on the stone buildings. I can smell the mountains, and that first arrival in the hills fills me with a rush of excitement. We are greeted by a scruffy, bearded figure wearing a battered old deerstalker who introduces himself as Hughie, the owner.

"The cottage is full, but I can take you in the barn." He motions to a low stone building.

Inside, the dimly lit barn has a medieval atmosphere. At one end stands an enormous three-tier bunk that could hold over eighteen folk crammed together on old foam mattresses. It's occupied by a mass of bearded youths and young women jostling around flickering gas rings where they struggle to cook their evening meals. Steaming pans fill the air with a mist so thick it's impossible to see more than a few feet. Walkers and climbers sit crammed together at trestle tables where they eat, drink and tell tales.

We find a table next to some Irish university students. One of them starts chatting to me. He's a blond-haired youth who tells us his name is Sean, and his flowing locks remind me of the Doors' frontman, Jim Morrison.

"See your man Hughie there. He's a tight one for sure," Sean says with a laugh. "Hell's gonna have to freeze over before he puts another log on the fire."

He's right, I realise. The temperature in the barn is struggling to rise above zero.

"We're climbing on Ben Nevis tomorrow, it'll be grand." He grins at me through his blond curls, eyes bright with enthusiasm. He and eight of his university climbing club have come across from Ireland for a taste of Scottish winter climbing.

We all find space on the bunks. I sleep soundly that night, glad for once that I'd mortgaged my soul and bought a decent down sleeping bag, while the others shiver around me.

* * *

Early next morning Glen Coe is gripped by a fierce frost and the air is filled with the sound of engines desperately turning over in vain efforts to start. I love my old Marina Van – it's the perfect climber's car. I bought it for a song and it can hold any amount of gear. Plus, you can also sleep in the back, handy for trips to the Alps. I drove all the way to Chamonix without any problem; provided, that is, I never took the ancient rust bucket over 55 miles an hour. That morning Joe and I hack the ice off the windscreen and climb inside, both of us wondering if after such a cold night the Marina will start.

I pull out the choke and turn to Joe. "Well, here goes nothing."

I turn the ignition key and, at first, the engine coughs and dies but then wheezes and stutters into life. As we drive down the glen we pass other folk lighting fires under their cars, trying to push them or heating them with camping stove. Cans of WD-40 are blasting away, prayers are being said and vehicles cursed in equal measure. Half a dozen times we climb out with jump leads and get other folk going but, in the end, we decide that if we are to get on the hill at all that day we would have to harden our hearts and leave the rest stranded.

Glen Coe is a spectacular place in summer but that winter's morning shows the place in all its intimidating glory. As the Marina chugs its way up the glen Joe and I watch the early morning sun tint the icy summits red. To our left towers the Aonach Eagach, a narrow ridge with a fierce reputation, long and committing to all who attempt it. To our right rise great ice-sheathed buttresses the look impossible to climb. My stomach churns in expectation of our first winter route. I'm excited and apprehensive at the same time. I don't know if I'll be up to the challenge and I'm not sure what kind of a test faces us.

* * *

Joe and I plod slowly, through knee-deep snow, into a glen known as the Lost Valley. This is a hidden gem of a place, a valley unseen from the road that only becomes visible once you climb through the jumble of huge boulders that guards its narrow entrance. Although this is not Arthur Conan Doyle's Lost World, a jungle populated by long-forgotten dinosaurs, it possesses plenty of monsters for me and Joe. Here we are entering a world of unknown peril. We're used to walking the ridges of hills in winter but venturing on to their steeper flanks and vertical faces is a new experience. It is already late when we stop beneath the cliffs and look for a climb to follow.

"That gully looks easy enough," I call to Joe as I stand at the foot of a short gully. A ribbon of snow rises up into the ramparts of the mountain at a 45° angle.

"Aye, okay. So it does. Don't want to do anything too hard for our first route," he yells back, uncoiling the rope.

"It looks easy. I don't think we'll need crampons, we can just kick steps in the snow."

It was easy, to begin with. I shoot up the first few hundred feet with no difficulty – at first.

"The last section looks steeper than I thought," I call to Joe seventy feet below me.

Now I am standing on hard ice, too steep to stop and put my crampons on. The situation is comical – now I desperately need my crampons I can't fit them, because they are sitting snugly in my bag. Unfortunately, with a couple of hundred feet of space below my boots, I don't see the joke. In fear and trepidation, I drive the pick of my Zero into the ice as hard as I can. It bites with a reassuring thud, which is fine until I try to move on.

"I can't get this bloody axe out of the ice."

Joe looks up, expression growing increasingly concerned. At least, out in front, I am master of my own destiny, doing battle with each demon as it arises. But Joe can only watch and has plenty of time to imagine the consequences of a fall. I inch my way up towards the crest of the ridge. I don't know it then, but this is the start of my winter climbing education. In the snow-covered mountains lessons are hard earned and knowledge is only gained by making mistakes, the price of which you must pay. I am on a learning curve and this curve is no graceful arch – it's vertical.

"Be careful." Joe's voice cuts through my concentration. "You are only standing on tiny nicks in the ice."

This is one of the many helpful comments Joe is wont to

call up under such circumstances. Other helpful comments he's made during our rock climbing expeditions include:

"Watch out, if you come off there you'll land on that spike and do yourself a serious injury."

"That rope will never hold you."

Or, my personal favourite: "A fall from there will probably kill you."

At last, I pull over the crest of the ridge and stand on horizontal ground just as the low winter sun is fading into darkness. We had been slow, incompetent even, but we are elated. We have, at last, completed our first winter climb. A world of possibilities stand before us as we buzz, full of the adrenaline high.

* * *

As we descend, in the deepening darkness, we meet the party of three and the young woman slips and falls into the void. All four of us career down the slope towards the dark mouth of the ravine, praying that we don't find a body in the depths. To our enormous relief, thanks to blind luck she had fallen on to a small ledge where she now sits dazed and bleeding from a deep scalp wound.

Despite her injury the young woman is tough. With the support of all four of us, she manages to make her way slowly off the hill. I can't help feeling her fall was my fault. I had suggested we remove our crampons. Despite that, the group shake our hands when we reach the roadside before setting off for the Belford Hospital in Fort William to get the young woman some stitches in her head wound.

We spend the evening celebrating our victory in the climbers' bar at the Clachaig Inn. No longer do we feel frauds amongst the hordes who populate that famous cradle of mountaineering; we had completed a route. The following day is clear and windless and the three of us teamed up once more to enjoy the ridge walking of Glen Coe. That night, tired and happy, we return to Hughie's bunkhouse full of beer and satisfaction at having completed our first real winter climb. I push open the rough wooden door and am instantly aware of the silence inside the barn. There's none of the usual drunken banter, no rattle of pans or voices clamouring for food. Martin is waiting for us and draws us towards him.

"The Irish guys haven't come back from the Ben," he says in hushed tones.

The Irish students cluster around a table, listlessly pushing teacups around, heads bowed. Instinctively I look for Sean but he and his partner aren't amongst the group. One of the young women looks at me and the look in her eyes makes me turn my head away.

I'd seen that look before, that morning in Chamonix, on the face of the young woman led away by the gendarme. Sean and his companion never did return. Six months later, when the snows of Ben Nevis receded, their bodies were found and returned to their homes in Ireland. I had learned something else about climbing.

9

Dangerous Days

It's 1983 and I'm living in Sheffield and working as a social worker in the South Yorkshire mining village of Goldthorpe. In the office, at lunchtime, I eat a local delicacy, a bread roll with currants in and cheese, followed by what's known as a Sore-Ear-Ole, a big biscuit with lemon curd and jam placed on the centre. I'll leave you to work out how the biscuit gets its name.

Browsing through the wanted ads at the back of the social work magazine I see an advert for a social worker post in Inverness. The advert sends a shiver of excitement through me; the thought of working in the Highlands has never crossed my mind. It's a place I visit for adventures in icy gullies or remote glens but I have never considered the possibility of moving there. There is a number to call for an application form and before I can think about it my hand is on the phone and a woman is telling me she'll put an application in the post.

By the time a brown envelope falls on to the mat in my Sheffield home I have developed a burning ambition to move north. It feels like an incredible dream – that I might be able to live in the place where I spend my holidays.

It's Easter. After a visit to the snowy Cairngorms, I travel north to Inverness in my old van and park in the town's campsite. I crawl into the back of my Marina, a scruffy, ill-kempt climber. Ten minutes later I emerge, as if from a chrysalis, transformed into a suited and respectable member of society. The advert offered an informal discussion. Determined to do everything I can to get the job, I make a big impression on the official who meets me, having demonstrated my commitment to the post by driving 400 miles to say hello. A couple of weeks later I am back in Inverness for the formal interview. Much to my delight, I land the job.

I remember 1983 for many things. It's the year that the Space Shuttle *Challenger* achieved nine missions, making space travel seem routine. It's the year that Michael Jackson first moonwalked and *The Return of the Jedi* was packing out cinema screens. The Red Hot Chili Peppers made their first concert tour. Closer to home, Neil Kinnock was elected leader of the Labour Party. 1983 was also a year ravaged by strife and acts of terrorism, the worst of which was the Nellie Massacre when over 2,000 East Bengal Muslims were murdered.

Such horrors are far from my mind on that Sunday morning in June when I cram all my worldly possessions into the back of my car and head out of a slumbering Sheffield. This will be different from all the other times I'd driven north across the border and into the Highlands. This time I won't be coming back. I am leaving everyone behind – few friends drop in when you are four hundred miles away, and I know that all the promises to keep in touch will mean nothing.

By now I have graduated from a series of geriatric Marina vans to a Marina estate car. It has plenty of room and a rather frighteningly powerful 1.8cc engine. It also has a rather disconcerting tendency for the whole body to twist when you jack one of the wheels up, suggesting an advanced state of rust in the chassis. Driving up the A9 this summer's day I try to put the car's obvious infirmity out of my mind and focus on the adventure of moving north. The A9 winds its way over the hills of the Highlands, through great tracts of endless open moor. At last I reach the crest of the final hill and can look down on to the Highland capital pressed against the shores of the Moray Firth, where Loch Ness empties into the sea.

I'm starting a new life, I think. Through the summer haze, beyond the town below me, the green hills roll on ridge after ridge, wave after wave, in an endless sea. I can't believe my luck. If you are going to do social work for a living, you might as well do it in a nice place.

I find myself a flat in the town centre, part of a row of old fishermen's cottages. It is stone built and shabbily furnished, with a shared toilet and a lean-to bathroom. On the plus side, it is pretty spacious, and right in the town centre. Opposite my front door is the River Ness, making its short, headlong dash from Loch Ness to the sea, its clear waters populated by salmon, seal and otters. I'd grown up beside the Mersey, a river so polluted it was a fire hazard – anyone carelessly tossing a cigarette butt into the water was likely to reduce the home of the Beatles to ashes. The Highland capital couldn't be more different from my home town. Inverness is a market town with one or two housing estates built outside the boundaries of the old capital. The bustle of the cities I've lived in, like Sheffield and Leicester, is absent. There is only one tiny supermarket – and even this closes at 5.00 p.m. and is shut all day on Sundays. I soon discover that if you don't get your groceries in on Saturday, you go hungry.

The town centre is dominated by two types of building:

churches and pubs. Most residents can be found in one or the other, and frequently both at different times on a Sunday. There's a 'God Rush' time at 10.30, when elderly followers of the almighty pile into cars that haven't moved all week and head for church. They are, by definition, Sunday drivers. They proceed slowly through the town centre and park anywhere they like. They take the view that they are going to church, and God, in his infinite wisdom, will overlook a little parking violation. It is as though there is a passage in the bible directly related to parking on Sundays.

And Jesus said unto the people, don't worry, it's Sunday; leave your donkeys and camels anywhere you like. Me dad'll sort the traffic warden.

The only problem with my new-found home is that, with all these hills on my doorstep, I am actually supposed to spend my time working – which feels like a terrible imposition. I join a small social work team. During one coffee break I ask a colleague if she knows anything about the local mountaineering club.

She turns to me with a horrified expression. "Oh I wouldn't go anywhere near them. They do dangerous things and drink a lot."

"Oh really?" I reply, thinking to myself, *Sounds like just the club for me. I wonder where I can find them.*

I hear that the club are to meet in a bothy one weekend soon. I don't really know what a bothy is, but my work colleague, who dabbles in hillwalking, tells me it is a disused cottage, open to all. Most have the barest of facilities. There is no electricity, no running water; but if you are lucky, there might be a fireplace and perhaps you might be able to scrape together enough wood for a fire. I'm intrigued by what sounds to be a world of mountain shelters I have never visited.

It is growing late as I approach Glenbeag bothy and the shadows have already lengthened in the glen. I left work early this Friday but it's taken me several hours to walk this far from the road. Evening is closing in. The valley I turn in to as I leave the Land Rover track is broad and empty and closed in on three sides by steep cliffs. It is remote and hidden away from the world, a place filled with silence and only a gentle breeze tugging at the heather. The path gradually fades away and soon I'm walking through bog, sinking here and there, as I try to pick my way through the peat. *Am I in the right place?* I can see no dwelling here, until I turn a corner and there, on the far side of a small river, is a low stone cottage with another green building close by. Smoke rises from the chimney and there is the faint glow of candlelight in one window.

I stand hesitant for a moment at the bothy door, wondering what kind of reception to expect from these northern folk. Will they accept me or snarl at me like the southern intruder I feel? The bothy is built of stone collected from the steep hillsides of the glen; rough, uneven, part man-made part organic. The wooden door stands twisted and battered, riven by a century of wind, snow and rain. I wonder if it remembers every hand that has pushed it open, eager, at times desperate, for the shelter within.

Inside the bothy, I can see very little – the air is filled with smoke from the smouldering wood fire. Gradually my eyes become accustomed to the gloom and soon I can make out a group of men and women, clustered beside the fire, drinking tea and sipping whisky. The ceiling is low, the floor made of earth, with pots steaming above the fire; the scene is medieval. They look a rough bunch at first in their ragged hill clothes but, as is often the case, the most ferocious of dogs shows a softer side with growing acquaintance. In minutes I have joined the circle and been absorbed into the group with the camaraderie of all folk who dwell in wild places.

One of the men introduces himself as Charlie. He's a big man, with broad, powerful shoulders, a shock of ginger hair and a wicked twinkle in his eye. He's surprised to hear that I walked in all the way from the road.

"Och, you should nae have done that." He laughs. "We got a key for the gate and drove up the track past Loch Vaich. Saved four miles' walking."

"How did you get the key?" I ask him, thinking of how less sore my knees would have been if I'd driven halfway there.

"Ah well," Charlie whispers to me conspiratorially. "I had a word with the ghillie. There's not a locked gate in all the Highlands a bottle of whisky can't open."

I meet the rest of the club. There's Charlie's diminutive wife, Ann, and a bearded Lutonian called Pete who is rapidly closing in on the last of his Munros. The Munros are a list of all Scotland's mountains over 3,000 feet. There are some 270-odd, all told, and a popular pastime for some folk is to climb all of them. I've never understood why people feel the need to complete a list of mountains compiled by someone else. What attracts me to the hills is their freedom and the fact that I can go anywhere I please without having to worry about rules and regulations.

The 3,000-foot contour doesn't exist; it's an arbitrary line drawn by man, imposed on the landscape. Perhaps there is a human need, when confronted by something wild and relatively untamed, to categorise it. I suppose it wouldn't do to have lots of folk wandering all over the hills, going where the please and enjoying themselves. Much better to have a list for people to follow so that the world can impose order on their lives.

As Pete talks about the difference between what makes one hill a Munro and another just a hill over three thousand feet, I gradually lose the will to live. I decide, that night, that I will never climb all the Munros, I will never keep a list of all the hills I climbed – I'll go where I want to.

The list was compiled by Sir Hugh Munro in 1891. It's a testimony to how unknown the Highlands were, even at this relatively late date, that the list surprised many mountain-goers – until Munro's list, there were thought to be only around thirty mountains in Scotland over three thousand feet. Sir Hugh's list is the first ever recorded case of Obsessive Compulsive Disorder.

* * *

As the evening draws on we sit around the fire and begin to tell tales. Charlie starts to tell me about other bothies he'd visited, names like Corrour and Shenavall conjuring visions of remote, wild places in my mind.

"I was in the Gelder Shiel once," he tells me, a wicked grin lighting up his craggy features.

Charlie goes on to explain that Gelder Shiel is a bothy on the Queen's estate at Balmoral. Legend has it that Her Majesty once visited the bothy and was so appalled by the debris left by visiting climbers that she took up a brush and cleaned the floor. One of her ladies in waiting was so amused she wrote in the bothy book, 'The Queen swept here.'

A few yards from the bothy is a small cottage used by royal parties for tea on shooting expeditions.

Charlie takes a sip of his whisky. "I noticed that one of the roof lights had been left open so I thought it wouldn't do any harm if I had a little gander."

Charlie had climbed on to the roof, opened the window and found himself staring down at the Queen's lavatory. Fortunately, the ruler of the realm was not sitting on that particular throne that morning. Overcome by curiosity he dropped from the window and into the bathroom.

"I had a wee sniff of the soap, sitting on an antique marble wash stand," he told me. "And then I used the facilities. Well, if it's good enough for the Queen's backside it's good enough for me."

All was well until he tried to leave, when he discovered, to his horror, that the bathroom door was locked shut. He made a few futile attempts to leap for the widow but it was beyond his reach. He was trapped! Looking around the room he found a beautiful marble Victorian wash stand, doubtless worth thousands, and did the only thing he could think of.

"I picked up the wash stand – it was so heavy it was all I could do to lift it. Then I hurled it through the glass door of the bathroom. What a mess it made."

Charlie shook his head, mourning the destruction he'd wrought.

"Have you been back since?" I asked.

"Christ no," he laughed. "If they ever catch me they'll put me in the bloody Tower!"

In the morning I awake groggy from the evening's festivities. Together with Charlie I climb up a hill with the romantic name of Seana Bhraigh. On our descent I look down into the coire on the far side of the mountain, and there below, beside the sparkling green lochan, is another bothy.

"That's Coiremor," Charlie reveals as we sit eating our sandwiches and admiring the view. The bothy looks lonely but inviting and we both decide to go there one day.

Back at Glenbeag, Charlie suggests we collect wood for the fire that night. Leaving the bothy, I'm mystified – there isn't a tree in sight. Charlie stops a few yards from the low stone building and begins to unearth sodden pieces of wood from beneath the peat. I can see no way this dripping wood will burn without weeks of drying out, but he assures me it will keep us warm. We return to the bothy with armfuls of moist timber. Once back at the bothy we set about building the fire and I resign myself to a long struggle trying to coax flame from these saturated logs. Much to my amazement it bursts into flame immediately, and in minutes we have a respectable fire going.

Charlie laughs. "You were expecting hours of entertainment trying to get that fire going, weren't you?"

He explains to me that the fuel we've collected is known as 'bog wood'. I had thought of the hills of Scotland as a natural landscape protected from the hand of man, but the truth, I learn, is very different. Once the Highlands were covered in forest, as was most of Britain. In their natural state the Scottish hills would be covered in forests with only the steepest crags and the very summits of the hills being much as we see them today. The landscape of Scotland is as manmade as its urban areas. The empty glens that we enjoy as hillwalkers are a recent development.

Charlie takes me further up the glen and shows me some rectangles of low stone walls.

"These were houses once," he explains. "People were kicked out of them and replaced by sheep. Mostly by landlords who didn't even live here. You know, English bastards." It takes Charlie a moment to realise that the particular bastard he is talking to is English – and a look of horror flickers across his face. I grin to let him know it's okay and we share the joke for a few moments. I am secretly happy to have been accepted as an honorary Scot.

That night we sit beside our fire of bogwood and swap tall tales of climbs we've done and things we've seen on the hills. I discover that something special happens when you light a fire in a bothy. The world with all its troubles fades away and all that seems to matter is the small glowing circle of flickering firelight. Perhaps this is something primeval. Millions of years ago primitive man must have huddled around a campfire and maybe, for a while, their worries vanished too. While the fire burned, it would keep them safe from the bears and wolves that stalked the forests of their waking lives. They could relax, enjoy the meat they had caught and swap stories about the big elk that almost ran them down or the bison's charge that sent them running for the trees.

It was around fires like these that stories began and legends grew. Around such fires religion was born as ancient eyes, staring out beyond the flames and wondering what terrors the darkness hid, began to look for a greater truth. Something of that dark, primeval time remains whenever climbers gather around a Highland bothy fire. They become kindred spirits, everyday lives only a distant memory as they share tales and memories and maybe a dram or two. Perhaps it is staring into the flames, as our ancestors did, that hypnotises them; or possibly it's the smell of woodsmoke that transports them far way. But most likely, I suppose, it's whisky that does the trick. I've heard it can do that.

* * *

I spend the rest of the summer walking and climbing. The weather is fantastic and I spend every weekend exploring the Highlands – I go to bothies, climb hills, stagger up some rock climbs. All this is great fun. I can't believe my luck in living here. Places that were once eight hours away are now accessible in under two hours. I travel to Torridon for weekends, Glencoe is a couple of hours away and the Cairngorms under an hour. I'm happy exploring and I soon feel at home in the Highland capital.

The truth, however, is that I'm waiting for the real action to begin. I'm waiting for winter. In Scotland winter is the great season, transforming gentle hills into savage mountains. Ice and snow turn the relatively minor crags of the British Isles into world-class arenas where even the best climbers will find themselves challenged. The summer slowly fades and autumn replaces it. October brings the stalking season, and the sporting estates – our usual playgrounds – don't welcome climbers and walkers on the mountains when they are taking wealthy clients out on the hills to shoot deer. Ghillies cruise up and down single-track roads, and Charlie and I play cat and mouse with them, trying to get on to the hills before they can catch us. October gives way to a wet and windy November when days are so short it's hard to go anywhere without ending up benighted and soaked to the skin.

One morning, as I leave my flat in the centre of Inverness, I glance towards Ben Wyvis, which I can see from my doorstep across the waters of the Moray Firth. The mountain has been transformed overnight. Its summit, green the previous evening, is sugar-coated white in the grey light of the morning. A thrill runs through my spine – the great season has arrived.

* * *

I wake up to the roar of a gas burner and a rattle of pans while muffled voices argue over the ownership of a packet of sausages. As I heave myself out of the bunk, my brain takes a moment to focus on where I am. I remember I'm in the Charles Inglis Clark (CIC) Memorial Hut, a climbing hut halfway up Britain's highest mountain, Ben Nevis. This realisation brings a knot in my stomach and a churning pulse of fear runs through me. So far, I've climbed a few easy ice routes in the Northern Corries of the Cairngorms and on the steep face of Lochnagar to the south of the Cairngorm massif. I've played at winter climbing but this is the real thing – this is what Charlie calls 'the big bad Ben'. I squeeze into my boots and struggle out of the hut to get a look at the beast.

The icy morning wind greets me beyond the hut door and

I stand shivering. But it isn't the cold that makes me tremble – it is the menacing sight of the North Face of Ben Nevis that raises the hair on the back of my neck. From the town of Fort William, sitting at the foot of the mountain, Ben Nevis appears a benign hump of a hill. This impression is a deception. There is another Ben Nevis hidden from the tourists, who climb from their coaches to munch shortbread and buy tartan tea towels. Millennia ago, ice and the elements tore into the northern side of the mountain, creating sweeping cliffs and sharp rocky ridges. As I cower outside the hut, this great frozen amphitheatre, over a thousand feet high, wreathed in ice and snow, towers above me. A big part of me wants to run down the mountain and head back to my safe flat where the demons of Ben Nevis can't get me.

"Well, Johnny, what do you think?" Charlie, swathed in his ancient fibre pile jacket with a woollen hat balanced on his head, is leaning against the wall of the hut smoking an evil roll up.

My mind drifts back to that day in the Glencoe bunkhouse when Sean and his friend didn't return from this place. I recall that it was months later, when the summer sun had melted back the snow, that their bodies were eventually located. I look up at the imposing cliffs for a moment, trying to comprehend their scale.

"Oh shit," I stammer. "Oh shit."

Charlie glances at me with an evil twisted grin, perhaps sensing the darkness of my mood. He yells towards the cliffs in a maniacal German accent, like the climbers of the thirties sent to their deaths against the North Face of the Eiger: "Conquer or die!"

Our laughter breaks the spell of fear and the knot in my

stomach eases a little – although I'm pretty sure Charlie's just as scared as I am.

* * *

"Opal Fruit?" Charlie asks, offering me the little packet of sweets.

Now, two hours later, we are high on the face of Ben Nevis in a world of ice and snow, huge drops all around us. I reach out to take the sweets but our woollen gloves are ice-covered and clumsy and the little tube of sweets slips from our hands.

"Shit."

We watch, with grim fascination, as the little yellow tube accelerates into the void below us. It is spinning away at incredible speed but it takes a long time to disappear from our sight, emphasising the drop below. Hanging in the silence between us is the realisation that, if we make a mistake, or the fates don't favour us, we'll follow the little tube of sweets in its wild ride to oblivion. Charlie has set up a belay below an ice pitch; it will be my turn to lead. He has driven a steel peg into a fragile crack in the rock to anchor us.

"Is that it?" I ask, hoping for more security.

Charlie is casual. "Och, if your number's up it's up. That's all there is to it."

I'm unconvinced by this fatalistic philosophy. Charlie has been unemployed for years. He is not constitutionally suited to employment, and spends his days climbing, fishing or drinking. As a result, he has little cash and his equipment is rudimentary, mainly acquired from jumble sales or passed on to him from kindly club members. His ice axe is an old Terrordactyl, an early short climbing axe with a straight pick invented by Hamish MacInnes in Glencoe. I tried it once and found it so insecure that I immediately understood why they put the word 'terror' in its name.

I've abandoned my faithful Zero ice axe in favour of a pair of Mountain Technology short ice tools with curved, drooping picks. They are lighter than my old Zero and have the advantage that you can remove them from the ice without spending half an hour waggling them about to free them. Mountaineering technology is beginning to move on apace now. The once tiny market for specialist gear is growing and that means serious manufacturers are now entering the race to design new and better equipment. I still have my faithful Superpro boots, for which I mortgaged my soul to buy before Joe and I climbed Mont Blanc. With their rigid soles, designed to hold crampons, they are as happy on Ben Nevis as they were in the Alps. Charlie's boots are a different story. They were handed down to him from a retired climber and bear the scars of battle; their soles now bend disconcertingly as he steps up in his crampons.

We have chosen to attempt Glover's Chimney, a famous climb high on the North Face of Ben Nevis. It begins with a long ascent up a broad fan of ice but, higher on the face, the course of the climb gradually narrows until it ends in a short, tight chimney of legendary ferocity. Charlie and I know the climb will test us and we approach the foot of the route with trepidation. I lead off up the ice pitch. It is long but not too steep although I am very much aware of how weak our belay is and very keen not to follow the Opal Fruits in their headlong plunge down the mountain. At the first opportunity, I hammer in a Warthog ice piton. The metal spike shudders under my hammer blows as it enters the ice, a good sign that it is solid. As I move on up the gully I'm increasingly aware of the yawning space below my feet.

Charlie joins me on the stance. "See, when I heard that ice screw going in I knew we were safe."

This must be a new use of the term 'safe', I decide – one that encompasses two men climbing thousands of feet up a mountain, secured only by a metal spike driven in frozen water. Soon Charlie is leading the crux of the climb, a short, very difficult chimney that leads up into a famous feature of Tower Ridge known as Tower Gap. 'The Gap' is a small notch in the rocky ridge, only a few feet across but sensationally exposed and renowned for its difficulty in getting in and out of. It's led more than a few climbing parties into serious trouble. The mountain has many features that climbers, sitting in the backs of pubs, talk about in reverential terms. Places like the Mantrap, the Eastern Traverse and the Curtain give the North Face of Ben Nevis a fearsome reputation.

"Look out," Charlie yells down as he teeters up the ice-glazed rock above me.

I hear something clattering down the rock face and look up just in time to catch one of his crampons before it follows the Opal Fruits down to the bottom of the cliff.

"Are you all right?" I call up.

"Yes, I've still got one crampon," comes a confident voice. There is more scraping from above followed by another clatter of an object falling.

I catch the tumbling spikes and clip them in to my harness.

"That's the second crampon then, Charlie!"

"Oh, Jesus!" I can hear the tremble in his voice and sense his fear as he battles steep, icy rock without crampons to give him grip.

A series of frantic scrapping sounds follow. There are grunts, and an assortment of obscenities.

"I'm up!" Charlie calls, his voice full of relief rather than joy.

Minutes later I follow Charlie up the chimney and into the Gap. Even with two crampons I find it difficult to squeeze and thrutch my way between the enclosing walls; how he made the climb on icy rock without spikes is beyond me. I suspect it was sheer terror that drove him up into the Gap.

A while later we are back in the CIC Hut, warm and comfortable amidst the hissing gas rings, cocooned from the big, bad Ben glowering down on us outside. Now that we are safe, after dicing with death on the mountain, life feels richer. The tea we drink from old chipped mugs is transformed to liquid nectar. With each cigarette, we inhale paradise. It takes a while for the fog of fear to leave our minds.

For days afterwards, my feet are in the street, but my mind is back on Ben Nevis grappling with the ice monster. I played the great game for a short time, high on those cliffs. My existence had been balanced on the points of my crampons, my fate decided by each second's throw of the dice. Journeying in high places is such an intense experience that it leaves its mark upon the traveller. On descending to the mundane world, part of us will always need to return to where life is lived on a higher plane. Once tasted, it is this thirst for life on the edge that draws us back again and again, that makes us mountaineers.

"Hello, is anybody there?" It's Thursday night in the Celt Street bar, and Charlie is standing over me with a pint in each hand.

His voice wakes me from my daydreams of climbing on Ben Nevis, and I jolt back to the mountaineering club's Thursday night session in the Inverness bar.

I laugh, embarrassed at being caught so distracted from reality. "I was thinking about the Ben."

"I know you were," he says, sitting down and putting a pint in front of me. "I could see it in your eyes, man. You've got the thousand-yard stare."

We both laugh and I know he is right. Winter climbing has seeped into my bloodstream.

10

Meeting the Reaper

So this is how it ends: alone, afraid, crouched on a ledge, a thousand feet of space below me, vomiting quietly. A large boulder crashes down from above and explodes beside me. That rock missed but I'm pretty sure the next one won't. The mountain is falling. Close by, a twenty-metre rock gendarme sways like a drunken old man before toppling forward and collapsing into the void. Then there is the noise. The roar all around me, so loud the mountain trembles and my ribs shake. I try to move but the rope tugs hard at my waist, reminding me that it leads down to Andy's lifeless body. He has already stepped into the darkness; I wait at the threshold. Something brushes my check, the gentlest of touches in all this mayhem – it is a leaf. Looking up I see a tree, hurled to its death by the monster, reaching out to me with its fingertips.

Through the fog of terror and despair, a thought struggles to be heard. At first the panic drowns it out but then I realise I am not dead, not yet. Somehow I have survived the last ten seconds. Maybe, just maybe, I can survive the next.

* * *

In the two years since I took my first timorous steps on to the North Face of Ben Nevis, I slowly gain experience as a climber, become confident and even comfortable in the Scottish hills.

From snowy gullies, I progress to ice faces and gradually master skills like front pointing (standing on the tips of my crampons) to get me up steeper climbs. I can't say I am an expert, but I am competent and getting safer all the time. The great cliff faces of mountains like Lochnagar, Creag Meagaidh and Ben Nevis still command my respect but no longer hold the terror they once had.

One Sunday night I'm sitting in my flat in Inverness watching the news. There's a story about a building collapse and then the TV cuts to a reporter standing shivering with the snowy Cairngorms at his back. Three hillwalkers are overdue and helicopters and rescue teams are searching for them in appalling weather. It occurs to me that I'm sitting comfortably at home whilst others are risking their lives. I should be doing something rather than idling away my time.

I am not certain if I am good enough to join the rescue team, but I know a member and he is kind enough to put me forward. A month later I join the Cairngorm Mountain Rescue team and I am immediately impressed by how professional their attitude is. I realise that being a member of the team is going to be a long way from the carefree jaunts I have enjoyed in the past. This is serious.

The provided training in rope techniques, first aid and search methods raises my game to a new level of competence. The learning curve is steep, but I am determined to rise to the challenge and learn everything I can about what it takes to get folk safely off the hill.

* * *

Three months later I'm sitting crammed into the back of the Sea King with the rest of the rescue team, heading into the heart of the Cairngorms. No one can talk above the roar of the engines. Every now and again the aircraft hits an air pocket and plummets towards the ground, and as we pitch sideways I catch a glimpse of snow and rock. There is something uniquely terrifying about flying in a helicopter. They are like bumblebees; aerodynamically they shouldn't be able to fly, but somehow they can. We fly on, balanced on a column of air. If the engines fail, we'll fall from the sky with all the grace of a brick. These are the thoughts that occupy my mind as we put down, much to my relief, on the summit plateau of the mountain.

When we land, the six of us spill out into the snow, clinging to our rucksacks and cowering as the Sea King's downdraft engulfs us in a vortex of spindrift. Seconds later the aircraft is hundreds of feet above and moments after that it has vanished into the cloud.

After the noise of the flight we find ourselves in the vast, silent emptiness of the Cairngorm mountains. Usually the body has time to adjust to the mountain environment as you climb up a hill into more extreme weather, but today we are parachuted on to the hill; the contrast between the warm metallic womb of the helicopter and the exposed mountainside comes as a shock. The team fight to zip themselves into cocoons of jackets and balaclavas.

Armoured against the cold wind and driving snow, we huddle together, as Peter, the team leader, gives us instructions. Peter is a clean-cut figure, an ex-Sandhurst officer whose calm, professional attitude always inspires me with confidence. We are searching for a young couple, both students, who should have returned from a day's hillwalking last night. If we can't find them this will be their second night out in the teeth of a Cairngorm winter. Concern for them is growing. Several other teams are searching in different areas and, all day, the big yellow Sea King helicopter has swept back and forth across this vast white landscape. In the poor visibility, the task of the rescuers has been a difficult one – a human is a very small thing in this savage landscape of empty corries and towering cliffs.

As darkness falls we line out across the plateau. We are far enough apart to only just be visible to each other, but sweeping yellow head torch beams mark the position of each man. We walk methodically forward, stepping into a surreal world where existence is reduced to the circumference of our torch beams, nothing beyond except the immense darkness of the mountains. Peter is to my left, making the centre of the search line. It's my job to ensure that I miss nothing in the space between us. Another team member is to my right in the line.

The darkness complicates things, but even in daylight it can be easy to walk past a body in the snow. Every few paces I do a 360° turn, scanning the ground behind me, double checking the ground I've covered. As I make one turn I step into a deep, snow-filled hole. I end up face down, spitting snow out of my mouth, in an undignified heap.

I hear Peter call over the radio: "Where's John? I can't see him, he's vanished." Although I only disappeared from view a few moments ago I've been missed already.

"I'm here!" I yell from the hole.

"Ah, skiving again. No time for a nap now, John." I hear muffled laughter, joining in the dark humour that many emergency services share.

I joined the team at the start of what was to become a dark period. For the last eighteen months all our searches have ended in tragic outcomes. We arrive too late to preserve the lives of the folk we are looking for. Sometimes climbers' fates had already been sealed by fatal falls; at other times the extreme Cairngorm winter conditions had left us with no time to find stranded hillwalkers.

Peter does his best to keep up morale. "Remember, no one we have reached alive has ever failed to survive," he would point out on training nights.

Despite Peter's best efforts there is an unspoken feeling of gloom pervading our searches. No one joins a rescue team to become a high-altitude undertaker; we all want to find this pair alive. We desperately need a win against the mountains.

We cover the pair's intended route but find no sign. Two hours in to the dark night, the lights of the Sea King once more loom down from above. We have been immersed in the natural world of spindrift and ice crystals, but as the great whirling machine comes out of the blackness it is a reminder that, beyond this white world, the neon signs of Aviemore's high street are only a few miles away.

We spend a few minutes in the warmth of the helicopter. The smell of its aviation fuel is comforting, reminding me of the old Primus stove my dad used to take with us on fishing trips. The smell of paraffin never fails to transport me back to the ponds where we used to fish, and heat up chicken soup over the ancient hissing stove.

Moments later the helicopter tips us out into the icy maelstrom and all thoughts of boyhood, soup and fishing are blasted from my mind. The mood of the team is low; we are all beginning to anticipate another long, fruitless search. Peter senses this.

"I was searching for a couple of naval cadets once," he announces as we prepare to move off. "One was called Hardy and the other Tough."

He pauses, fastening on his rucksack for dramatic effect.

"I came across a snow hole occupied by two guys on Ben MacDui and shoved my head in the door. I said 'Excuse me but are you blokes Tough and Hardy?'"

Peter pauses and checks his radio. "And one of them says, 'Well, I dunno but we do our best.'"

Everyone bursts out laughing.

We resume our search. In one of the remote corries of Braeriach there is a small, rough shelter. This is an improvised old hut, known as the Garbh Choire shelter: an ancient howff, one step down from a bothy, built of stones piled against each other. A half-broken wooden door, wedged in place, serves to keep out the worst of the Cairngorm winds. The shelter will only take around two people and has more holes than walls. It isn't much – but it is a lot better than being outside, completely exposed to the elements.

Peter pushes open the rickety door and, huddled together, cold and shivering, are the two people we've been looking for. They are hungry and tired and were not relishing the thought of trying to survive a second night in that lonely shelter. Most importantly, they are alive – and we can take them to safety.

That night we all go home satisfied. At last we have won against the mountain and there will be happy phone calls made to worried relatives that night.

* * *

Over the next few years I gradually expand my experience in the Scottish hills, climbing and taking part in rescues. One of the many things I learn from taking part in rescues is just how inaccurate press reports are. I barely recognise press reports for some of the rescues I participated in. They report the wrong mountain, the wrong events, and, misquote team members.

"It's there in black and white," my dad used to say whenever I argued over what the *Daily Express* said was going on the world. Now I know that if it is in black and white it is almost certainly not what happened.

The press delight in calling folk who get into difficulties in the hills 'idiots'. In all my time in Mountain Rescue I never came across an idiot. I came across people who had made mistakes, who were inexperienced, or caught out by unexpected changes in the weather, but never idiots. In everyday life we all make mistakes and no one notices; in the hills, such errors can be costly and high profile. I once met a party of police officers who got lost and came down the wrong glen. The press had a field day and misquoted one of the team's members, saying they had made a 'pig's ear' of the navigation. Clever pun that. Anyone can make a mistake on the Scottish hills and sometimes, more than anywhere else in Britain, you pay for it.

The press have promoted and developed a blame culture.

Every accident, every fall or missing party, according to the press, has to be someone's fault. The media love nothing better than to pillory some poor soul and if they can't find a reason they simply make one up.

* * *

I think back to all the mistakes I made in my early hill days and shudder at how narrow my escapes were. Ten years before I move to Scotland, one snowy weekend in the Lake District, Martin, Joe and I decide we are ready to tackle an easy gully on Scafell Pike, having grown confident on the Lakeland hills. Looking up at the cliff face on the mountain I can see a few easy-looking gullies that might offer us some good experience without being too taxing. Standing at the foot of one of these small ravines that cut through the sheer rock, I can see a few hundred feet of easy snow until the passage turns and obscures my view. I assume that the rest of the climb is just as straightforward.

"This one looks okay," I call to the others as they approach.

Martin is less confident. "Are you sure?"

"Ah come on, it doesn't look too steep." Joe sets off, plodding up the easy-angled slow.

We climb on, kicking steps with our boots, growing in confidence. But soon the angle grows more formidable and sheer rock walls rise up around us, enclosing the gully on either side.

"Don't worry," I call down from my position in the lead. "It's okay as far as I can see."

In truth, I am now a lot less confident; but since we are unable to climb down what we have come up, I have no alternative but to try and bluff it out. Then I turn a corner and a short rock step bars further progress. We can't go forward and we can't descend. We are trapped – and this is before Joe and I climbed Mont Blanc, so we have no rope. Our inexperience has led us to take on something beyond our capabilities. I can feel the press sharpening their pencils.

I have been introduced to rock climbing in Sheffield so I am a little more confident than the others on steep terrain. I can see an escape route to easier ground to the right of the rock step.

"I think I can get round here, maybe get help. Someone with a rope," I call down.

Martin looks dubious but there is little alternative. I make a couple of moves and suddenly the external tubular frame of my Karrimor rucksack jams alarmingly and begins to push me off the rock face. The climb is technically easy, but a fall from here would be serious.

"I can't do it with this rucksack," I declare and step back down, relived to get back on to the snow.

Everyone used external-framed Karrimor rucksacks in 1979. They had a straight, rectangular aluminium frame, designed by someone who had never seen the human body. To this frame a pack was strapped. They were strong and practical and just about the only robust rucksack on the market. The only people who didn't use rucksacks like these were climbers – because as soon as you left the horizontal it was like having your body strapped to a bed frame. I give the rucksack to Joe and try again. As soon as I begin to climb up the side of the gully the drop below becomes obvious. Mercifully the climbing is straightforward and suddenly I'm back in the easy snow at the top of the gully.

"I'll get help," I yell down and moments later I'm amongst the crowds on the top. I know what to look for: someone who isn't carrying a framed rucksack. I find a friendly climber and soon he's bringing up Joe. Martin appears next.

I look in horror at the knot at Martin's waist. "What the hell's that?"

"It's a bow. It's the only knot I know," he protests.

Back then we were incompetent, inexperienced, the sort of folk the *Daily Mail* like to get their teeth into. Experience would have told me to take a rope and some gear, and I'd know that what appears simple from below can often have hidden difficulties. Experience, however, isn't something you can walk into a mountaineering shop and buy.

"Here you are sir," the assistant says with a grin. "This experience is a day lost in a Cairngorm blizzard. It's only £25, reduced from £35. After this, your navigation will be much better."

Experience doesn't come encased in shiny packages. Experience is grubby, cold and wet, and it comes wrapped in exhaustion and fear. Experience is more about getting it wrong than getting it right. You don't learn much from bright sunlit days when everything goes to plan – you learn from howling blizzards, hours lost in mist when the compass needle seems to lie. You learn from days in cloud and rain wandering in despair, from climbs that defeat you or leave you clinging on by your fingernails, trembling in terror. Fear is a great teacher.

No one in the rescue team considered the lost or cragfast people we helped stupid. We rescued people who lacked experience, and whose mistakes, in gaining it, had come to haunt them. Every member of the team, even the best climbers, had tales to tell of their own mistakes, of things they had done. All of us detested the newspaper headlines that attacked the people we rescued. The newspapers called them 'fools', 'idiots', 'morons'; we just called them 'people like us'.

* * *

The Cairngorm Mountain Rescue team comprises forty-odd folk, which sounds a lot until you realise that at any one time we might only be able to put a third of that number out on a rescue. I should say that there were forty men and women plus one dog. One of the team members, Dave, is a police officer based in Aviemore. Dave often brings his police dog Rocky on rescues: a great brute of an Alsatian whose aggressive nature fits his name exactly. Although he's a very keen search dog we are all a little afraid of Rocky. One poor hillwalker got lost in a blizzard on Cairn Gorm, and was found by Rocky close to the ski shelters on the mountain. On being located by the barking, ice-encrusted Rocky, the man took refuge in a maintenance hut and refused to open the door until the dog was taken away. At lunch breaks on rescues or exercises, when Rocky asks for piece of your sandwich he gets it, no questions asked.

Being part of a mountain rescue team is a serious business, but like most of life there are lighter sides. One evening we were called out to an accident at a local crag. The cliff is almost two hundred feet high and near vertical. The foot of the cliff has what climbers term a 'bad landing': a jumble of huge jagged boulders which make the consequences of any ground fall very serious. I've always thought the term 'bad landing' to be an odd one because it implies that there can be such a thing as a 'good landing'. I would have thought that pretty much any impact with the ground, after you have fallen two hundred feet, is likely to be unpleasant.

That evening there was a report of two climbers going to the aid of a young boy trapped on the crag. According to what we were told, the boy had been successfully rescued from the cliff, but one of the climbers had unroped and fallen the full height of the crag. There was a grim silence amongst the team as we assembled the stretcher and began the short walk to the foot of the climb. Going to collect a body is never a pleasant task. We had only covered a few hundred yards when a dishevelled young man came staggering down from the crag.

"I've broken my bloody tooth," he announced on seeing us heaving the stretcher up the path. None of us could see how he had survived. I did ask him if he fancied doing it again so we could see how he did it but he wasn't keen to oblige.

* * *

Winters come and go quickly in Britain and, even living in Inverness, I have to snatch ice climbs from the jaws of westerly gales and sudden thaws. I always feel a tingle of excitement as winter approaches. Only in winter do the Scottish hills really come alive. Only swathed in snow and ice do the hills of the Highlands transform into serious mountains, drawing climbers to them from all over the world.

On dark November nights I spend hours planning the climbs I hope to complete when January and February bring real snow and proper winter conditions. Great climbs take place in the imagination as much as they do in reality. *Cold Climbs* by Ken Wilson, a book of great winter climbs, is my bible. I turn its pages reverently, reading over and over again about the challenges offered by this magnificent, frozen world. It's a place known only to the tiny brotherhood of winter climbers, populated by monsters and demons, where men were devoured in spindrift avalanches and risked life and limb to achieve the most esoteric of things. The photographs in Wilson's book capture the atmosphere of this other world with the exhausted, rime-encrusted faces of men like Tom Patey, one of the heroes of Scottish mountaineering, bearing testament to the ferocity of the battles they faced in the mountains. Weekdays pass in mundane work in my job with a small social work team while I dream of days in the hills.

Charlie and I are contrasting climbers. He is fatalistic, casual in his approach to safety, believing that you only die when the fates decide. I study belaying methods and rope techniques, learning everything I can to minimise the danger, and take infinite care with belays. One day I try to encourage him to be more safety conscious.

"Look at this belay, Charlie." I'm proud of my technical excellence. "That's how it should be done."

"Och, man, you're wasting your time," he snarls in response. "If your number's up it's up and that's all there is to it."

I was determined to make sure that my number didn't come up. He and I had a great time on the hills and shared a ribald sense of humour. This didn't ingratiate us with many of the climbers we met, but since we spent most of the time laughing that really didn't matter.

The famous American climber Alex Lowe once said, "The best climber in the world is the one having the most fun!" If that's true, Charlie and I must have been amongst the world's elite. We certainly weren't the best climbers but I'm pretty sure we had more laughs than any others out there.

One morning we head down to Creag Meagaidh, a massive mountain between Fort William and Newtonmore. There we plan to do one of the climbs on the vast Post Face that rises above Coire Ardair on the mountain's southern flank. I have never been to this cliff, although I've read about it in the pages of *Cold Climbs*. Despite what I have read nothing has prepared me for the sight of that face as we plod our way into the coire. We turn a corner and are confronted by a vast sweeping cliff rent by shallow gullies and glittering icefalls. The cliffs are topped by colossal cornices, great lips of snow that hang from the summit of the hill like wave crests frozen in time. Only Ben Nevis can rival this place for sheer scale and it's only when I spot some climbers, tiny dots on the face, that I begin to appreciate the true size of the cliffs.

The line we choose is a steep gully that sweeps up through the vast white face, gradually steepening to a wall of sheer ice until the gully finds its way through the enormous, overhanging lip of snow at the top of the cliff and on to the summit of the mountain. My stomach churns with fear as Charlie and I rope up and begin to climb the first few easy pitches. Soon the way is barred by a steep ice cliff that we will have to avoid to the left, although even that route does not look easy. It's my lead and Charlie is uncharacteristically quiet as I begin to move out of the gully and on to the face. Just as in the gully on Scafell Pike, it's only now that the space below my feet becomes apparent. Far, far below me, ant-like figures move in the corrie, silent reminders of how insecure we are and how serious a fall would be.

The climb becomes steeper and more difficult as I traverse right. In the confines of the gully the enclosing rock walls provide an illusion of security, but as I move out on to the open face and the sheer drop beneath me dispels what little confidence I possess and leaves me feeling very small and vulnerable. I'm climbing the steepest ice I've ever climbed, at the limit of my ability and my mind focuses down on the picks of my ice tools and the points of my crampons.

Charlie's voice breaks my concentration. "You should be okay if you can get an ice screw in there."

I switch my mind back to the ice and the steel, the only things in the universe that matter to me right now. Charlie's voice breaks into my mind again. Although I am concentrating so hard on what I'm doing, I can hear the anxiety in his tone.

"Keep your thoughts to yourself right now, Charlie." Conversation is a distraction I don't need.

I make it over the ice pitch and follow a set of footprints to the right. What I don't realise is that these prints are taking me off route. Charlie follows.

"I had to leave your ice screw in there," he tells me.

"Why?"

He's unabashed. "Och, too much hassle to take it out."

After the next pitch I set up a Deadman belay: a kind of metal plate that acts as a snow anchor. I keep climbing but can't find anywhere secure to belay. I'm on steep, insecure snow when I run out of rope. Now we have to move together with nothing but the rope between us, no anchors in either snow or rock. I can't hear Charlie but I know that he is as tense as I am. A slip here could see us plunging into the corrie a long way below. At last I find an anchor and bring Charlie up; minutes later we are on the summit, glad to be away from that yawning void.

Charlie lets out a long sigh. "Jesus, I was a zombie there. If you'd come off we'd have been brown bread."

Darkness falls as we head off the mountain and by the time we arrive back at the car we are overdue. Charlie's mum has alerted the police. Just as we are driving away a police car rolls into the car park.

"Are you okay, boys?" the burly sergeant asks.

"Aye, just a bit late," I reply through the window.

"Och, well that's okay then." And the patrol car heads away into the night.

I hope no one in the rescue team hears about this. I've been late on a climb and almost triggered a call out. The ribbing will be merciless.

* * *

Charlie doesn't work, he takes life as it comes and his only problems occur when the DHSS decide, for reasons beyond his understanding, that he should be in gainful employment.

"So I go in to the dole office," Charlie tells me as we are driving to the Cairngorms one morning. "And the fella says to me, 'Now then, Charles, what kind of work do you think your experiences make you suitable for?' I had to think."

He laughs, taking a draw of one of his special (and evil) roll-up cigarettes.

"So, what did you tell him?" I ask, my eyes watering in the smoke.

"Well, I said to him, I spend most of my time climbing, drinking and fishing." Charlie pauses for a moment, deep in thought. "I don't think he wanted to hear that."

"What did he say to you then?" I'm curious as to the response of bureaucracy in encountering such a free spirit as Charlie.

"Oh, he didn't look best pleased the fella. And then he says, 'I'm afraid, Charles, there aren't many jobs that fit your skill set.'"

"Well, he's not wrong there, is he Charlie?"

"I suppose not," Charlie laughs. "Now they want me to go on a training course. What could they teach me?"

"Nothing, Charlie, absolutely nothing." I can't argue with that.

Few relationships in sport, or indeed life, are as intense as the relationships between climbing partners. There are not many situations in which two people are dependent on each other for their very survival in extreme situations. This codependence creates a bond that transcends friendship. But like all relationships, there are tensions – and much as I enjoy Charlie's company I am becoming uneasy with him as a climbing partner.

Partly as a result of my time in the rescue team, and my experience of what can happen when things go wrong, I find myself becoming more and more worried about climbing with Charlie. We are both moving into higher-grade winter climbing and the risks are increasing. Walking back from a climb on which Charlie had shown his usual casual attitude toward safety, those worries begin to niggle away at me.

This guy is gonna kill me one day, I think.

* * *

One evening in March, the phone goes in my little riverside flat in Inverness. It's Hugh – a young, fit, enthusiastic climber.

"I climbed Crowberry Gully yesterday," he says. "You should try it. It'll be in condition [climbable] for a while, I think."

Crowberry Gully is a climb in Glen Coe I'm familiar with by reputation, having read *Cold Climbs* time and time again over the years. It's not a hard climb, but it takes a spectacular line up the face of one of the most striking mountains in Scotland, Buachaille Etive Mòr, and aims straight for the summit. Buachaille Etive Mòr, Gaelic for the Great Herdsman of Etive, is a pop star amongst Scottish mountains. It's featured on more shortbread tins than any other hill and possibly even rivals little Scotty dogs and dozy Highland cows for the top place in Highland calendars.

I am shaking with excitement at the thought I might get a chance to climb it. I hang up the phone and then hesitate, my fingers hovering over the dial – I know Charlie is as keen as me to climb the route, but my doubts hold me back. I make my decision and dial the number.

"Hi Andy, it's John. Hugh tells me Crowberry is in nick. Do you fancy doing it this weekend?"

Andy is a climber I met through a friend in Inverness. He's a tall, bearded guy from the Midlands who works in the town as a joiner. Andy is a perfectionist in everything he does. I know I'll be so much safer with him but I can't help feeling I've betrayed Charlie. Climbing partnerships are intense, and once broken are hard to mend. I know I'll probably never climb with Charlie again. A big part of me regrets that, but there is only one way to win this climber's game of ice and iron: survive.

On Friday night we make the two-hour drive over to Glen Coe and stay in the bunkhouse of the King's House Hotel. British mountaineering has a few places that are iconic in its history – the hotel in Wasdale Head, the Clachaig Inn, and the King's House further down the glen, which has its own place in mountaineering folklore. In walking through these corridors we are conscious that we are walking in the footsteps of our heroes. Men like Don Whillans, Joe Brown and Dougal Haston stayed here. They were the legends of our youth, climbers whose names and exploits were featured in the press and whose courage was legendary.

The next morning it is bitterly cold and the sky a vivid blue. Our breath mists the air and the snow crunches beneath our boots. This is perfect climbing weather, the kind of day that makes up for hours of frustration when you sit and watch the rain running down the window. The mountain is a great white pyramid sparkling in the morning sun. Running from the base of the peak to its summit is the great cleft of Crowberry Gully. Climbers talk about 'lines', or the routes that climbs follow, and Crowberry Gully follows one of the finest lines I have ever seen: it is direct, simple and elegant. There is beauty in this line and it calls to the climber in me.

The lower part of the gully yields easily to us and soon I am standing below a short, vertical ice cliff: the crux of the climb. In my hands I hold a pair of brand-new ice axes. These differ from other tools that I've used in that they have picks that curve up, known as 'banana' picks. These are Chacals, made by the French company Simond, and are state-of-the-art ice tools. At first the odd-shaped pick looks counter intuitive, as though it shouldn't really work. Its design was invented by mistake, when a worker put some ice picks in the tooth-cutting machine upside down.

I swing the axe into the steep ice. It bites hard, and I realise that I have no excuses now – these tools can climb anything, so if I can't get up a climb it'll all be my fault. The tools give me confidence and soon I'm over the bulge and we are on easy ground. Crowberry is ours.

Andy and I make a good team. I am confident in him and he is with me. That winter we move up through the grades and break into the magical Grade V, close to the hardest routes around. As always in Scotland, the weather is fickle; in subsequent winters we are less lucky with conditions and as climate change begins to take effect it becomes increasingly difficult to find good ice to climb.

One January, we are sitting in Andy's van watching the rain run down his windscreen.

"Of course, you know where it is cold don't you?" he remarks casually, between bites of his cheese and pickle sandwich.

"Where's that then?" I'm thinking he knows some hidden glen I am unaware of.

"Canada. There's got to be ice there."

* * *

It's 1988 and Calgary is hosting the Winter Olympics. The crowd falls silent as a lone figure, dressed in the red, white and blue of the British team, appears at the top of the ski jump ramp. The man on the ramp is not a typical ski jumper. Eddie is a plasterer from Gloucester. He's too big for a ski jumper, nearly 20lbs heavier than any of the other competitors, and he has another handicap, even more serious: he can't see the end of the ramp. Eddie is short sighted and his bottle-rim glasses mist up in the cold air so he's almost blind.

Eddie and I have two things in common. The first is that, as he stretches and psyches himself up for the jump of his life, he is afraid. He knows that this jump, right at the edge of his abilities, could be his last. That's exactly how I feel as Andy and I head towards the foot of our first Canadian ice climb above the town of Banff. Eddie nervously slides the skis backwards and forwards across the icy slope. He breathes heavily, sucking air into his lungs, trying to convince himself he's going to make it. As the red, white and blue figure begins his run down the ramp the watching crowd holds its breath; they know how close to disaster he is. The Canadian authorities, worried for Eddie's safety, tried to prevent him from competing. Eddie, however, is a determined man and his determination to compete overcame them all.

I don't know it yet, but as I start to climb the first pitch of our route, Andy and I are about to need all the determination we can summon just to survive.

We are high on an ice climb called the Cascade, just outside Banff, and it's warm – way too warm for ice climbing. High on the icefall everything is melting. I peer into the dripping ice and notice it's honeycombed with melt holes. Suddenly I feel very vulnerable.

"I don't like this, Andy," I yell down.

"No?" he calls calmly back from the belay.

"The whole thing is rotten. It might collapse."

"Come down, man, it's not worth it," he shouts, and I can hear the concern in his voice.

I gingerly reverse the climb back to Andy and then on down to the belay below. Off the steep ice, the climbing is easy. We are on a frozen waterfall only a few hundred meters across from a golf course on the main road into Banff. In Scotland, you have to walk up a remote mountainside for several hours to get to a route; in Canada there's an ice climb behind the local supermarket. I relax in the warmth of the sun and let my eyes wander across the panorama of forests and snow-capped mountains that stretches endlessly towards the horizon. The place is beautiful and so calm I can hear the birds singing in the woods below.

I clip in to the belay and Andy begins the short climb across the icefall towards me. Looking down I notice something odd. A line of birds is leaving the woodland, heading away from the foot of the cliff. This isn't a flock; all the birds in the forest are leaving together. Songbirds, birds of prey and woodpeckers have forgotten their differences and are heading out of the woods. I've never thought of birds being terribly bright but now I can see they know something I don't. They know that thousands of feet above me and Andy something is moving.

Eddie begins his run. His legs bent forward he accelerates down the slope, every bump in the snow sending jarring shockwaves up his legs. The cold air rushes past his face. Mist forms on his glasses.

Now he can't see and isn't sure where he is, but all he knows for certain is that the end of the ramp is coming.

As I watch the birds my brain registers that something else is happening. A few moments ago I was in bright sunlight; now, I realise, it is going dark. Then Andy says something I don't quite hear. I turn to ask him what he said and in that brief moment, in the time it takes to turn my head, the monster is on us. It leaps down from hundreds of feet above, bringing with it hundreds of tons of snow, ice and rock. It is belligerent, angry and bent on the destruction of everything in its path. In that moment, the world explodes.

I am slightly out of the creature's path. It ignores me but grabs Andy and hurls him down the mountain. I have the rope round my body using an old technique that will allow me to arrest any fall gradually, to place as little stress as possible on the belay. I can't see Andy; he is somewhere in the thousands of tons of snow roaring past, but I can feel him. He's about to go over the cliff below us. I have to stop him. It's now we live or die.

When I lock off the belay the shock will hit me and if the belay fails I'll be catapulted into oblivion. I hesitate, transfixed by fear, afraid to stop the running rope but knowing I must. Suddenly I am watching from a distance, as though from far away; then my arm, as if controlled by someone else, swings slowly across my body and locks off the belay and stops the rope.

Eddie gathers speed. The end of the ramp comes and he leaps into space. There is a moment when he feels he is flying. A time when the crowd floats away below him and he is in his own world, like a superhero, invincible, powerful, godlike. Then he feels the air catch one of his skis and twist it. Now he is not flying – now he is falling incredibly fast.

I had been on a winter climbing course at Glenmore Lodge when they told me to use a body belay, to hold a fall by gradually slowing the climber down in order to protect the belay from a sudden shock. What they hadn't told me is what it feels like to hold a falling climber in the grip of a monster. The moment I lock off the rope I am convulsed with pain. The rope is trying to separate my pelvis from my chest. It cuts deep into my body, cracking my ribs, and just when I can hold on no longer the rope snaps. I collapse on to the ledge, gasping and vomiting, waiting for death.

Eddie's first contact with the snow is hard, jarring his bones and knocking the breath from his body. Now he is spinning over and over, bouncing on to the snow and then rising again in a jumble of legs and skis. A woman in the crowd screams. There is a final, shuddering impact and the darkness comes.

I'm dead, I'm dead, I'm dead. Rocks, lumps of ice and fragments of tree pulverise the ground around me. Something hits me in the stomach and I double over, convulsed with pain.

It's coming, it's coming. I'm sure the fatal blow is imminent. The rock that will shatter my skull, the lump of ice that will break my neck. Andy has already gone; I am waiting to follow him.

Eddie wakes from the dream and the pain greets him like a familiar friend. Around him are the white coats, the concerned faces. He is alive, he has survived the big jump.

The monster leaves as quickly as it came, the sun returns and the birds even begin to sing. I lie coughing and gasping for air. My hand is bruised and bleeding, fingers broken but I am alive.

Perhaps I dreamt everything. Perhaps this is a nightmare from which I will awake.

The tight rope that runs to what has to be Andy's lifeless body is heavy and reminds me that I did not dream. My bruised hands fumble with the rope. Eventually I manage to tie a friction knot around it and set off down towards Andy, dreading what I will find at the end of the rope. My crampons graze across the rock and I jingle down, festooned by karabiners and all the gear I can carry. It seems so utterly pointless, so stupid, to have come all this way to die on a piece of ice. I don't call down to Andy; there is no point in shouting at a corpse. Just beneath a small overhang I find him.

"Jesus Christ, you're alive." I'm almost crying with relief.

Andy grins back at me.

I can see a small dot in mid-air coming down the valley towards me, then I hear the drone and know it's a helicopter. A ranger spotted us, passing in his car on the highway below, and called in the rescue service. I'm expecting a Sea King but what arrives is a much smaller aircraft. It carries Andy away, slung below it in a stretcher, then the chopper comes back for me. I clip in to the rope. They lower me and I wait to be winched into the aircraft but this doesn't happen. Instead the helicopter takes off down the valley and plucks me off the face where I swing like a spider on a web. There are two thousand feet of space below my feet. This is the ultimate bungie jump.

Eddie is dazed and bruised. Perhaps he'll never jump again but that doesn't matter – he's made his Olympic jump, he's realised the dream.

If it had ended there, would it have been worth it? Every

time you tie on to a rope, every time you make the first move on a climb, you take that chance. The years of climbing in Scotland, seeing the starlight sparkling on the summit of the Ben, the mates, the laughs we had, the good times and the bad, would all have come to an end there. Somehow, we had cheated the Grim Reaper; he had us on his list but we escaped him.

As Charlie would have said, my number was up, but I'd wriggled out of it. I doubt if the Reaper was troubled; after all, I'm sure he has pencilled us in for another day.

Next time I'm climbing, if I notice it's going dark and I see the birds are leaving, I'll know the Reaper's back.

11
Death by Armchair

I can hear the phone ringing at the other end of the line. It rings for a few seconds and then it's picked up.

"Hello?" a man's voice answers with an Edinburgh accent.

"Hi Peter, it's John." I can hear an intake of breath on the other end of the line.

"Yes?" Peter is not one for small talk.

I hesitate for a moment, wondering how to ask the question and fearing rejection. "I wondered if you fancied climbing Point Five at the weekend?"

"No," he says, without the slightest pause for thought.

I try to sweeten the pill. "I'll lead it."

"No." Quicker this time, like a gunfighter making the draw.

In my heart, I know it's all over – but I'm desperate. Point Five is a world-famous ice climb on Ben Nevis that I've dreamed of climbing all my career. "The weather forecast is really good."

"No." This time Peter says it firmly, like he's talking to a badly behaved dog pestering for crumbs.

"Okay Peter, thanks anyway."

I hang up, take a pen and cross his name off my list. It's a very short list and all of the names are crossed off now. I take the paper, crumple it up and hurl it into the bin, together with my aspirations.

Let me tell you where I am now. I've just fast-forwarded fifteen years. I've spun the video of my life through marriage, children and divorce. I don't know if you wanted to read about those things but, to be honest, if I wrote it down it would be much the same as everybody else's. A catalogue of good intentions shipwrecked on broken promises, surrounded by the flotsam and jetsam of human failings. I'll leave writing about those things to the people who do it much better than I can, and concentrate on what I do best: telling tales about lads from Merseyside discovering the hills, and journeys in places populated by dreams.

I'm pushing fifty now, still climbing and getting into the hills, but everything around me is changing. Now it's harder and harder to find people to climb with. Andy doesn't climb now. The Canadian avalanche took a greater toll on him than it did on me, both physically and mentally. His life was saved when he rolled below the overhang but he didn't get away completely free. His ribs were broken and one lung punctured – even now, years later, his side aches when the weather is cold. He climbed a couple of easy winter routes once his injuries had healed but the desire just wasn't there for him. We never climbed together again.

Something happens to your mates when you get towards fifty. I think it's something to do with armchairs. Armchairs have hidden dangers. You sit in them, watching TV, having a beer, and maybe even thinking of the hills. But there are invisible tendrils hidden in the soft furnishing. As you sit watching *EastEnders* or dozing beside the fire, the tendrils grow. They silently wrap themselves around your nice corduroy trousers – you know, the ones with the comfy elasticated waist. Then they sneak up on you, while your attention is diverted to what's happening behind the bar of the Queen Vic, and pin your arms to the sides of the sofa. You get to fifty and don't know it, but the man who strode across Snowdon and climbed hill after hill all those years ago is dead. He's still alive in your head and dreams and talks of the things he'll do, but what he doesn't know is that the armchair's got him. It holds him down as surely as if iron chains bound him. Years ago weekends were filled with frenetic hill climbing, but now Tesco, gardening and days with the in-laws fill your life.

As I go through my little list I hear a string of reasons why my potential partners can't make it out that particular day.

"We are shopping that day."

"Ah, sorry it's the garden."

"I would love to, of course, I would, but you see…"

It's not them I'm talking to; the armchair is a ventriloquist. I resort to putting notes in climbing shops looking for partners, like some climbing whore, advertising my services.

'*Experienced climber seeks partner for climbing at Grade…*'

That advert gets me nowhere, so I drop my grade restriction. Now I simply seek someone to climb with, at…

'*…any grade.*' I now have no self-respect.

I'm a climbing prostitute who'll go with anyone who has the price. If you can tie on to the end of a rope I'll climb with you; in fact, if you can't tie on I'll do it for you. I end up climbing with a variety of punters. All of them are fit but inexperienced in the mountains. I am an old man with a young novice, a recipe for disaster. I still manage to get out but all my peers have long since sunk into the interior springs of their divans. I'm not as fit as I was but I can still, just about, keep pace.

My peers now expect me to phone on a Thursday night when the weather is right. I suspect they keep a list of excuses pinned up by the phone and tick them off one by one so they don't accidentally repeat them.

"But you went to your mother-in-law's funeral last month!" I cry down the phone in despair.

Such are the trials of aging climbers. I wonder what the future holds for me. I see a vision of myself in future years seated at the foot of Point Five Gully, the wind tugging at my long grey beard as I sharpen the spikes on my specially adapted ice climbing Zimmer frame. Perhaps I'll wave the end of my climbing rope at passing climbers with a note around my neck.

It says, 'Please help an old man achieve his last ambition. (Frequent urination stops may be necessary.)'

I've become a climbing anachronism. Because there are so few climbers my age I am now one of Robert Service's 'men who don't fit in'.

I miss being part of a community. From my early days as a hillwalker and then as a climber I'd been part of a generation of climbers, a brotherhood. When we had bad times, failed on climbs or were sent scuttling back to the valley by torrents of hail or snow, we could sit and lick our wounds together. I could talk to other climbers and know that they shared my frustrations, my concerns at my shortcomings and even my fears. It's this support that sustains you as a climber through the bad times.

* * *

One Sunday morning I'm on Ben Nevis again, heading towards Vanishing Gully with a guy called Graham I met through the climbing shop notice board. I'm slow; it's taken me longer than usual to walk up from the North Face car park. The snow looks good, the face in great condition for climbing, but something's wrong and I can't decide what it is. Graham races on ahead. He's climbing with a slow old man, me. As the snow steepens we put on our crampons and begin to climb to the foot of the gully. I can't understand what the problem is; something doesn't feel right. The thought of the ice pitches to come fill me with dread but I can't understand why.

As we climb I hear a whirring sound from above and instinctively I plunge my face into the snow. A football-sized piece of ice embeds itself in the snow near me with a heavy thud. Climbers are dislodging lumps of ice from the cliffs above us – something unavoidable in ice climbing, one of the many hazards. Usually I would accept such a risk with a shrug but today I find it disconcerting. Another whirr and thump into the snow, closer this time. The knowledge that a climber was killed here, only weeks ago, when a brick-sized rock fell from the cliff and broke his neck, doesn't add to my confidence. I keep going but somehow I feel no eagerness to get on the climb. It's not fear that I feel. I understand fear. I've been scared at one time or another on every climb I've ever been on – I'm no hero. This is something different. Another lump of ice crunches into the snow a few feet away. I press my face into the snow and then head on up. As Graham plods beside me a thought comes to me; I try to push it away but it persists.

Then it forms clearly in my mind: *I don't want to be here.* I can't believe what I'm thinking. I've been climbing for years, it's what I do, the thing I love.

Another thought registers: *I can't do this any more.* It's louder this time and the instant the thought enters my head I know it is true. In that moment the illusion is shattered. Instead of being elated at being on a climb, I feel cold, vulnerable and being here seems utterly pointless. I can't go on.

"Graham, I'm not feeling good," I lie. "I had flu a while ago, thought I was over it but I'm not."

He looks at me and I can see the disappointment in his face. I think he knows I am making an excuse. Climbing isn't like golf or table tennis – you can't just have a bad game. I know if I go on it'll be dangerous for both of us. Climbing is more than anything else an act of will. You have to force yourself to go into places that no sane person would ever visit. You have to be prepared to push the fear into the back of your mind, control your body and your head at the same time. I suddenly see myself climbing this ice slope and it all feels ridiculous.

We drive back in silence and I am alone with my thoughts. Perhaps over the last few years I've just been going through the motions. I've been climbing out of habit. There has been a quantum change in my head I can't come to terms with. I feel like a priest who suddenly realises he has lost his faith. I have fallen from grace. There is a saying: 'For those who believe, no explanation is necessary; for those who do not believe, no explanation is possible.'

I no longer believe.

* * *

Christ, this is worse than climbing. I'm shaking, my mouth is dry and my palms are sweaty. Thanks, body, that's just what I needed right now.

It's three years after I quit climbing. I haven't been near a hill since. I don't regret it at all, but its left a gap in my life, and I need that adrenaline fix somewhere – I can't just sit down and let middle age take me. I can't give in to the armchair, at least not without a fight. I started writing poetry. In my teens on Merseyside in the seventies I'd cross the Mersey and visit the Everyman Theatre in Liverpool. At the time the theatre was a sea of denim flares and long hair, reeking of petunia oil and cannabis.

The interval was a race to get to the tiny bar. If you were not at the head of the stampede you didn't get time to buy a drink in the ensuing rugby scrum. Those who understood this would be out of their seats and sprinting down the aisle even before the interval was announced. Because the Everyman was the only theatre I knew, I assumed that all theatres were the same. When I went to university in Leicester I visited the Phoenix Theatre which sadly closed many years ago. Knowing that a bar break was imminent, I tensed, determined to make it for an interval pint. Moments later Hamlet said his last line before the break, and turned to leave the stage. As he did so I left my seat with the urgency of Usain Bolt going for gold. No one else moved – including the actors who remained on stage, startled by the disturbance. The entire auditorium watched in stunned silence as I sprinted across the front of the stage and out to the bar. Propelled by my own momentum I careered through the foyer and slammed into the front of the drinks counter like a train hitting the buffers. The young woman running the bar leapt back in shock – never had she seen a thirst like it. To my intense embarrassment it was several minutes before the rest of the audience arrived, having left their seats in a civilised manner.

Only the bold got a drink at the Everyman. I would listen in awe as Roger McGough would perform his clever, funny poems. Then a trembling, nervous individual with a mass of dark curly hair would take to the stage. From this figure would emerge gentle, sensitive poems of incredible beauty. This was a young Brian Patten. When I began writing poetry I thought all poets performed their work, because the poets of the Mersey scene were the only ones I knew, so I looked around for somewhere to perform. I think it's fair to say that performance poetry came as a bit of a shock to the Highlands of Scotland. In the Highlands men aren't supposed to have feelings – and if they do have them they are supposed to drown them in alcohol and certainly not talk about them.

Not surprisingly I found that there was nowhere north of the Central Belt that catered for performance poetry, so I established my own group: Mad Poets Society. Remarkably a local landlord allowed me to run a night at a pub called Blackfriars in the town. My only problem was that although I'd written some poems I had no idea how to perform them. I turned up at the local theatre and their drama teacher, oddly a Liverpudlian called John Batty, agreed to help me.

"I'm going to have to teach you how to act a bit," John told me.

"I'm not sure I can do that," I replied, having never so much as played a donkey in primary school nativity play.

John laughed. "Well, I'm sure we'll manage something."

In a few short, intense lessons he put me through the basics of acting. At the end of it I wouldn't say I was an actor but I had some rudimentary skills. Once a month, on a Thursday night, I would perform my poems in front of confused boozers in the town centre bar. I even managed to attract a few other like-minded folk who would stand up with me and bare their souls to the unwitting Inverness populace. Poetry nights in places like Glasgow and Edinburgh were taking off, but Inverness is a long way from Glasgow – and when you drive up the 150 or so miles from that metropolis to the Highland capital you also drive back twenty years or more in time. If you head over to the west coast of Scotland, it's possible to arrive some time in the 15th century. I exaggerate, but those who know the place probably won't argue. It's not that long ago, perhaps ten years, since the swings in children's play parks were chained up in Stornoway on the Sabbath to prevent children playing on them. I find it hard to believe that the almighty would be offended by the sight of little Jimmy MacLeod swinging his grubby knees into the air on a Sunday morning. I would have thought God would have more important things to do. Galaxies to collide and suns to build, that sort of stuff.

I achieved some moderate success as a performance poet, no mean feat in the Highlands. One night I was asked to perform in Glasgow where they even paid me a fee. I performed in a pub to a small audience who seemed to enjoy it. When I left the gig I walked out of the venue into city streets alive with music and song. I'd played to about twenty people in the only gig I could get for months. Around me the air was alive with people singing and bands playing. I even managed to get a poem or two published in a magazine. By way of payment the editor sent me half a dozen first-class stamps. Fortunately, I'd not booked a week in Las Vegas or ordered cocaine from the local dealer.

Poetry, I realise, is a cul-de-sac. The vast majority of people would rather watch a slug die than listen to someone performing a poem. It dawns on me that I'm working in a dead medium. If I want to scratch a living from my writing or performing, poetry just isn't an option. If I work really hard over the next few years I might end up as a half-decent poet, but when I arrive at that pinnacle no one will give a damn. I have to find something else to replace climbing in my life.

I've come to understand that sometimes inspiration gets planted in my mind and lies dormant for many years until something stirs it up. The poets I saw as a teenager in Merseyside left something inside me that only emerged years later. When I first moved to Inverness sometimes I'd come in from the pub late on a Saturday night and flick on the TV. Through a haze of beer I'd watch the Red Rose of Montreux a selection of comedians featured from the Canadian comedy festival. One stood out in my memory: Emo Philips. A long-haired spider of a man, he performed as a character filled with nervous anxiety whose hands wandered about his body, plucking his hair and exploring his ears as he spoke. His jokes were clever and surreal and I always sought out his TV performances. By accident, I picked up a copy of the Edinburgh Fringe programme and opened a page at random. There, beaming out at me, with that same spider-like awkwardness, was Emo Philips, performing that August at the Gilded Balloon. A couple of weeks later I'm queuing outside one of the many converted venues that become theatres during the Fringe. The support act is a disappointment who crumbles under the first assault from a heckler but then Philips himself takes to the stage. He's a little older than I remember; I expected the skeletal 20-year-old to appear before me as though he's been in some TV-induced cryogenic state. He's older, hair flecked with grey, and then I remember this is 2004 not 1984. He's older and so, of course, am I.

For almost an hour he delights the audience with his weird humour. He has an incredible skill in wrong-footing you and saying something completely unexpected that tricks you into laughter. What fascinates me more than anything else is that he entertains the audience for all this time simply by talking to them. He doesn't sing, he doesn't dance, he just talks.

Sitting in the fourth row watching Emo Philips sweat his way through his routine, I think, *I can talk. I could do that – how difficult can it be?*

By the time the next Edinburgh Fringe comes around I have obtained a grant from the Arts Council to go on a stand-up comedy course run by London's Amused Moose comedy club. After the usual pleasantries, the lady from the Arts Council told me they were happy to offer me the grant but warned me that "Stand-up comedy audiences can, at times, be rude and even hostile to performers and are a long way from those you might expect to meet at poetry readings." She obviously imagined me as a pale, fragile poet about to step into a bull pit. Perhaps she couldn't imagine what it was like to walk in front of a crowd of drunken Invernessians and recite a poem that betrayed some vulnerability and even talked about how I felt. I was well used to the bull pit.

In stand-up I find something that replaces the adrenaline rush of climbing. In comedy, you walk across the stage and pick up a microphone. I never get used to that walk – it's a long walk no matter how short the distance is – and you never know how an audience will react. In the few seconds it takes for you to take that microphone from the stand and say hello, somehow the audience decides if they are going to like you or not. If they don't like you, the next twenty minutes are going to feel very long indeed. In stand-up I find the kind of community I miss from my climbing days. Comedians face fear just as climbers do. When comedians talk about bad times on the stage, when the audience just stares at you blankly, they say, "I died out there tonight."

When it goes well they say, "I killed them tonight."

It's the struggle between life and death I'm familiar with from the mountains. There is something primeval in this battle for the comedian. Deep down, in some elemental part of our consciousness, we fear rejection by our own tribe more than anything else. For the cave man, to be cast out by his own people must have been a death sentence. The struggle for life in a harsh environment, surrounded by predators much larger than you, can only have been survivable with the support of your fellow humans. When the comedian steps out on stage he is walking out into the centre of primeval firelight; around him sit his peers, and if they reject him he is doomed to walk out into the darkness alone and face certain death. Of course, no comedian actually gets killed by his audience – although I did do a gig in the Gorbals where someone in the audience disliked a comedian's act so much he threatened to stab him. To be fair, the guy was so bad I was surprised someone hadn't stabbed him before.

Comedians, like climbers, face danger together. I perform in smoke-filled rooms above pubs in Soho, in comedy clubs in Manchester and in late-night venues in several Edinburgh Fringes. I perform wherever I can, when I can. Somehow, though, success as a stand-up comedian proves elusive. My main problem is my location. In around 2005 one of the local pubs, Hootenanny, starts a comedy club. At first Highland audiences are as confused by stand-up comedy as they were by poetry. The only time most of the visitors had been in a theatre was when they were six at panto time. Their only experience of humour is the banter they have with their mates, so they heckle constantly. Sometimes the heckles are good and I can work with them but the worst kind are odd guttural sounds that mean nothing and leave us comedians with nothing to work with. It takes several months for the crowds of Friday-night drunks to get the idea that if they listen to what we say we might actually be funny.

There's a saying, 'What doesn't kill you makes you stronger.' I owe a lot to those early nights, tough as they were; the experience definitely helped me. The manager paid us in beer tokens which says a lot for the respect he had for performers. The odd thing about stand-up is that you get to work with a lot of people in the early stages of their career. I performed with Kevin Bridges at a football club in Aberdeenshire where the show was paused for half an hour to allow a charity waxing event to take place. I also shared the stage with Sarah Millican on her first professional gig.

I was sitting backstage with Sarah, who had a streaming cold. "I've just given up my day job," she told me.

"Oh God," I replied. "You better be funny."

She looked at me for a moment and then said, "Fuck off!" with just the right amount of venom. I'm sure she meant it.

Being told to fuck off by Sarah Millican remains my major claim to fame. Kevin and Sarah have gone on to greater things whilst I am still performing for beer tokens. I'd like to say the reason behind that is the lack of comedy clubs in Inverness where I can develop my act. The trouble with being a comedian in Inverness is that the nearest regular comedy clubs are all in the Central Belt, so you are faced with a three-hundred-mile trip for a ten-minute spot. That sort of journey can sap the will of even the most ardent of performers. Just as pilots need their flying hours, comedians need stage time. You can write all you want and prepare what you think is the funniest material ever, but it's only on stage, in front of an audience, that you become a comedian. It's only on stage that you can watch as your best joke nosedives into the ground in front of a silent audience. I'd like to think that it was the distance between me and comedy clubs that stopped my career as a stand-up rocketing into the stratosphere but I suspect the truth is different. I suspect that I lack the kind of hard work and discipline that made Kevin Bridges and Sarah Millican stars – but more than that I think I lack the talent.

If stand-up isn't going to be the key to my performing career then what is? I can't sing, I sure as hell can't dance, so what am I going to do? I could have given up but I have tasted some success and giving up is not in my nature. If stand-up isn't going to be my adrenaline dealer then what is? I begin casting around for some other way to harness my creative drive. I remembered that when I joined the Inverness Mountaineering Club they had a book that members wrote their exploits in. Glaring from the book with a ferocious stare was a bald-headed man that club members told me was Aleister Crowley, whom the club had adopted as a mascot.

No one knew much about Crowley. They told me he was a madman who practised black magic, had been some kind of mountaineer and had lived not far from Inverness in a house on the shore of Loch Ness. It occurred to me that Crowley and I looked quite similar; we are both bald and have the same kind of round face. Perhaps, in the life of this man, I could find a one-man play I could perform. As I began to delve, a fascinating picture emerged. Ask any climber about Aleister Crowley and those who know a little of the history of this least sensible of sports will be able to dredge some bizarre fact from the dark corners of their memory. You'll likely be told he was a madman, that he threatened to shoot a fellow climber who wanted to descend Kangchenjunga or that he broke a Sherpa's leg with an ice axe. Those are the more moderate tales. Others will tell you that he was a black magician who practised child sacrifice and experimented with drugs. They will probably all tell you, however, that he was 'The Wickedest Man in the World' who revelled in the nickname 'The Beast'.

Crowley's life is surrounded by myth, lies and half-truths. Crowley himself was more than creative with the truth concerning his own life, and others, including the *Daily Mail*, have happily bestowed fantastic tales and helped to build a reputation that has made Crowley more famous in death than he was in life.

In researching the play, I discover a complex man whose early life as a mountaineer had been as controversial as his later life became when he turned increasingly to the occult. His achievements have been largely forgotten, but Crowley was one of the foremost mountaineers of his generation. He began climbing in his late teens as a way of escaping the brutality of Victorian public schools. Crowley had been a model pupil, but on the death of his father, when he was 11, the boy's life changed forever. The loss of the man he idolised plunged him into dark despair. He became unruly and was expelled from a number of public schools, finally being taught by a succession of tutors – all of whom struggled to contain their rebellious charge.

In his late teens Crowley discovered a freedom in the outdoors and began his climbing career on the chalk cliffs of Beachy Head. There the friable rock shaped his climbing style.

Crowley describes his technique: 'One does not climb the cliffs. One hardly even crawls. Trickles or oozes would perhaps be the ideal verbs.'

Crowley pioneered a number of routes on Beachy Head, one of which he describes in this article he wrote for the SMC Journal.

We ran up a grassy slope which hid the lower portion of this formidable obstacle, and a fine sight burst upon our astonished eyes. Behold the entire mass of Etheldreda's pinnacle [E.P.], with the cliff, here fissured with the magnificent 'Cuillin crack' [C.C.], some 200 feet high, overhanging it, and the distant sea behind; above, a mass of fleecy clouds framing the picture, and gorgeously lit by the afternoon sun. The effect was superb. We stood for a moment entranced.

His words exude a love of climbing that any climber can empathise with. Soon Crowley was visiting what was then, in the closing years on the 19th century, the cradle of British mountaineering: Wasdale Head in the Lake District. There he met the pioneers of the day including the Abraham brothers, Sir Martin Conway, Norman Collie and Tom Longstaff.

Longstaff said of Crowley's ability as a climber, 'a fine climber, if an unconventional one'.

It was at Wasdale Head that Crowley met Oscar Eckenstein, the man who was to be his greatest influence as a climber. Eckenstein was sixteen years Crowley's senior and already a Himalayan veteran. Eckenstein, a railway engineer, was almost as eccentric as Crowley and was noted for strolling around the streets of London, his beard wild and unkempt, and wearing a pair of straw sandals in all weathers. Despite his eccentricity he was also a man of considerable talent. He is said to have pioneered the technique of balance climbing, a technique we would recognise today. In the Victorian era climbers frequently hugged the rock and used the friction of their tweed suits to keep them in contact with the mountain. Crowley and Eckenstein were advocates of bouldering as a way of improving climbing skills – a practice that was relatively rare at the time. Eckenstein is also credited with developing the first modern crampon, upon which all future crampons have been based.

In 1898 Eckenstein and Crowley began climbing in the Alps where, over a number of summers, Crowley claimed to have become an expert alpinist. Although he made few notable first ascents he was clearly a climber of some ability and repeated many of the toughest routes of the day. It is the prerogative of youth to challenge the preconceptions of the elders; so it was that Crowley came into conflict with the Alpine Club. Crowley and his companions climbed without guides, in contrast to many stalwarts of the Alpine Club who relied upon locals to help them find their way to the summits of mountains, as was common practice at the time. When Crowley poured scorn on their achievements, as they had only been achieved with support, he was ostracised.

Crowley had little regard for the formal structures of such institutions as the Alpine club. Although he was a member of the Scottish Mountaineering Club for a time, he is unlikely to have sought membership. His growing reputation as an anti-authoritarian figure, coupled with rumours about his magical practices and homosexuality, would mean that his achievements as a mountaineer were never properly acknowledged.

Eckenstein and Crowley began to turn their attention away from the Alps towards the Himalayas and, in preparation for their expedition to K2 and Kangchenjunga, they journeyed to Mexico where they climbed a number of volcanic peaks in record time. On Iztaccihuatl Crowley claimed to have achieved a world record for the greatest pace uphill over 16,000 feet: 4,000 feet in 1 hour 23 minutes. If true, this would clearly have been no mean feat – although I doubt such records are maintained today. It is a measure of Crowley that in all his climbing accounts he never mentions that both he and Eckenstein were severely asthmatic. He does talk of his health breaking down at points, but never once discusses his breathing difficulties that must have made high-altitude climbing difficult to endure at times.

He relates having to retreat from one active volcano when he and his partner's boots actually began to melt as a result of the heat from the rock. On another occasion a local journalist cast doubt on the claims he and Eckenstein made for their ascents, so they invited the man to join them on a climb. This, of course, was a trap. He and Eckenstein tied the man between them on a rope and set off at enormous speed, dragging the gasping writer between them. After pausing for only a moment at the summit, they then dragged their exhausted and now terrified victim down the loose and dangerous mountain at an even greater speed. His pen never challenged their feats after that.

It is for his attempts on Kangchenjunga and K2 that Crowley lays claim to fame. In 1902 he and Eckenstein joined an expedition to K2. The attempt was dogged from the outset by divisions within the team and the machinations of outside forces keen to frustrate their ambitions. Eckenstein himself was detained in Rawalpindi, allegedly as a result of a plot by Sir Conway who had previously been on an expedition with the climber and held a grudge against him. Eventually Crowley gained Eckenstein's release but it delayed the expedition. There were then arguments between the team members, one of them caused by Crowley's baggage far exceeding the specified limit – he insisted in bringing a small library of books. After enduring searing heat and bitterly cold temperatures the party established Camp 10 at over 18,000 feet and attempted to make Camp 11 at around 20,000 feet. Here the weather and team morale began to break down with fierce arguments about the route. Crowley later claimed that on K2 he had experienced some of the worst weather in his life, and it is certainly the case that he was forced to endure extremes, spending an incredible 65 nights on the Baltoro Glacier.

One of the great Crowley legends originates from this expedition. I was told he forced an exhausted climbing companion to continue climbing by threatening him with a revolver. The truth is slightly less dramatic. In his tent and suffering from malaria, Crowley began to hallucinate and feared he was being attacked by his companion, Knowles, who was sleeping in the tent with him. At this point Crowley drew a revolver and Knowles had to overpower him and take the weapon. Why Crowley had a pistol with him on the mountain is never explained. Perhaps Edwardian gentlemen abroad didn't feel properly dressed without a gun. At the turn of the century and at such altitudes they were climbing into unexplored territory and perhaps feared that, lurking in the snow, might be hostile creatures.

On this expedition Crowley displayed an advanced understanding of the human body's response to high-altitude climbing. One of their party fell seriously ill with pulmonary oedema, a respiratory condition that can afflict climbers at high altitudes. The practice at the time would have been to treat him for pneumonia – which would have had no effect on his condition. Crowley insisted that the man be taken to lower altitude, a move that saved his life. In that era there was a debate raging amongst mountaineers – the belief that a climber could acclimatise to any altitude, given sufficient time, was widely held. Crowley maintained the view, held today, that above 20,000 feet the body endures a slow decline and that periods above such an altitude should be kept to a minimum. The attempt on K2 was eventually defeated by bad weather.

Crowley's final attempt at high-altitude climbing was an assault on Kangchenjunga. Significantly, Eckenstein declined the invitation to join the party, perhaps fearing the worst. The team made good progress until tragedy struck and four people were killed by an avalanche. Here Crowley's conduct is controversial – he is alleged to have refused to descend to help his fallen comrades despite hearing their calls. That he did not help them is a fact but his motives are obscure. That Crowley was courageous is, I think, beyond doubt; if it was not fear that prevented him from going to their assistance then what was it? Here I think Crowley's belief in the occult plays a part. Perhaps he genuinely believed that for those who had fallen he could foresee their fate and could do nothing to change it. Possibly, however, a stronger psychological issue restrained him. Crowley was traumatised by the death of his father and found death impossible to face. I believe that deep memory prevented him from going to the aid of those in the party who had perished. He was never to attempt a major climb again.

Despite the fact that Crowley's two major expeditions failed, they were considerable achievements at the time and Crowley's status as a mountaineer should not be overlooked. It was only several decades later, when knowledge of such mountains and how to climb them had increased considerably, that both peaks were finally climbed. As Crowley, I relive his attempt on Kangchenjunga in possibly the most dramatic part of my play. In bringing Crowley to the stage I have gained considerable respect for this man whose reputation was destroyed as much by himself as anyone else. Crowley was many things – a master of the occult, a poet, a traveller, a linguist – and his life is surrounded by controversy.

* * *

So, I wrote the play and here I am, in the Edinburgh Fringe of 2010, standing behind a curtain sweating gently. I am about to walk on stage as Aleister Crowley, but I feel like an imposter. I've just been sharing a dressing room with people who trained at RADA.

People who say things like, "Break a leg darling."

People who can actually act and have the certificates to prove it. I don't have any certificates and my performing experience consists of telling knob gags above pubs in Soho. Once I step through that curtain it's me and the audience for fifty mins. If I forget my lines, fall over, or just run away in sheer terror it'll all be my fault. Somehow I get through the first few shows and, amazingly, people like the play. More people come to my show than come to see the Darlings. Audiences don't know I'm faking it; I'm getting away with it.

Anything can happen throughout an Edinburgh Fringe run and frequently does. At one point I was in mid-performance when I noticed a pale yellow liquid forming a pool on the stage. At first I thought one of the audience had given me the ultimate accolade and actually peed themselves. Then I realised someone has spilt a pint of lager. In another show I was halfway through when I realised that a dagger, a vital piece of stage equipment with which Crowley kills himself to end the play, wasn't on stage. I spent the performance trying to work out how I was going to get off stage at the end but was saved by a miracle. The technician realised that the knife was missing and plunged the theatre into darkness just before the death scene. In pitch black I ran backstage, found the knife and was so relieved I did the best death scene ever. A one-man play is said to be one of the biggest challenges in acting; fortunately, nobody told me that.

* * *

After the Fringe of 2010 I begin looking for another writing project. One day, in a second-hand book shop, I come across a book about the Scottish hills and nights spent in bothies.

After reading it, I think, *Maybe I could write something like this little book. I've had loads of experiences.*

That's how this book started, as a farewell to the hills. I've spent over forty years walking, climbing and just living in the Scottish mountains.

It's time to say goodbye to all that, I thought.

So that is where this little book you are holding started out. I'm still not too sure why, but that's not where it ended up.

12
The Bothy Hunter

I am leading a group of elderly people through Anagach Woods near Grantown-on-Spey. They move slowly and I count the minutes until the walk will be over and I can go home, back to my writing. There is something about the woods that makes me feel uneasy. The scent of the old Caledonian pines pervades the air; I can hear the wind in the trees above me and feel the moss on the path beneath my feet. It feels as if I am visiting a house where I once lived that is occupied by strangers. I feel as if I know the place but it is different from the pictures my memory holds.

I have a job many would die for. I'm the organiser for a Highland-wide charity that aims to help people improve their health by encouraging them to walk. We run thirty-odd groups involving people with chronic illness, mental health problems, learning difficulties and obesity. I establish groups, plan walks and risk assess routes. In short, I'm paid to walk in the most beautiful part of Britain and there's only one problem: I hate it. My mountain rescue experience and social work skills got me the job but I don't feel comfortable. This is the kind of thing the old me would have done.

Every Thursday I drive down from Inverness to the village of Grantown-on-Spey in the Cairngorms National Park and there take the small group of elderly people for a gentle walk in the area. Sometimes we walk beside the River Spey where it passes the village in a broad sweeping arc of sparkling, clear water. Occasionally we see one of the local fishermen catch a salmon (a rare event). Mostly the fishermen stand thigh deep in the cold water and spend fruitless hours gracefully casting their flies. It's less about landing a fish and more about simply being out in the deep swirling water of this big river as it makes its way from the high tops of the Cairngorms towards the sea. At other times we walk in Anagach Woods, which has everything from 230-year-old Scots pines to seedlings that only germinated the year before. All around us the woodland teems with life from red squirrels to industrious ant colonies.

The walking groups are normally led by volunteers whom I recruit and train. For some reason this proves difficult in Grantown, and so for several months, through the autumn and winter and then on into spring, I have to lead this small group myself. In groups like these it is the older people I like to talk with as they can look back to a time beyond my experience. One woman tells me tales of her father who worked on the railway when it ran through the village. His job was to constantly walk the line to ensure that the steam trains had not left sparks in their wake that would smoulder into fires in the tinder-dry moorland. The line is long gone now, the tracks ripped up, but the little huts where her father and his mates would have their tea are still there, slowly sliding into decline. The station in Grantown is derelict, its platforms silent and overgrown with weeds. Years ago they must have been the heart of the Highland village, alive with people travelling to Inverness, the capital of Edinburgh or possibly on as far as London. The rail lines have gone, torn up during Dr Beeching's notorious cuts of 1968, leaving nature to reclaim the line.

The group finishes its walk with cake and a cup of tea in a local cafe – undoing most of the good the walk did them with calories and sugar, but the chance to spend half an hour with friends and talk about the weather and the things they saw today does as much good as the walking. Some days, I find myself sneaking back to the woods before heading back to Inverness. I am fascinated by the minutiae of things and notice tiny fungi growing in the leaf litter, and the tracks made by ants as they scurry through the woodland floor. In the autumn the place is a riot of fungi. Decay is an amazing process. Without the work that fungi do the world would slowly die, the soil deprived of nutrients.

There is such a variety of fungi I can't begin to identify all of them but there are a couple I know. On quiet Thursday afternoons, I pick strange-looking wrinkly yellow fungi I hope are Chanterelle. At home, when I fry them in butter, the smell takes me back to fishing trips with my father. In the early morning, we would walk through fields made silver by the dewy webs of a million spiders woven in the grass. On the way back to our fishing hut we would pause to pick mushrooms. At the hut my father would take out the old Primus stove and go through the mysterious ritual of lighting it. First, he would burn methylated spirit in the little trough around the burner until it was hot enough to vaporise the paraffin. Then he pumped the brass piston to pressurise the stove and then, if everything had been done right and the paraffin was hot enough, he would light the stove and it would roar into life. He'd fry the mushrooms with a few sausages in a battered old frying pan. No restaurant in the world could compete with those fry-ups, consumed in the early morning amongst rows of fishing rods on an old dusty table.

I am discovering a new Highlands by organising the walking groups – a world that exists below the two-thousand-foot contour. It makes me realise that the Highlands I knew as a climber and hillwalker are the high Highlands, but there are huge areas that I have never explored. This is brought home to me more than ever when some of the more able walking groups want to walk part of the Dava Way, a walk that extends along the disused railway track and over Dava Moor. Even though the moor is not mountainous, it is high, remote and can be exposed to some fierce weather. I set off to plan the route and do an all-important risk assessment.

It is May in the Highlands and there is still snow on the moor. I'm following the route past an old railway cottage and between some gorse bushes when something moves in the snow a few yards ahead of me. Something tiny darts about like a minuscule apparition, almost invisible in the snow. A little white creature, not much more than six inches long, darts in to view. It is a stoat, dressed up in his Sunday best winter ermine, as worn in the House of Lords. The snow deadens my foot prints so he can't hear me and dances through the snow with quick, furtive movements oblivious of my presence. I discover later that not all stoats turn white in winter. Only a few shed their brown coat and adopt the white raiment with its distinctive black-tipped tail. No one knows why some change and others do not. Oddly it does not seem that the more northerly individuals are more likely to change, as one would imagine. I stand entranced, watching the little creature as he explores every aspect of the world around. At last he turns and sees me and does a Buster Keaton-style double take, then vanishes in a flash of white fur.

As I drive back to Inverness, the image of the stoat replays in my mind. I feel privileged to have witnessed such a sight in that wild place. In the distance, I can see the Cromlet hills, the foothills of the Cairngorms, white in their snow cover on this sunlit day. Those few moments in the snow watching the little stoat have crystallised something that has been growing inside me for a while. I wonder what it would be like to walk those hills again. Am I still able to walk in to a bothy? Could I do that?

Somewhere deep inside me an old urge is stirs.

* * *

Everything feels wrong. I'm not quite sure why I am here. Perhaps I should turn around now. I am heading up into the Cairngorms with a pack on my back, making for Ryvoan bothy. I feel ridiculous, an imposter; any moment some passing mountain-goer will emerge from the forest and double over with laughter.

"What the hell are you doing here? You crazy old man." He will look over my ancient gear, my outdated plastic boots, battered old rucksack, and shake his head sadly at my foolishness.

I'd struggle to find words to explain to him and myself what I'm doing. "Well… you see I just thought maybe I'd try it again. The hills I mean."

My imaginary tormenter looks at me, puzzled. "But you gave all this up – it's twenty years since you last slept in a bothy. You don't do this any more. You are too old, too fat. Why don't you go home now while you still can?"

It's May in the Cairngorms. It's supposed to be spring but mountains don't care about dates and this May winter retains its hold on the landscape. The path before me winds its way up through the narrow glen, snaking between Scots pine, some of the last few survivors of the ancient Caledonian forest. These trees are twisted and contorted into odd shapes, their limbs formed in countless Cairngorm gales. Above the tree line the hills are white with feet of snow and the still air carries the rasping calls of ravens that echo off the small crags above me.

The walk in to Ryvoan is far from challenging. It's only two or three miles up an easy path, the kind of walk I would not have even thought about thirty years ago. Now it feels like a major challenge. I'm struggling to remember the last time I walked in to a bothy with a sleeping bag, my stove and a quantity of whisky. It feels like a long, long time ago. Perhaps it wasn't me who walked in to Shenavall bothy more years ago than I can recall. That was a different person, someone actually capable of making such a journey – this is me now, and I'm a fake. The confidence I once felt in these hills has long since evaporated, replaced by uncertainty and even a hint of fear.

Fraudulent or not, after a mile or so of sweating I'm standing looking into the depths of Lochan Uaine, the Green Lochan. This small lake is named as you might imagine, by someone with stunning imagination. Its waters are a deep green – a colour I have never seen anywhere else – and it marks the halfway point of this little walk/mighty challenge. I expect to collapse at any moment, my heart strained to breaking point by the heavy load

I'm carrying. Fortunately, that doesn't happen and part of me is actually enjoying the walk. Not far from the bothy I leave the forest and walk out on to the moorland that is typical of the high Cairngorms, a rolling, heather-covered expanse watched over by the big sky I recall from my days of climbing here. The sky feels bigger here than anywhere else in Scotland. The open glens and rolling hills that characterise this place allow your eyes to wander across an endless sky.

I'm not sure how long it has taken me but eventually the chimney pot of the little shelter I am seeking rises from the heather. I begin to imagine myself warm beside a roaring fire, swapping stories and sharing a dram with fellow bothy-goers as I did in days past. I tell myself there is something magical about the closeness one feels to one's fellow man in these remote shelters. Ryvoan is a modest little bothy. The little stone building sits stoically at the foot of a minor hill, as if bracing itself to repel the raging Cairngorm weather.

I stand for a moment beside the bothy, kicking the shallow fringe of snow that clings to the foot of the stone walls.

Doubts race through my mind. *Am I really going to stay in this place tonight? It'll be cold and miserable. Go home, you idiot.*

Inside, the one-roomed shelter is less than inviting. Below a small step is the fireplace, blackened by years of use, its soot-stained cavity gaping black like some great open mouth. The walls, once white, are stained by woodsmoke. The room smells of smoke and sweat: the odour of a thousand nights of tired walkers huddling beside a smouldering fire. It's a smell I remember. Once, everywhere people lived had that smell; once, everyone lived in need of a roof and a fire however basic. Now we sanitise ourselves and our homes. Rather than woodsmoke our houses bear a less honest smell – of last night's takeaway curry or some chemical device pumping out the perfume of simulated roses. There is a low wooden sleeping platform that is elevated to keep the bothy visitors out of the cold draught that steals beneath the bothy door and nags at your ankles. At one end of the sleeping platform a couple of sleeping bags lie neatly folded. I'm pleased I will have company tonight – at least I won't spend the night alone reading my book in an empty bothy. Then I notice that beside the fire there is a collection of wood for burning, obviously gathered by the current occupants. The wood has been gathered into three neat stacks according to the thickness of the branches. The first pile is tiny twigs, the second is the thickness of a finger and the last pile slightly thicker than my thumb. This level of order disturbs me. I've never met bothy-goers that ordered and it looks to me as though this wood can only offer a meagre fire.

I'm just laying out my sleeping bag when the door opens and in walk a couple in their late twenties.

"Hallo," the young man says.

I can tell from that one word that they are German. He doesn't look too pleased to find me standing there. The couple's English is limited although much better than my German. I attempt a little conversation but this proves fruitless. I decide attempting humour of any kind will probably be the social equivalent of the charge of the Light Brigade and lead to the same level of disaster. I retreat to my book. The couple hunch over the fire – or at least a few smouldering twigs on which, to my amazement, they attempt to cook. Clearly they want to minimise the environmental impact of their journey. This, as far as I can see, involves burning a microscopic amount of wood, eating something that looks like dehydrated sawdust and being as miserable as possible.

I take a sip of whisky. *No bothy craic for you tonight, my boy.*

As the couple crouch over the flickering fire I decide it's time to cook my evening meal. I will show them how it's done. I unpack my paraffin stove. This is the bothy beast, three and a half pounds of brass and steel, capable of punching a hole in the ozone layer the size of a football pitch whilst making a cup of tea. There will be no eco-friendly sawdust for me. The stove has two different settings using interchangeable burners. The first setting burns at a gentle hiss and disperses the flame evenly through a mesh. The second spouts forth flame like the exhaust from a Saturn V rocket and is aptly named The Roarer. The couple are watching me in amazement as I assemble the beast. I smile at them reassuringly. Normally I use the burner that emits a gentle hiss, but today I decide nothing else will do and fit The Roarer. They watch with obvious disgust as I light the meths, filling the room with toxic fumes, and pump the pressure handle. Just as they return to stirring their sawdust The Beast reaches ignition temperature and I open the valve that releases the paraffin.

Instantly the bothy is filled with a tremendous roar and the Germans leap in alarm.

Normal conversation is now impossible so I yell, "It's all right. It always does this." The couple don't look too convinced so I add, as I pump the pressuriser furiously, "It's okay. These things hardly ever explode."

I open my can of stewed steak and it sizzles happily when it enters the pan. As they watch me do this I can sense, without a word being said, that both my companions are staunch vegetarians. It's the way they try not to vomit that gives the game away.

I'm happily stirring my pan of charred corpse when I notice a clear liquid forming a pool across the table underneath my stove. This turns out to be paraffin. I realise it's so long since I used my Primus that the washers have dried out and shrunk. Although the stove always roars it doesn't normally spout paraffin. I'm trying to hide my alarm and decide what to do when the pool ignites, swallowing the whole stove in a ball of flame. The Germans shrink into the far corner of the bothy and I try to look nonchalant while I wonder how long it will take before the paraffin tank explodes and takes me and the Europeans on a quick tour of the Cairngorm plateau. I manage to get the valve shut and the conflagration subsides just as my dinner comes to the boil.

"Quick these stoves aren't they?" The whole process took about forty seconds, during which period I aged three years.

After my meal, by way of apology for almost killing them, I offer the Germans a drink of whisky.

The young man accepts. "Oh, it is too strong!" he responds, having taken his first sip.

"Yes, I thought it would be."

The evening passes in silence, the Germans huddled together for warmth over a flame the size of a candle, and me drinking my whisky immersed in George R.R. Martin's *A Song of Ice and Fire.* At one point it occurs to me that I might bring a little levity to the proceedings by using soot from the fire to paint a Hitler moustache under my nose and jack booting around the bothy. After a little consideration I decide that this might not be the best way of breaking the ice.

After all, I'm not completely insensitive.

At about dusk I hear odd sounds outside the bothy, and sneak out to see strange birds dancing on an open space about fifty meters from the door. The birds are slightly larger than pigeons and mostly black with a white chest. It dawns on me, as I peep round the corner of the stone wall, that these are black grouse and I'm watching their mating dance. I crane to get a better view, but one of the birds spots me and issues a warning cry; instantly the birds scatter. They vanish into the undergrowth and it's as though they and the dance never existed. I don't know much about birds but I remember these places where birds gather are called leks. It's pure coincidence that I have come at the right time of year and I feel as though I have had a glimpse into a hidden world. After a few minutes the birds return and, by keeping myself well hidden, I can watch them at my leisure.

The following morning, at dawn, they return only to vanish again when the sun is fully risen. I've passed this spot many times over the years but never realised the black grouse existed. You would never see them unless you spend time out at night in this place. I didn't much enjoy the company last night but the birds more than make up for it.

* * *

The following morning the Germans head off, doubtless happy in the knowledge that the carbon footprint of their bothy visit is small enough to match their sense of humour. It's a bright, cold day as I walk along the broad footpath that leads through the national park towards the summit I am seeking. It feels more like March than May; my feet break through the thin veneer of ice that covers the puddles on the track. I'm moving slowly, I feel awkward and cumbersome but at least, I tell myself, I am here – although I still feel like an intruder in an alien landscape. A long, well-made path, cut every few metres by stone drainage channels, climbs gently towards the shoulder of the mountain. I can see that the hill is still wrapped in snow and soon my feet are sinking through inches of crisp snow. I have neither crampons nor an ice axe with me today.

It's May, I tell myself. *The snow will be soft; I won't need them.* Besides, I wasn't too sure if I could handle the extra weight of mountaineering paraphernalia on top of having to haul in my sleeping bag, stove and food. At first I have the mountains to myself. My advantage of having started from the bothy, a few hundred feet up the hill, means that I'm ahead of the day trippers. This isolation doesn't last long, however, and soon figures begin to appear behind me on the path. I quicken my pace, hoping they won't be able to catch me up and pass me. Somewhere deep in my subconscious, a mountaineer's pride lingers and I cling to the illusion that I can move with speed through these hills.

After ten minutes I am sweating and blowing hard in my efforts to keep some distance between me and my pursuers. My brain still thinks I am the lean, fit mountaineer I was twenty years ago; my body harbours no such illusions. My legs are aching and chest heaving. Minutes later I come to a grinding halt. The figures behind are much closer now.

Well, at least the people catching me up are, young, fit guys, I console myself. *I can't be expected to compete with them.*

I have forgotten that it is ten years since I did anything like this. A few minutes later the 'fit young guys', who are actually a retired couple from Wigan, smile happily as they pass me on the path.

"Nice day," I call, as I pretend to be taking a photograph and try to exude a sort of 'well I'm only out for a stroll and not in any hurry at all' kind of attitude.

These are only the first of a number of walkers to pass me that day, and over the next hour or so their numbers increase dramatically. After a while I become immune to the ignominy of being overtaken. None of the cheery, super-fit outdoor fanatics who pass me are young. Most, it transpires, are my age or older. I reach the inescapable conclusion that I am completely unfit. Something will have to be done.

Eventually I reach the shoulder of the mountain, a point where the ridge narrows and steepens for the last few hundred feet. Below me the glen sweeps wide and open all the way back to Ryvoan bothy where I had watched the black grouse dance the night previously. On the far side of the glen, Cairn Gorm itself towers over the landscape, a great white mass dwarfing everything around it. I wish I could say that Cairn Gorm is an elegant mountain with towering ridges reaching up to its shapely summit. Unfortunately none of those descriptions apply. Cairn Gorm is a great white lump of a thing. Impressive is the most flattering word I can come up with. That the summit of Cairn Gorm can claim the worst weather in Britain is its principal claim to fame. In this temperate isle, nowhere else are the temperatures as low or the winds as ferocious. Hurricane-force winds frequently scour the peak, sweeping on from its summit to wreak havoc across the exposed plateau of the highest and most savage mountains in Britain.

"Don't fight the wind," Peter Cliff once told me as we plodded back from a rescue on Ben MacDui, Cairn Gorm's neighbour and the second-highest peak in Scotland. "You ever get caught out in a blizzard and howling wind, don't struggle against it. That's what gets people killed. Go with the wind. You might have turn a cliff but you'll get off the plateau and that's what counts. When it's really bad up here no one can survive."

If Cairn Gorm is not an aesthetically striking mountain, the view from its summit more than makes up for it in grandeur. I have stood many times on that top and stared in awe into the kingdom of bleak snow and rock that is the heart of the Cairngorms. When the hills are wreathed with snow the view south, across the Loch Avon basin and over the mountains beyond, holds an untamed wildness that no other view in Britain possesses.

Memories of such days flood through my mind as I begin the last short climb to the summit. Here I begin climbing even slower than I had before. I expected the snow to be soft and allow me to kick into it, but as it steepens it grows harder. My light summer boots won't make any impression on the icy surface. Without ice axe or crampons I'm forced to admit defeat. I've failed on even this modest hill.

As I head back to the bothy I assess my achievements over the last couple of days. On the upside I managed to walk in to one of the easiest bothies in Scotland – not much of an achievement really. I've just been passed by a bunch of geriatrics and failed to get up an easy hill. The humiliation is intense. The only consolation I can find is that I managed to terrify the young German couple in the bothy with my incendiary paraffin stove act. It is from such small things that old men take comfort. Near the Lochan I meet a group of young people, the first I have seen. These folk are clearly not hill-goers, I can tell that from their mismatch of ordinary street clothes and shiny new hill gear – they remind me of how I must have looked when I first set foot in the hills. They are led by a woman closer to my age, clearly revelling in leading her charges into the Cairngorms. I wonder why they are in a group. Perhaps it wouldn't do for young people to be out on their own, would it? Anything could happen.

Did I enjoy myself? I am really not sure. At least I have proved I am capable of walking in to a bothy without collapsing under the weight of the rucksack. Perhaps I'll to do this again.

* * *

That summer my confidence grows as I begin to find my way to increasingly remote bothies. I start to seek out bothies that are hidden away in remote glens, finding a delight in spending nights in their seclusion. On this cold November day I am following the little path that leads up from the tiny hamlet of Strathcarron (which is really just a station, a hotel and two or three houses), over a high ridge and on to Bearnais bothy. I've done this before, I remember; it's easy and the path is obvious. I once raced one of my friends in here, jogging in, each refusing to allow the other to pass. Now, as the snow begins to fall and the light fades on this short winter day, I struggle to recognise the place. It seems even harder to fit the landscape to the map. As I climb higher, blowing heavily beneath my rucksack with its load of coal and whisky, I remember something. The race I had with my friend was thirty years ago. Then it was my summer; now it's the autumn of my life, and my legs, like my rucksack and the rest of my gear, have seen better days.

I thought I was ready for the long climb over the ridge to Bearnais bothy; my legs, however, take a different view and are increasingly unsteady with every step. The path is now obscured by snow and the light fading fast. I left home too late. I always leave home too late. There seems to be a curse that afflicts me whenever I am packing to leave for a bothy. There is always something I can't find. A pair of socks will inexplicably vanish into the ether. My compass dives down the side of the settee and, without a word to anyone, my plastic mug will go and hide in the back of a cupboard. Then, when I think I have everything ready and I'm about leave, those masters of escapology, my reading glasses, leap from my pocket and, using the black hole they obviously have at their disposal, travel to another bloody universe. Such is the curse of middle age.

My rebellious belongings, coupled with the fact that walking in to the bothy always takes longer than I expect, inevitably lead to a frantic race to get to the bothy before darkness shrouds the scene. Something odd happens to bothies when darkness falls. They become invisible, and I'm not totally convinced they don't actually move about. Bothies are usually built from the stone of the hillside upon which they sit, so as the light fails they can quickly blend in to their surroundings. Perspective vanishes in twilight, and boulders and broken walls look like they might be part of a shelter, only to vanish, mirage-like, as you approach.

I have experienced all these tricks in the past and this is why I am now hurrying along, desperately trying to get to Bearnais before it is completely dark. At last I head down in to the glen to the waiting bothy. The only problem is that the bothy isn't there, and the glen is the wrong way round. It takes me a long time to accept that my years away from the hills have not only eroded my fitness but my navigational skills too. No matter which way I look at it, the inescapable facts are I'm high in the Scottish mountains, alone and lost. I try to stifle the rising panic, telling myself that, though tonight I'll be denied the comfort of the bothy, my survival isn't in doubt.

All prospect of toasting myself beside the bothy fire has gone. In disgust at my incompetence, I hurl the bag of coal from my rucksack and, realising I'm too tired to walk back out to the road, I resign myself to a night in the cold. I search in vain for some shelter in the glen but there isn't even a boulder or a ruined wall I can huddle behind. I stop by a small stream and climb into my sleeping bag. I remember the old survival articles I used to pore over in magazines, and recall reading somewhere that I should put the foot of my sleeping bag into my rucksack and cover my head with my cagoule.

I climb into my makeshift shelter. It's finally happened: I am about to endure my first enforced bivouac in forty years of hill-going.

At this point my luck changes: the snow ceases, and the night sky clears and comes alive with a myriad of stars. The moonlight picks out the silhouettes of the hills in the broad glen and soon the Milky Way girdles the sky like a great band. It is cold and clear but at least I'll be dry. I feel isolated and vulnerable here. I had expected to be safe within the walls of the bothy by now yet here I am, alone and out in the cold of this great dark glen with only the stars above me.

I settle down into my sleeping bag, expecting to endure an endless cold night, then something unexpected happens – I start to feel warm. My sleeping bag is cheap. Unable to afford the luxury of a down sleeping bag, I had to get myself a heavy synthetic alternative but, despite its economy, it does the job. I pull my cagoule over my head, take out the little computer tablet I carry for company, and watch a film I downloaded at home. The titles of *March of the Penguins* roll across the little screen. The irony of lying in an icy glen watching a bunch of birds doing pretty much what I am doing right now, trying to keep warm in a hostile environment, is not lost on me. If I'd known I'd be spending a night out in the frost I'd have downloaded *Priscilla, Queen of the Desert*. Under the cover of my cagoule I feel as if I have walked into my own TV lounge and, gradually, I forget where I am and enjoy the film. A couple of whiskies help me fall into an untroubled sleep.

The next thing I know a thin light is filtering through the cagoule that covers me. Pushing open my shelter I find myself in a sparkling world of hoar frost as the weak winter sun ushers a new day into the empty valley. I realise I've been warm and comfortable all night. The long, cold ordeal I had expected never happened; putting my feet in my rucksack has somehow worked. The wide glen is motionless and silent, still held fast in night's mysterious spell. No wind disturbs the ice-encrusted blades of grass inches from my face. Here, in the early morning, there is a peace I've rarely experienced before. I have woken in a secret place. How many dawns have passed this way unobserved by hurrying humanity? I rest, content in the warmth of my bag, as the sky comes alive with ribbons of pink clouds. The hills, reduced to dark outlines by the night, slowly emerge like images developing from a photographic plate. Soon I can distinguish patches of heather, ridges and rocky crags, as colour returns with the growing daylight.

Sitting up, I realise I am not alone in the glen. Only a few feet away to my right, hearing the disturbance as I rise, a young hind raises her head from the heather and sits blinking at me in the morning light. Moments later another hind to my left pops her head up, ears twitching, and scents the air. She is followed by another ten or so, all encircling me and my little nocturnal shelter. As I slept the herd must have descended from the hills and come, silent footed, down into the glen to sleep. They must have known I was here. I may have snored or, even if I slept silently, my scent would have filled the air like a beacon, pointing out my presence to their sensitive noses. Strange that these timid, wild animals so accepted my presence among them that they were happy to abandon themselves to sleep within touching distance of the apex predator. Now, in the morning light, the truce suddenly breaks and the herd rises as one before galloping off across the heather. As I make my breakfast the roar of my paraffin stove feels sacrilegious. I stir porridge and prepare to return to the world that passes for civilisation. Bearnais bothy will have to wait for another day.

Back home, surrounded by technology and central heating, I

write in my blog about my quest for the little bothy.

Someone makes a comment on my musings: "It made me realise how comfortable you are in the hills in winter."

I read that sentence over and over again and realise he is right; I am comfortable there. In the vast silence of that dark glen, I returned, at last, to the place I lost.

* * *

It's mid-June when the phone rings in my flat in Inverness.

It's Martin, calling from his home in Blackpool. "Fancy a weekend camping in Shiel Bridge? The weather forecast is good."

I remember our nights, forty years ago, in the hotel in Shiel Bridge, the place packed to the rafters with young hikers like ourselves. I remember walking the hills and being in awe of the spectacular scenery.

"Yes, of course, why not?"

As I throw my sleeping bag and rucksack into the back of my car I try to recall the last time I spent a night in a small tent. I realise it was a very long time ago – and then I recall how hard the ground was, and the struggle of simple tasks like cooking a tin of beans or getting my trousers on. On the drive down past Loch Ness I realise I have been lured to my doom by nostalgia.

When I arrive at the little campsite in Shiel Bridge, Martin is waiting beside the tent. The last time he and I camped here we were in our twenties. Now we are both closer to our sixties. It is July so I expect the campsite to be bursting with folk, but in fact it is fairly quiet. There are a few men in our age group; each has his own tent. They are not in a group, but individuals probably, enjoying their early retirement. There is a group of Germans.

Everywhere I go there seems to be a group of Germans. I've no objection to their presence but I do find it odd that they seem so drawn to the Highlands. Surely Germany has mountains and, probably, better weather. The Dutch are common hill-goers in the Highlands – them I can understand, having no native hills of their own – but the attraction the Highland hills hold for the groups of German folk eludes me.

Martin speaks before I can even manage to say hello. "We're going to the pub."

"Okay, let me get my kit unpacked first," I respond casually.

"We are going to the pub now," Martin states.

I am puzzled by his insistent tone when the explanation literally bites me in the throat. I feel a sudden pinprick, not painful but annoying. This is closely followed by another. I realise instantly the cause of Martin's distress: he is being devoured by midges. Whist I detest the Highland midge with a passion I can at least tolerate them for a while and protect myself with insect repellent which renders their attacks bearable. Martin's skin erupts with large red spots when he is attacked and, as though the little insects actually know this, they clearly prefer his flesh to mine. Insect repellent is also on Martin's list of things that will kill you, and therefore he refuses to use it, despite the fact that the entire midge nation is intent on stripping his flesh to the bone.

We head for the pub. We remember this pub from the days when we were in our twenties. Then it was crammed with folk our age, mainly students but also bikers and other degenerates. Getting to the bar was an ordeal as you fought your way through a seething mass of drunken youth to get your fizzy Scottish beer at the Formica altar. Everything was made of Formica in those days, even some of the people.

The hotel in Shiel Bridge, the Kintail Lodge Hotel, has changed little since we visited thirty years ago in our student days. The hotel – a white-painted jumble of a building, a mass of extensions built on to extensions – sits in a spectacular position at the head of Loch Duich. Here, the mountains of Kintail fall headlong into the sea as the old drove road squeezes between their feet and heads on towards Skye. Martin sits scratching while I go to get some beer. By the time I return from the bar, the psychosis induced in him by a million biting midges is beginning to subside and I can risk conversation.

"This place hasn't changed much," Martin declares through sips of beer.

He is right – the place remains essentially the same. The Formica has been replaced by wood and the fog of cigarette smoke that clouded the place in our younger days has been cleared by legislation. Where there was once a gleaming cigarette machine, now a blackboard with a menu of up-market pub food stands proud, offering such delicacies as local mussels and venison. Years ago pub food consisted of crisps and, if you were lucky, a packet of salted peanuts. Then, hotel bars in the Highlands weren't places you went to eat – they were places you went to get drunk before falling out into the rain at 10.00 p.m. Although the building is much the same there's something different about it that I can't identify at first.

Then it comes to me. "Where are the students?"

Martin pauses mid scratch and looks at me puzzled. "What do you mean?"

"There's no one in here under forty."

We survey the patrons. The tourists are mostly middle-aged folk out enjoying their evening meal, engaging in polite conversation. A few locals lean against the wooden bar drinking whisky, but the bikers and hikers who once filled the place to its rafters have gone.

"Perhaps they are all still here," Martin says with a laugh. "They just got older like we have."

I laugh with him, but there seems to me a serious point here. "Things have changed. No one in their twenties goes for a fortnight's walking holiday in the Highlands any more. Why would they, when they can fly to the Alps or Spain or the Pyrenees?"

"The scenery is just as good here," Martin retorts. As ever he is a staunch defender of the British Isles. He refuses to fly, due to the possibility of instant death, and never goes abroad.

"Maybe the scenery is, but the weather isn't. You could quite easily spend two weeks in the pouring rain on Skye when you could be climbing warm dry rock in Spain," I say, thinking aloud.

Martin is unwilling to concede the point. "Why would anyone want to go abroad? There are so many things to do here!"

"And there are no midges!" I've got him now.

Martin takes a long, thoughtful pull on his pint. "No midges? Really?"

"No. I've climbed all over the world – the Alps, the Rockies, Africa, the Pyrenees – and nowhere have I encountered anything half as annoying as the Highland midge."

"You mean you can sit outside in places like that, and…" He

pauses, trying to grasp the implications of what I've said. "And enjoy the view without being eaten?"

"Yes!"

Martin looks longingly through the pub window. Outside, the place is deserted, everyone having been driven inside by the flying hordes of insects.

"Imagine this place without midges," he muses.

"Well it wouldn't be Scotland unless you are freezing to death or soaked by the rain or something is trying to drink your blood, would it now?"

13
The Last Hillwalker

In the beam of my head torch the river boils and hurls white spray up into the dark night. As I walk up and down the bank, trying to find an easy way to cross, the rain increases in its intensity. I have crossed a mountain ridge and descended into the glen, and now I must find a way to ford the river to get to Glencoul bothy. In the darkness of this winter's night, it is impossible to tell how deep the river is. Here and there boulders offer the possibility of stepping stones but the gaps between are long and the rocks wet and slippery. In the torrential rain the river grows deeper with each moment. I must move soon. The possibility of climbing back over the ridge and to my car, several miles away, is remote – I am tired and saturated. The bothy is no more than three miles away and the prospect of night in the warmth of its fireside makes it worth overcoming the torrent.

A younger man might leap athletically from one boulder to another and arrive dry-footed on the far bank, but I am not that younger man – and I have a heavy rucksack full of coal, tinned steak, and whisky. An old man's comforts. If I slip from the rocks and fall in, I might break a leg and never resurface so in I wade. Icy water fills my boots and soaks me to my thighs but at least there is no danger of a bone-crunching fall. Out in the river the noise of the rushing water blots out all other sound. It's deep – rivers are always deeper than you think. I feel my way cautiously across the riverbed, fearful of some hidden hollow. A waterlogged shuffle brings me to the far bank but here I am confronted by an overhanging peat wall I cannot climb. I follow the bank downstream until I find a point I can attempt, but the black peat is soft, and saturated with water. I drive my fingers deep into the oozing mass, clawing my way up; the water sloshes about in my boots as I kick into the mush and begin to haul myself, trying to get some traction. I'm three feet above the water, inches from solid ground and escape, when the peat bank crumbles and dumps me unceremoniously into the water.

What the hell am I doing here? I am a sixty-year-old man, standing in a river in the pouring rain. I'm cold, wet and rapidly tiring and there isn't another human being for miles. Everyone else in the Highlands is in a house or perhaps a pub, somewhere dry where there are lights and food and there isn't icy water running past their knees.

I make another try at the bank. I'm touching the grass at the top, inches from freedom, when it collapses again, hurling me into the water a second time. I swear a lot, at this point; it makes me feel better. I'm glad that no one can see my ridiculous attempts to get out the water. People would pay money to watch this. You could put it on TV right after *Strictly Monkeys Singing* and *Dancing for Fame and Peanuts*.

Whole families would watch, sitting stuffing themselves with crisps. "Mother! Come and see, he's fallen in again. He'll never get out of that river."

I takes two more failed attempts before I stand dripping beside the river and can head downstream to where I hope I'll find the bothy. There is no path – so few people come here that the ground is not marked by the passage of human feet. The water in my boots quickly warms up and I'm oddly comfortable, although soaked to the skin, as I follow the river down towards where it meets the sea and the bothy sits at the shoreline. The glen is vast and dark but I am not alone as I wander through the night. My head torch picks out glowing eyes watching me through the incessant rain. Red deer have come down to find what shelter they can in the base of the glen. Deer lose their fear of humans at night, and I pass by so close I catch the smell of their misting breath and the pungent scent of wet fur. I am glad of their presence; at least some other warm-blooded creature is finding its way through this foul night.

After a few hundred yards I hear an ominous sound. *Oh God, what's that?* It is the roar of a powerful cascade of water somewhere in the darkness ahead. It is the unknown that holds the darkest terror. I look at my map and see that I have another stream to cross before I reach the bothy. Logic tells me that this cannot be as deep or as wide as the river I have already crossed, yet as the sound of the torrent fills my ears I walk on into the night with growing apprehension.

A handful of years have passed since that cold May night when I frightened the German couple with my Primus stove in Ryvoan bothy. Since that Cairngorm night I have come to love Highland bothies. I have explored many of them, sleeping in them in all seasons. There have been long winter nights when I have shivered in icy glens and summer evenings when I have watched the sun dip below the horizon as the heat of the day gives way to the cool of night. I have explored the high bothies of the Cairngorms, including remote Corrour where, forty years ago, I slept on the earth floor as a blizzard raged. I have bathed in the luxurious heat of the new wood stove in Gelder Shiel, remembering how Charlie and I shivered through a winter's night before the stove was installed by the Mountain Bothies Association. I have travelled the remote bothies of the far north, walked around the long coast route to Kearvaig, where the small white-walled cottage sits with its face toward the wild Atlantic. I've found my way through trackless bogs to bothies with names like Strabeg, Strathchailleach and Achnanclach.

I find myself drawn to these places, enjoying glimpses of wild things. I watch eagles hunt their prey, see white mountain hares running long-legged through the bracken. I love to find the tracks of a fox outside the bothy in the morning. There are the small things too; the delight in the dew on a spider's web or the sight of a silver flash as a trout leaps from the clear river. Despite the soakings and leg-weary walk-ins, despite the cold, the hard beds, the weight of the coal and the infernal midges, I find myself returning to bothies I know and am always seeking out new and remoter places to visit. Glencoul bothy has been somewhere I have wanted to come for a long time, so here I am walking through the rain and the darkness, plodding steadily into the unknown.

The roar of the water is growing closer. Its sound makes the ground tremble and I grow increasingly alarmed. *If that torrent is between me and the bothy I'll never make it. I'll have to spend all night out here in the cold and wet.* Then I reach the edge of the stream as it cuts across my path. To my relief, it is not the savage beast that I can hear roaring in the blackness. The river has burst its banks but I cross it easily, even though it fills my boots with even colder water. I realise that the monster in the darkness is the Eas a' Chual Aluinn, the highest waterfall in Britain at 658ft, plunging over the cliff face. I cannot see it but, with this volume of water passing over it, it must be an impressive sight. Fortunately the falls are on the far side of the glen and I won't have to pass through them on my way to the bothy.

I continue my waterlogged march, feet sloshing in my boots and trousers sodden. My great fear is that I'll walk past the bothy in the darkness. In the blackness of this rain-soaked glen I become the bothy hunter. Robbed of sight I use all my other senses to track the creature down. Once, completely lost in mist, I followed the smell of woodsmoke right to a bothy door. Now I become the Sherlock Holmes of navigation. Looking down I notice a few strands of seaweed in the clumps of grass.

"Ah, Watson, we must be near the sea!"

I peer at my soggy map and plot the distance to the bothy. I have sworn never to use a GPS device. I'm no technophobe and spend as much time glued to iPads and laptops as everyone else but I refuse to use a screen for navigation in the hills. I'm here because I want contact with wilderness, to feel the earth beneath my boots and the wind on my face. For me, to see the landscape reduced to something digital behind a screen would lessen that experience. Right now I am dependent on my own skills. My ability to read the landscape and the flickering compass needle will decide if I reach the bothy. Adventure is made of uncertainty and risk – both of which would be reduced by a GPS system in my hand. It's not that long ago I failed to find Bearnais bothy and spent a night under the stars, but the experience was all the richer for that failure. Nothing sharpens your navigational skills like having to sleep out 500m from the comfort of a bothy!

In the darkness, I unleash my secret weapon: I count paces. At night, you always think you have travelled further than you have.

It's easy to become confused by distance. *I must have passed the bloody place!*

Counting paces is a skill you must acquire over time. All kinds of things affect the length of your stride and only experience will allow you to adjust the count for the length of the grass or the hardness of the ground. My pace-counting skills are still rudimentary but they give me great reassurance in the blackness: by counting paces I know I haven't gone far enough, I know I haven't passed the place.

561, 562, 563. Maybe I should start looking for the bothy now.

My head-torch beam picks up a low stone wall, long since fallen into disrepair. It's not the bothy but it is the first man-made thing I have seen for miles – a sign I am close. There are other signs I look for in my bothy hunts. Things like Rhododendron bushes are planted to decorate gardens and usually grow close to dwellings. Peat was used as a fuel for generations in the Highlands, so old peat cuttings can point to the presence of a bothy. I keep following my bearing and suddenly my feet hit something hard. Tarmac! There is no road to this place but the map shows a small jetty and a little track heading to the bothy. *So, the bothy must be over there.* I turn to the direction of the bothy and a small white elliptical shape shines back at me. The Mountain Bothies Association sign on the bothy door. *I've made it!*

In the bare, wood-lined room an old table sits by the window with two rickety chairs to keep it company. The fireplace is cold and empty and someone has left a flimsy camp bed in the corner. The room is frigid, dark and smells of damp; it is not an inviting place to stay. Despite this outwardly unwelcoming appearance I unpack my stove, candles and coal eagerly, because I know a secret.

I go into a well-rehearsed routine. With my wet clothes dripping from hooks on the walls, I slip into the lightweight, dry clothes. I light the candles and kneel for a few moments at the fireplace, blowing on the embers, kindling the fire into life. I pour my tin of stewed steak into the pan – together with instant mashed potato it is my favorite bothy meal – and light the stove. It's then that it happens, just like I knew it would. It's then, in the candlelight, as the flames in the hearth begin to rise, that the bothy transforms. A few minutes ago, it was a dusty, empty room but now, as my dinner begins to bubble in the pan, it becomes a haven from the lashing rain and the howling wind. As I eat my simple meal, made delicious by hunger, the fire smokes and little jets of flame emerge from black lumps of coal. The heat of the fire begins to reach me and ease the ache of my legs. Fed and warm, despite the rain beating against the window pane, I begin to relax – and as I sip my whisky the warmth comes from within.

Later I sit, watching the endless permutations of colour and light in the flames dancing in the fire. This is the bothy TV; it has only one channel, but on nights like these, it's the only one you need. In my mind I replay the day's walk, knowing I must repeat the challenge on the way back to my car, but at least that will be in daylight and I won't have the coal to carry. They say that the best bothies are hard gained; if that's true, then Glencoul must be one of the finest there is. I am cocooned in the firelight, lulled by whisky into a state of gentle contentment in this timeless place, where the cacophony of everyday life cannot reach. In this basic shelter, among these wild hills, I am in tune with the land around me. My mind and body drift into a simple rhythm set by the traverse of the sun and the dwindling firelight. Here is peace, a peace not purchased by wealth or property or power. It is the simple contentment of a man who is fed, warm and dry and who, for a few fleeting moments, has all he can desire.

The next human being is several hours' walk away and I have no means of contacting anyone yet I never feel alone in places like this. In fact, I seek solitude. In travelling here, I have had a conversation with the land, with the hills, the river and the wind. If you listen the landscape will guide you. Solitude is, of course, a choice; loneliness is not, and that makes all the difference.

* * *

It's late May and spring is giving way to summer. The winter was mild, wet and windy, like so many winters in recent years. With the effects of global warming, these are the kind of winters we can expect in the future. For those of us who wander these hills the demise of winter is a terrible loss. The snows and the icy winds elevate these hills to mountains. Winter is the great season, before which all must bow. It is a tremendous joy to walk through a magical landscape, transformed by snow and cold, to kick the snow from your boots at the bothy door, and finally sit by the fire whilst the wind rages through the icy glen.

These days you sit dripping as moisture works its way into your underpants. I have a secret longing for climate change to do its worst and to switch off the Gulf Stream that warms these islands, plunging us into Arctic winter. I know that's a selfish thought as most of Britain would be shut down by snow. Perversely, such cold weather would probably kill the Highland skiing industry as no one would be able to get here and a glacier would gobble up the ski centre on Cairn Gorm. It'll probably never happen – it's the dark fantasy of an old mountaineer – but if it does come at least I'll have the right socks.

The deer are fat this year. They have benefitted from the mild winter; their coats are sleek and they look healthy. In other years, when winter comes late or lingers longer than usual, I have seen the herds of deer ravaged by starvation, desperately waiting for the grass to grow. This winter the living has been easy for them and most have made it through the colder months. I'm trudging up this long glen, weighed down by food and coal, heading for one of the remotest bothies in Scotland. It has been a dream of mine to make my way to Maol Bhuidhe bothy for almost two years now, ever since I began to travel to these simple shelters. Maol Bhuidhe is situated deep in the Highland hills, a long, tough walk from any direction and the place also has a secret weapon: it is guarded by rivers. No matter which direction you come from, you have to ford a river – and, as I have already learned, these can be formidable obstacles.

I have chosen to walk in from the south via Glen Elchaig. Long though this walk is, at least the gradient is easy. After five or six miles, I meet a group of huge beasts with great fearsome horns and wild shaggy coats. Fortunately, despite their warrior-like appearance, Highland cows are placid creatures and they regard me with mild curiosity as I pass amongst them. A few even amble aside to let me by. I suppose when you look as tough as they do you don't need to be aggressive; no one is going to mess with you.

After several hours' walking a small house comes into view. This is the romantically named Iron Lodge. Sadly, despite sounding like something out of Game of Thrones, it is little more than a small modern house, sitting incongruously in this remote spot and slowly falling into disrepair. I have reached the head of the glen and now hills crowd around me like schoolyard bullies, each looking more menacingly steep than the last. It's here that I leave the gentle track and head up the path that climbs into the mountains, over a pass to descend to where the bothy lies, isolated from the world by miles of trackless moorland. When I drove to the start of the walk, I passed a small corrugated-iron church that proudly displayed a sign promising 'JESUS SAVES US FROM SIN'. My eyes follow the path as it climbs higher and higher over the hills and I shift uneasily under my heavy rucksack. It occurs to me that I will pay for my sins in the next few miles.

Walking to Maol Bhuidhe is a legendary feat. In the accounts I've read it is the breaker of hearts, the blisterer of feet. It is on this path that old men, carrying too many luxuries, finally succumb to the Grim Reaper's scythe. After a few hundred feet my legs – which, after the distance I have already walked expect to be at rest in the bothy by now – rebel furiously and I come to a grinding halt. As I sit on a boulder, gasping for breath, I notice a movement in the glen below me. There is a figure following me up the path. Not wishing to be overtaken I gather what strength I have and forge on. Well, 'forge' is perhaps a bit of an exaggeration, but I head on up. Every now and again I look back and with each glance the figure seems closer. A few minutes later a bearded figure in a wide-brimmed hat saunters into view. I am dripping sweat and gasping for breath; he looks as though he just stepped off a bus.

"Hello, are you heading for the bothy?" he asks with a cheerful grin.

I try and look as though I am sauntering along today and in no rush at all. "Why yes, nice day isn't it?"

"Good. See you later," he says and shoots off in the direction of the bothy.

He is younger than me, perhaps thirty; he is cheerful, his pack is half the size of mine, his waist is slimmer and his legs are stronger. Following him slowly up and over the pass I have time to mull over these facts. I'm not sure which of these characteristics make me hate him the most but I am certain of one thing, I do hate him. Eventually I reach the head of the pass and I am, at last, able to look down at the glen in which the bothy sits. Below me a long loch cuts through the landscape surrounded on every side by rolling hills. I can see nothing man made as far as the horizon, and standing here it is easy to feel as though the rest of the planet has ceased to exist. At last the white walls of the bothy rise from the heather. The weather has been dry over the last few days and the river between me and the bothy is only ankle deep. The bothy is fairly basic with a wooden bench, table and blackened hearth; it's a long way in to bring anything so I am not surprised it's quite spartan.

My young friend, whose name is Alec, is already in residence. It's been quite a while since he passed an old lumbering man on the trail. He's had time to write a short romantic novel, rebuild the bothy or perhaps translate the Koran into Yiddish, possibly all three. He looks bemused as I drop my rucksack on to the bothy floor with a thud that brings down dust from the ceiling, then watches in silence as I unpack stove, flask of whisky, steak dinner and lastly my bag of coal.

He watches in astonishment as I slowly fill the small table. "You've come well equipped, haven't you? I travel light myself."

It's then that I notice he's eating something that looks like chicken feed from a small bowl. "What's that you're eating?"

"This?' he says, waving the bowl at me. "It's Couscous."

"Couscous? What the hell is Couscous?" I have a fairly wide repertoire of culinary knowledge but I've never heard of this stuff.

He stops, mid spoonful, and pokes at the semi-congealed mass in his saucepan. "I don't really know what it is. But it's very good."

I glance at my tin of steak. I'm a little worried the sight of real food might overexcite him. "Couscous? How do you cook it?"

"I don't," he explains. "I haven't got a stove. Travelling light, you see."

I'm incredulous. "No stove! How do you make tea?"

'I just drink water… unless someone offers me some tea, that is," he says, eyes lingering on my stove. I've renovated myself as a walker over the last few years. I loved the smell and the roar of my old Primus but at three and half pounds the old brass monster was too heavy for my legs to lug around any more. I now have a little folding gas stove.

I set up the stove and screw on the canister. "You do have a mug I suppose?"

He looks hurt, and produces a little blue plastic mug. "Of course."

We sit in silence while the water boils. I can't understand how anyone can stay in bothies without the ability to keep out the winter chill with a hot brew. Sharing the tea thaws the atmosphere and we begin to relax. It turns out Alec is walking the Cape Wrath Trail, a long, arduous route that begins at Fort William and takes in some of the wildest and most rugged landscapes in the British Isles before it ends on the north-westernmost tip of mainland Britain. There are a variety of routes to the north but all pass by this bothy, making it an obvious stopping place on the trek. He tells me of the endless rain he encountered when he tramped through Knoydart and of terrifying river crossings that I can sympathise with. Despite his refusal to carry anything heavier than a teaspoon it's clear that Alec is a hillwalker of some experience.

It's then that I notice his feet. "Good God, man, have you nae boots?" He is wearing a pair of battered old trainers.

"These are walking shoes. I don't need boots," he explains cheerfully. "I have waterproof socks."

I had not known waterproof socks existed; they are a dream come true. "Do they keep your feet dry?"

"Well no, but they are warm in the wet."

No boots and waterproof socks that aren't, how does he survive?

Later that evening darkness descends on the little white-walled shelter. Inside, the candlelight and the coal fire work their magic, and we both relax watching the flames dance in the semi-darkness. He is the youngest person I have met in a bothy for a long time. Emboldened by the whisky I decide it's time to impart on this young man some of my old-man-of-the-hills wisdom.

I lean over to him and whisper as if someone had their ear pressed to the door. "Hillwalking is dying out, you know."

He glances up at me from his steaming mug and gives me a sceptical look. "What makes you think that?"

On my solo bothy trips I get to think a lot. In fact, thinking is pretty much all I can do. As a result of too much time spent in bothies on my own I have developed theories about the future of hillwalking and, since I have an audience, it's time to rehearse them. I tell him about when I started hillwalking all those years ago in the Lake District. I tell him how there seemed to be more folk on the hills year after year. I tell him about how Martin and I had returned to the Kintail Lodge Hotel and found no one under forty there. I explain that, as there is no younger generation of hillwalkers coming up to replace my generation, in thirty or forty years the hills will be empty.

Alec sits in silence, amazed at my pronouncements. "There may be some truth in that, but when were you last walking in the Lake District?"

I'm ashamed to admit it must be twenty years ago now.

Alec shakes his head. "The Lakes are full of young people walking the hills. I think there's plenty of interest."

I try a different argument. "You rarely see people your age in bothies. When I started going to bothies thirty years ago you'd see a lot more folk. And I often go to bothies now where there aren't any mice. There were always mice in bothies when I started. That's because there aren't enough folk passing through. Not enough crumbs to keep a mouse alive these days."

Alec grins. "I don't think the mouse population of bothies can be considered a scientific measure of their use."

I can't argue with that and we both laugh.

"Besides, lightweight camping is much more popular and affordable these days," he adds. "You see lots of folk doing that."

I sense I'm not going to win this argument. I know I'm right, but being right doesn't always win arguments. I decide on one last try.

"Climbing walls are another thing. Loads of people only climb indoors – that's not real climbing. The problem is we are losing touch with nature. Climbing outdoors is an adventure. Me and my mates had lots of tales to tell about being caught in foul weather and trapped on ledges. What can indoor climbers talk about – the day the cafe closed early?"

Alec shoots me a glance. Perhaps I've gone too far. "It's okay for you, you have the time to get outdoors. A lot of younger people have to work and can't afford to get to the hills."

I realise I'm a baby boomer – I've had it all. I didn't have to fight a war, my dad did that. When I went to university they actually gave me money. I didn't leave with student debt or have to work my way through college. I got to retire early on a decent pension. My mates and I have spent all the money. And, while we are on the subject, you know the environment is knackered? Well, that was us too. It occurs to me that I might have lapsed into an old man telling the next generation how they are doing everything wrong.

I pick up his empty mug. "More tea?"

As the night passes we talk of the places we've been. We talk about hills and glens and remote bothies and it's clear that he takes as much pleasure as I do in travelling these places. Perhaps I'm wrong, perhaps hillwalking is not becoming extinct, perhaps it's just changing. I'm glad to hear that he enjoys these wild places as much as I do but perhaps in a different way.

The next morning Alec wakes early and eats his breakfast, which appears to me to be dog biscuits. He declines my offer of tea, drinks only cold water, and sets off on the next leg of his journey north. No doubt when he gets home he'll tell a story of meeting a cantankerous old man in a remote bothy. I sit on a flat stone, drinking tea and scratching, as I watch his wide-brimmed hat heading towards the horizon. Despite what Alec said last night, I still think I'm right – one day these hills will be empty.

Maybe I just met the last hillwalker.

Postscript

It's dark now. Inside the bothy our candles flicker and the fire casts a warm glow across the wooden floor while the world is entombed in darkness outside. This is not the darkness of cities where perpetual light invades the blackness at its corners; this is the profound, tangible darkness of the hills. The wind is rising. Now and again it picks up the tumultuous rain and hurls it against the bothy window. At intervals, the wind retreats, rebounds off the hillside opposite and runs full force against the walls of our small dwelling. The roof creaks and shudders in the storm; at times it sounds as though the wind will tear it apart but, in the end, it holds.

The three of us have been sitting, talking and drinking for hours, safe in the bothy while the storm rages. Now Joe is snoring gently in his sleeping bag. Martin and I sit enjoying the last of the wine and watching the flames in the fire. I tell Martin about meeting Alec in Maol Bhuidhe and all about his lightweight approach.

"No boots, really?"

I nod.

Martin shakes his head in disbelief. "Good grief."

"Remember how little gear we had when we walked the Pennine Way forty years ago? You didn't have boots then."

Martin laughs, almost spilling his wine. "And we didn't have a proper tent."

"I don't know how we did it."

"I wonder if we could do it again?" Martin asks, and the question hangs in the air.

I blame the wine and the heady dose of nostalgia. Whatever it is, I'm not thinking clearly. "Well, there's only one way to find out."

So that's how it happened – that's how we decided to walk 270 miles of the Pennines forty years on. I don't know if we'll do it this time, but I'm sure we'll have adventures along the way.

That, however, is another story.

~

The Journey Continues

If you would like to follow more of John's journeys to bothies and wild places, and his adventures in the world of theatre, visit johndburns.com where you can read his blogs and listen to his podcasts.

If you have enjoyed the book, please share a review on Amazon.co.uk. Reviews are vital in boosting the visibility of good books and helping writers to succeed. Most importantly of all, tell other people about this book!

~